A Diamond
in the Dust

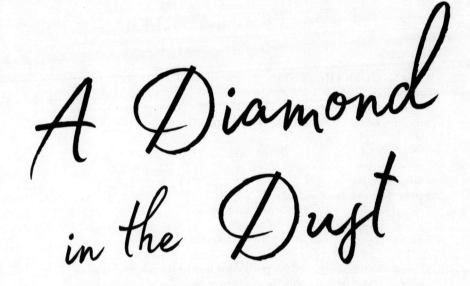

A Diamond in the Dust

FRAUKE BOLTEN-BOSHAMMER
WITH SUE SMETHURST

SIMON &
SCHUSTER

London · New York · Sydney · Toronto · New Delhi

A CBS COMPANY

A DIAMOND IN THE DUST
First published in Australia in 2018 by
Simon & Schuster (Australia) Pty Limited
Suite 19A, Level 1, Building C, 450 Miller Street, Cammeray, NSW 2062

10 9 8 7 6 5 4 3 2 1

A CBS Company
Sydney New York London Toronto New Delhi
Visit our website at www.simonandschuster.com.au

A catalogue record for this
book is available from the
National Library of Australia

Cover design: Christabella Designs
Cover photograph: Chris Magnay Photography, www.magnay.photos
Internal design: Christabella Designs
Typeset by Midland Typesetters, Australia
Printed and bound in Australia by Griffin Press

The paper this book is printed on is certified
against the Forest Stewardship Council®
Standards. Griffin Press holds FSC chain
of custody certification SGS-COC-005088.
FSC promotes environmentally responsible,
socially beneficial and economically viable
management of the world's forests.

Land of Forrests, Fleas and Flies,

Blighted hopes and blighted eyes

Art thou hell in earth's disguise?

Westralia.

Allan Deuchar

To the spirit of the people who have called Kununurra home

Contents

A Diamond in the Dust

Prologue

APRIL 1981, PERTH

The flight attendant raised an eyebrow as she locked eyes on our tickets.

'Do you know what Kununurra is like?' she asked smugly. I suppose it was understandable she'd be curious about anyone with a one-way ticket to the most remote part of Australia – especially a young couple who barely spoke English, with three small children in tow.

As she placed our luggage onto a trolley, already piled high with newspapers, sacks of flour and bibs and bobs of machinery, I lifted the baby a little higher on my hip, confidently pushed a stray brown curl off my face and summoned every ounce of false bravado to plaster a smile across my face.

The stubborn German blood that ran through my veins was not prepared to give even the slightest hint of the crippling fear that had stolen my sleep since my husband

Friedrich dropped a bombshell six months earlier: we were moving to Australia.

Flights from Perth to the outback were a rarity, and so were passengers on them. Flight MV 392 from Perth to Kununurra via Derby, known as the 'milk run', delivered much-needed supplies to the remote cattle stations and tiny settlements that dotted the vast desert. For the people who lived there, it was a lifeline to the outside world.

There was no fancy cabin service, no message from the captain to 'sit back, relax and enjoy the flight'. We were cargo, of the human kind, to be delivered to the furthest part of the desert.

With our tickets checked, eleven-year-old Fritz and ten-year-old Margret raced across the tarmac and up the metal stairs to find their seats, while the last of our luggage was placed into the cargo hold. We didn't bring much with us. The thick woollen coats and hats needed to survive the winter at home were packed into the attic of our farmhouse in Seedorf, in Northern Germany, awaiting our return. A handful of suitcases and the clothes on our back were all we would need for our adventure.

We were on our way to one of the most remote and isolated areas of Australia, possibly the world. A crocodile-infested corner of the outback, eight hours' drive from the nearest major town. Our new home was to be a farm I'd not seen, in a place I'd never heard of, with a name I could hardly get my tongue around, 3200 kilometres from Perth, on the border of the Northern Territory and Western Australia; in the middle of nowhere.

I buckled myself in for the ride of my life.

Chapter 1

The state of Schleswig-Holstein, where I was born and raised, is known for its picturesque rolling hills, rich green fields and secluded lakes that look like scenes straight from *The Sound of Music*. I confess to getting a little homesick every time I see that movie.

My mother was the love of my father's life. They got engaged on the eve of the Second World War, and when he was enlisted to serve in the German army they wrote more than four hundred love letters to one another to keep in touch.

Every one of my father's notes began, 'My darling Lotte! Our thoughts return to each other.' There are pages and pages in the most perfect pen, sharing tales of life in the trenches. My mother would write back, offering comforting words from home. They married when he was home on leave, but the honeymoon had to wait because he was shipped back to the front line. They hated being apart.

After the war, my father returned and they began their married life living and working on my grandfather's farm in Neuheim. Then along came my brother, Juergen, in 1943 followed by my sister, Dorte, in 1945. I was born Frauke Seemann on 3 October 1947. Frauke means 'little lady'.

Not long after my second birthday, my mother, Liselotte, died from cancer. She was just thirty-four years old. I never knew her, and it breaks my heart to this day that I have no memories of her that are my own. My memories belong to others, recollections borrowed and cobbled together from stories and snippets I begged my family to share. With their help, I've pieced together a patchwork picture of her, a treasured image I've locked away in my heart.

I have one precious photo of us together, a fading black-and-white picture that sits in a frame in my bedroom. I wake to her face every day. She was very sick from the cancer when the picture was taken. Thin and pale, she shows no resemblance to the robust German women of my family, but I'm grateful for that one image; it gives me something to cling to.

My father, Johannes, was bereft when she died. Her coffin was lined with her favourite flowers, so she was buried resting her head on a thick bed of dark red and crimson carnations. When the coffin was sealed, huge garlands of flowers were draped over the top. My brother and sister and I weren't allowed to attend her funeral – we weren't even told she'd died until after she was buried. We never got to say goodbye.

In his eulogy, my father proudly declared that they had a great love which grew every day, and called her his 'dear partner in life'. He recalled how sad it was to say goodbye to her in the rare times he was home on leave during the war. 'It was difficult for me never knowing if we would see one another again, but her silent prayers, her bravery, her love; everything contributed to me surviving the war.'

In the final hours of her life, she squeezed his hand while he tenderly cradled her, until 'death was stronger and she no longer had the strength to defeat it,' he told the congregation.

Years later I was told that he broke down in tears reading his final words: 'My only wish is that the children and I could see you just one more time.' I've read his eulogy many times; it's clear he adored her. I believe his heart and his spirit were broken the day she died. He kept a lock of her hair with him for the rest of his life.

After she died, we barely spoke about my mother; it upset my father too much. Whenever one of us would mention her, he'd cry. We could see how sad it made him; he was heart-broken. We didn't want to upset him too much, so we just stopped talking about her. It was like she never existed.

My father struggled to look after us without a wife; at that time it was not considered a man's job. He was a very traditional man, a stout German farmer whose role was to provide a home for us, a roof over our heads and food on the table – and he did all of that, but he struggled to show us love.

What we craved most was affection, a father's gentle hug, someone to wipe away the tears and tell us everything would be okay, but he was trained to keep a stiff upper lip and soldier on. That's what he expected of us too; he sternly reinforced the belief that children were to be seen and not heard.

Every day before lunch or dinner we had to stand behind our chairs, silent, with straight backs, as my father entered the room; we couldn't sit until he gave us permission.

One particular day we were being fussy, screwing up our noses at the food on our plates, and he was trying to get the message through to us to be grateful for what we had.

'You children don't know how difficult it was during the war,' he bellowed before storming out into the garden.

He came back inside with a limp-looking sparrow in his grasp. He'd killed it with his bare hands and we were going to eat it. We were horrified as he took it into the kitchen.

'That's how soldiers survived the war,' he told us when he returned and swiftly cleared our plates to make way for the roasted bird.

4

We never complained about our dinner again.

Dorte's only real memory of my mother is of the last Christmas we had with her, just a month before her death. When I was around four or five years old, Father decided we didn't need a Christmas tree. He told us Christmas was cancelled; he couldn't deal with it. We were so sad. Eventually, he gave in and got us a tree at the last minute, but his misery seeped through us all.

By the time I was six, my father felt I was ready to begin helping on the farm with Juergen and Dorte. After school we worked out in the fields bringing in the crops. We hoed the leaves off sugar beets, which was painstaking but nowhere near as difficult as gathering the potatoes. During late autumn, early morning and late at night we had to walk along the field following a grader that dug up the potatoes, picking them up as they broke through the soil. Potatoes can't handle frost because they rot, so we had to gather them quickly before they spoiled. We collected hundreds of the near-frozen potatoes, so cold they were painful to hold. At times I felt my tiny fingers would snap right off.

This was all part of Father's plan to toughen us up; we had to learn how to weather difficult times.

Still, there was also time for play, and as children we enjoyed a lot of freedom. The only other kids that lived nearby were boys on a neighbouring farm, but that didn't worry Dorte and me – as long as we had someone to play with we didn't care if it was a boy or a girl. We had a sprawling barn for the hay and with the help of the boys, we dug a secret cave, a *Höhle*, at one end of it and lined it with wood. It was something to behold. The cave was hidden behind the haystack, so you had to climb through the hay to get into it. I clearly remember us taking candles into the hay *Höhle* one day and lighting them! Nowadays, I shudder to think about what could've happened.

Each day we walked two-and-a-half kilometres to and from our *Grundschule*, or primary school, in Mehlby. I was a terribly shy child and more comfortable sitting back quietly in the classroom than seeking attention. To bring me out of my shell, my teacher singled me out, which of course had the opposite effect. When I did pluck up the courage to put my hand up, he'd make snide comments like, 'Oh, she speaks,' or if I got the answer wrong, 'What would I expect from little Frauke?' I was made to feel stupid, so I just gave up.

My father employed home economics apprentices from the nearby school to help around the house. They were young women whose job was to cook, clean and keep the house organised. They did their jobs well, but we longed for nurturing and the mother we didn't have. Adele, my maternal grandmother, was wonderful and Dorte became a mother to me. She was the one to comfort me and hug me when I needed it, but she was only a child herself.

Salvation came into our lives the day a middle-aged East Prussian refugee arrived on our doorstep. She became known as Tante Banta, or Aunty Banta.

After the Soviet Union had taken control of her town and she had to flee with her daughter Ursula, she knocked on our door looking for a place to stay. My father welcomed her into our home and into our lives, and we quickly came to love her. This tall, thin woman with her round wire-rimmed glasses, thick stockings and sensible lace-up shoes gave us random hugs, baked biscuits and read us stories; she warmed our hearts. We knew she couldn't stay forever, but we clung to every precious moment with our very own Mary Poppins.

When I was eight years old, Father remarried. We were very happy for him and hoped that Frieda would bring some sunshine back into his life. But it was a loveless marriage; he wanted someone to help him with the children.

Frieda tried her best with us but she wasn't an affectionate woman and my father saw affection as a sign of weakness, so it wasn't encouraged. He felt it would spoil us. Thankfully Tante Banta settled nearby and remained very much part of our lives.

My upbringing would shape the sort of parent I would become. I promised myself I would smother my children with affection and shower them with love. You can never spoil a child with too much love.

My future and my fate were sealed in 1965, the day I was sent to work at the Bolten family farm at the age of seventeen. Just as my mother had done, when I finished school I took on an apprenticeship in home science, or home economics, as Australians would call it. We learnt all sorts of domestic duties such as ironing and cooking and gardening – everything a woman needed to know to run a household.

It was customary that we served part of our apprentice-ship working with a family on a farm, just as the young apprentices had done with us. Along with another young girl, Elisabeth, I was sent to the Bolten family, who ran a very successful farm, Suenderuphof, just outside Flensburg, about 45 kilometres from Kappeln where I grew up.

As we approached, from the road we could see that this farm was something special. An enormous thatched roof poked through the treetops and then the sprawling white brick home appeared at the end of a long meandering driveway bordered with thick green hornbeam hedges.

The moment I stepped inside the Boltens' beautiful house I fell in love – in love with their home and in love with them. The sense of family warmth and welcome was overwhelming.

Their home was a beautiful big traditional German farmhouse. It had fifteen rooms, all decorated in different styles and colour schemes, overlooking rich green pastures. The original house was bombed during the war and burnt out, so the family had rebuilt it exactly as it was on the exterior, but inside they had installed every modern appliance you could imagine, including decadent central heating, which our house never had. I would never feel cold while I lived here.

Elisabeth and I were given bedrooms upstairs and our job was to help Mrs Bolten with the domestic work. The farm was busy and our day began at 6.30am preparing breakfast for the men who were headed out to the fields, and traditional German milk soup for Grandmother Bolten, who lived there too.

When the evening's dishes were done and put away and the house chores complete, Mrs Bolten invited us to stay downstairs and chat with the family. I enjoyed their company, particularly Mr Bolten's, as he was very generous and made me laugh. Mrs Bolten could be demanding – she expected everything to be perfect and to meet an exceptional standard – but she also offered a warmth I'd longed for since

I was a small child. She taught me many things, including how to enjoy a glass of good wine, and she made us feel like we were part of the family.

About a month after we arrived, the Boltens' daughter, Hedi, got married. The reception was held at the house, so in the days leading up to it Elisabeth and I were run off our feet making sure there wasn't a speck of dust to be found. Glassware sparkled, linens were starched and pressed until they were crisp, flowers filled vases in every corner of the house and cutlery was polished until you could see your reflection.

We prepared a feast fit for kings, poured champagne, waited on guests and made sure everything ran like clockwork so Mr and Mrs Bolten could entertain their guests. Later in the evening, when all of the food had been served and the last of the guests were sipping their drinks, we could relax. Most of the older people had left at a sensible hour, but a few younger ones were still there dancing late.

Hartwig, the Boltens' youngest son, stretched out his hand to me, asking if I'd like to dance. He was charming and more confident than any other young man I'd ever met. Mrs Bolten encouraged Elisabeth and me to join in the dancing, so we did.

That evening Hartwig became my boyfriend. It was a very sweet courtship. Sometimes he took me to a local dance or the cinema, and we'd hold hands or kiss every now and then, but that was the extent of it.

We'd been dating for about a year when Hartwig suddenly broke it off. I was heading to the Frauenfachschule, the Women's College, in Flensburg, to continue my studies. He explained that he didn't want the relationship to deepen too far, because, 'I don't want to marry my first girlfriend.' He wanted to sow his wild oats.

I was sad, mostly because I thought I might not see the Boltens again, and I loved their family.

After college I moved away, to Hamburg and then further south, to Bad Nenndorf, near Hannover, where I had a position at a sanatorium that had four hundred patients. It was a rather depressing place – a big old brick building full of very sick people – but it had an enormous kitchen and they needed large numbers of domestic staff to keep the place running.

It was hard work and I was exhausted at the end of each day, but I learnt an enormous amount during this time. I was now earning my own money and financially independent, which was something to be very proud of.

Shortly after my nineteenth birthday, Mrs Bolten invited me back to the farm to visit. Friedrich, the eldest son, happened to be home. After doing army service, which he detested, he had gone on to study agriculture in Soest, five hours away. Friedrich's fate was determined at an early age: as the eldest, he would inherit the Bolten family farm. Great expectations were on his shoulders.

Friedrich was a blond string bean. He was tall and thin with a thick head of hair, the spitting image of his father, both of their lithe bodies carved by hard work. That day, we got along well and he paid quite a bit of attention to me. Shortly after that, he plucked up the courage to ask me out. Years later he confessed that he'd always been keen on me and was annoyed his little brother had asked me out first.

We were great friends and enjoyed one another's company. Friedrich wasn't confident like Hartwig. It took him a couple of months before he dared to kiss me, so it wasn't a heart-racing romance, but we grew to love one another very naturally. He was never going to sweep me off my feet, but that's what made me love him: he was patient, gentle and kind, thoughtful and considerate; and he was strong and sensible.

Friedrich wasn't a big talker and he wasn't showy, but he was a big thinker. He had big dreams and he was determined to make his own mark on the world, to earn his own reputation.

His family was very successful in farming and in business. His great-great-grandfather August Bolten co-founded the Hamburg-America shipping line, which later became the company Hamburg Süd, Germany's second-oldest shipping company.

It would've been easy for Friedrich to just plod along until he inherited the family farm, but that was not his way; he'd inherited their entrepreneurial spirit. He was proud and he was smart; he had dreams and a restless spirit; he wanted to work hard and suck the marrow from life; he wanted to push himself to see what he could achieve through his own hard work, not just accept what would be handed to him as a birthright.

The way I found out that Friedrich wanted to marry me was anything but typical.

His sister Hedi quietly sidled up to me in the kitchen of their farmhouse one day and asked, 'Has Friedrich talked about your future?'

I knew what she was hinting at and suspected she was doing research on Friedrich's behalf. I smiled back at her and said 'no'.

Armed with the reassurance I would say yes, she scurried off to her painfully shy brother and said, 'Friedrich, why haven't you asked her yet? Hurry up!' With matchmaker

Hedi's words ringing in his ear, one afternoon a week later he asked me if I would like to take a drive to the seaside town of Flensburg when he finished his farm work.

We found a quiet spot looking out at the Baltic Sea. We'd been there before, to celebrate after the crops had been harvested and Friedrich had some time to relax – although farmers never really relax; they've always got one eye on the sky and the other on the earth. Sometimes we came here just to be alone. We'd smooth out a picnic blanket and lie staring at the sky, counting the stars while the ocean breeze soothed our skin.

I knew something was brewing in his mind that late summer evening. Friedrich was curious about life – there was always something more to see, someplace else to explore, something new to learn. He could be very shy and at times quite serious, but when his mind was in full flight he was exciting to be around.

He took my hand and locked his sharp blue eyes on mine, and with the peaceful sound of water lapping at the bows of fishing trawlers moored near us, he asked if I would be his wife.

For a farmer, his hands were always so soft and his fine pale skin remarkably unblemished by the sun, even though he spent long hours in the fields tending to crops day in, day out.

I squeezed his hand. 'You know my answer,' I said, grinning from ear to ear.

Asking me was the easy part. After he proposed, Friedrich had to formally ask my father for my hand in marriage, so the next day we took flowers for my step-mother and while I went off to make tea for us all, Friedrich plucked up the courage to ask my father if he could marry me.

This was far from a fait accompli: when my sister's boy-friend asked him twelve months earlier, he said no. Dorte's boyfriend was a teacher and my father didn't approve; it was only when they announced there was a baby on the way that he suddenly gave his blessing.

I carefully carried the tea tray back into the room, trying to tiptoe so I could overhear their conversation. I needn't have worried: as soon as I saw Friedrich sitting at my father's card table, I knew he'd given his approval. My father never invited anyone to sit at his precious card table – you had to be very special – so this was something akin to a papal blessing!

'You'll have to learn to play cards,' my father told him.

Friedrich and I went together to a local jeweller and I chose a small diamond engagement ring and a wedding band. Having both was extravagant for post-war Germany.

I was so proud to wear the rings on my finger. In Germany, tradition dictates you both wear rings on your left hand to signal you are engaged and when you marry you swap them to your right.

One month after my twenty-first birthday, in November 1968, we became husband and wife. First we visited the registry office in Mehlby and signed all of the legal papers. As custom dictates in Germany, you must marry in a civil legal service first. By mid-morning, technically we were husband and wife.

Then in the afternoon we were married again in a beautiful service at a Lutheran church in Maasholm, overlooking the Baltic Sea. My wedding preparation had been very low fuss. At lunchtime I began to get ready, with Dorte helping me. She was married the year before, so I wore her dress. An empire line with a high waist to accommodate her growing shape, it was a little too big for me, but my father had no money to buy a new gown. It was white organza with a lace overlay, or *Spitze* as we call it, over the bodice. My veil was pinned high on top of my head with a flower to hold it in place, and it fell just past my shoulders. I carried a long teardrop bouquet of red roses and white freesias.

Hartwig, who was very happy for us, drove us through the pretty little fishing village, lined with cobblestone streets and traditional half-timbered German homes, to the church.

CHAPTER 1

There were no nerves or butterflies, just a sense of peace as I made my way up the stone steps of the white brick church. Friedrich would look after me, and I was thrilled to be able to look after him.

The only tinge of sadness I felt on an otherwise happy day was the absence of my mother. I longed for her to be sitting in the front pew waiting for me to walk down the aisle. Although she wasn't with me, I felt some sense of her spirit being there.

We stood before a small group of family and friends and vowed to be faithful until death part us; we promised to better understand ourselves, the world and God, through the best and worst of what was to come, 'as long as we both shall live'.

There was no wedding cake or banquet – that just wasn't how things were usually done in Germany at that time. It was understated. Our reception for thirty close friends and family was held at my father's home, and at midnight Friedrich and I left for our honeymoon on the windswept island of Sylt, off the west coast of Germany, near the Danish border.

On our wedding night, as the wild Baltic Sea pounded the coastline outside our cabin, Friedrich cuddled me up close and kissed me tenderly, and for the first time we truly became one.

Almost nine months to the day of our wedding, on a warm August morning, our honeymoon baby, Friedrich Georg Bolten, arrived safely after a home delivery at the Boltens' family farm, Suenderuphof, where we had been living in our own small cottage since our marriage. He was the fifth Friedrich Georg in the Bolten family, another heir to the farming dynasty.

I've never seen Friedrich so emotional. Tears ran down his cheeks as the midwife lifted the red-faced bundle up for his father to see. '*Wunderbar, Frauke. Wunderbar!*' he cried.

While the nurse wrapped up baby Friedrich Jnr, or Fritz as he would be known, in a blanket, Friedrich raced outside and began yelling our good news to all of the farm workers.

'*Es ist ein Junge!*' – It's a boy! – he screamed, running through the sheds, waving his arms with glee. Watching him through the window, we giggled as he then climbed to the top of the silo, continuing to shout, '*Es ist ein Junge!*'

I'm sure all of the workers on the Boltens' farm and every other farm nearby heard our joyous news. They also heard Friedrich's deathly screams as he lost his footing on the way back down and fell 5 metres onto the concrete-hard earth below.

After a sickening thump, there was silence.

The midwife raced outside to find Friedrich's limp body

lying in the dirt and for a split second she thought he was dead, but after a few deep gasps, getting air back into his winded lungs, he shook himself off and started laughing. She helped him inside, his ribs and his ego bruised, and tucked him into bed beside me and our new baby.

'Friedrich!' I cried. 'You silly man!' He was white. The fall had sucked the colour from him and he spent the next few days recovering.

The Boltens were so proud that we'd produced another heir that they gave me a precious diamond ring, an heirloom Friedrich's father had given to my mother-in-law when Friedrich was born. I treasured it.

When Fritz was six months old, I fell pregnant again. Like her brother, Margret Liselotte Bolten arrived safely at home. It was just before Christmas 1970. Two babies in two years was quite a handful, but motherhood was precious and I loved every moment of it.

Like my father had, Friedrich adopted a very traditional approach to parenting. His role was running the farm, while mine was taking care of the household and family. He adored his children but he never once changed a nappy, and I didn't complain – that's just how it was back then. It worked for us: we were running a successful farm and the household was very organised. We made a great team.

We had 170 hectares of wheat, barley and canola planted, produced 200,000 chickens a year for meat and at one stage we also had ninety milking cows. But Friedrich was never content to rest, always looking for the next opportunity to do things bigger, better; always finding new ways and learning more about farming. So I guess I wasn't entirely surprised when he very casually told me over dinner one evening that we were moving to Africa.

Chapter 2

'*Mhoro, mauya*, hello and welcome to Salisbury,' the captain said. After an exhausting eighteen-hour journey via London with two lively toddlers in tow, we had finally arrived.

The intense blast of hot air when we stepped down onto the tarmac instantly woke our travel-weary bones. The humidity was thick and stifling, nothing like we'd ever experienced in Germany, not even on the hottest days. But I relished the sun on my back and the warm air filling my lungs.

A carpet of thick purple petals welcomed us to Rhodesia, now known as Zimbabwe. It was the beginning of the wet season and the jacaranda trees were still in full bloom. Roads around the international airport were lined with the sprawling trees. Their majestic blossoms showered brilliant mauve petals onto the scorched red earth every time a breeze from the Indian Ocean blew across Mozambique. A sea of purple ran to the cloudless horizon.

I thought I'd arrived in heaven.

I was so excited when Friedrich told us we were going to Africa. The furthest I'd ever travelled was a trip to Frankfurt after I finished school. I knew when I married Friedrich that a world of adventure awaited us, but Africa was beyond my wildest dreams. I also looked forward to skipping the freezing German winter.

Friedrich had been offered a ten-month placement working on a property outside Salisbury, now Harare, with farmers George and Lyn Matsukis. George, who was friends with a German family we knew, had earned a reputation for his uncanny ability to grow crops in arid, subtropical climates.

His invitation was a wonderful opportunity for Friedrich to learn how to adapt crops to challenging conditions and a chance for us to see a part of the world I thought I'd only ever see in books and movies. It was, in many ways, like a long working holiday.

Before we left Flensburg, I found pictures of Rhodesia and other African countries in old magazines and library books and tried to help the children create a mental picture of where we were headed. They were very small – Fritz was three and Margret not quite two years old – and I don't think they really understood what was happening. We were all wide eyed with wonder when we landed in Salisbury.

The colours of the landscape changed rapidly as we drove out of town to our new home in Shamva, an hour north of the city. The rich red earth, covered with miles and miles of thorny savanna, painted a very different picture to the endless rolling green pastures of home. So too did the Rhodesian people, an eclectic mix of pale-skinned expat Brits and exquisite dark-skinned Africans who spoke sixteen different languages.

Our home for the next ten months was a rustic two-bedroom weatherboard farmhouse nestled among hectares of crops. The view from the veranda, which swept all the way around the house, was of endless rows of thigh-high green cotton plants to one side and the mountains of the nearby Shamva gold mine curtaining the horizon on the other.

The farmhouse was basic but comfortable; we hadn't expected luxury. Fragrant frangipani trees dotted the garden and gave us much-needed shade. My prayers for sun and warmth were well and truly answered in Rhodesia. We had arrived during the hottest wet season in fifty years and enjoyed day after day of cloudless skies and sunshine – sun, glorious sun.

I adapted very quickly to the weather – I absolutely loved it – but it was quite difficult for Friedrich, who found himself working in intense heat, without all of the comforts of home. It was virtually impossible to get any sort of electrical goods because of sanctions against Ian Smith's government, which had declared independence from the Common-wealth in 1970. The iron was an old heavy metal one that you heated on the stove, there were no fans to help cool us and our refrigerator was primitive by comparison to what we'd had back home. We'd left arguably the most modern country in the world and arrived in a place where time had stood still.

Early one morning while I was chasing the children around the garden, I spotted one of the young farm workers walking rather intently towards us, armed with an enormous silver weapon over his shoulder.

It was a metre-long object, razor-like and so obviously sharp it sparkled in the sun. My stomach squirmed and I was uneasy.

'Time for morning tea, hurry along!' I cheerfully chimed, lifting Margret onto my hip while shooing Fritz inside the house. I carefully slid the bolt on the door behind us and looked out the flywire door – curious, if not slightly alarmed – to see where he was going.

The strapping man, who looked no older than fourteen or fifteen, stopped just inside the gate to our house. He unhooked the leather strap he had been using to carry the heavy object, then took his place, standing squarely in the grass.

With one enormous heave, he swung the piercing blade up over his shoulder and furiously sliced it towards the ground, beginning a rhythmic swaying movement backwards and forwards. The weapon, a cross between a machete and a sickle, with a huge and fierce-looking hook at the end, was in fact a lawnmower, African style.

For hours I watched, almost hypnotised by his smooth, ancient movements; it was as if he was engaged in a beautiful, almost spiritual dance; the taming of the wild grass.

Apart from a handful of little shops and a tiny bakery in Shamva, most of our shopping was done once a month in Salisbury and it was quite a big adventure. I needed Friedrich's help because everything came in bulk and we had to buy enough to last a month, so we had huge hessian bags of flour and boxes of powdered milk, but sometimes we got fresh milk from the Matsukis' farm, which was wonderful. It was our first taste of what life is like when you live in a remote place.

Fritz and Margret loved to roam and explore, and they took great delight in heading down to the channels at the back of the farm. The Mazowe River was nearby but we were warned not to swim there because the water was unsafe. Bilharzia, 'snail disease', was common in the rivers around the area, which were infested with parasites that could cause the internal organs to completely shut down. Even on the hottest days, when our farm workers used the river water for irrigating, they had to wear raincoats and boots to protect themselves.

The river locals also weren't the most welcoming.

On our first trip to the river, we could spot him off in the distance, his leathery back just skimming the top of the water as he rolled around in the shallows.

Then he lifted his enormous head and spotted us too.

Staring straight at us, the enormous hippo opened his cavernous mouth as wide as he could and bellowed a warning that we were not to come any closer, this was his turf. Fritz's eyes were as wide as saucers as the hippo slowly waded through the muddy water, two calf-like ears cocked, listening, and his eyes following our every move.

He was majestic but hippos are aggressive. We sat painfully still in thick grass high up on the riverbank and watched from a safe distance, as the hippo eyed us off while skulking his way along the edge of the river. With one eye trained on us the whole time, he carefully procured his lunch by stretching out a long pinky-grey tongue and picking off leaves from the scrub lining the muddy riverbank. It was exhilarating watching this majestic creature in his natural environment.

I longed for little adventures like this because I had quickly become quite bored during the day at the farm. It was an unwritten rule that farmers had to employ local workers, not just for farm work but to help with the household too. We had a wonderful group of people who worked for us, including a housekeeper and a nanny to care for the children. While it was a luxury to have so much help around the house, I was used to running a very busy household and raising my children myself. Suddenly I was out of a job.

It was the same for the other farmers' wives on neighbouring properties, so we would visit one another, and I made some wonderful friends. Every Saturday a group of us gathered at the farm of Mr and Mrs Muton, our neighbours. Mr Muton taught us how to shoot so we could protect ourselves in case we were ever attacked. I enjoyed the company of the women and we had a lot of fun learning how to navigate a rifle, but I prayed I'd never need to use one.

Political tensions had been bubbling for some time in the country, which was run by a largely white government. Although many farm workers were well looked after, some black people were still oppressed. The Zimbabwe African National Liberation Army (ZANLA) wanted freedom for their people and were waging a brutal and bloody guerrilla war.

It wasn't long after we arrived that we got our first real taste of what it meant to be living in the middle of a civil war, when ZANLA insurgents with grenades and assault rifles attacked a tobacco farm owned by a white family about an hour's drive from us. The next night another property was shelled with mortar fire.

Most of the country's farms were run by white people and were very well run. But the shadows of darker days lingered and the ZANLA had drawn up a list of farmers they intended to attack. Our farm relied on the help of our workers, who we treated as family, and we were confident our good reputation would protect us.

I immersed myself in learning the local languages, which were tricky. Most people spoke Shona or Ndebele. Friedrich got up at 4am each day and practised learning the language before he went out into the fields so he could communicate with the farm workers.

At the tender age of three, Fritz mastered Shona almost immediately and was fluent within weeks of us arriving.

For months I watched the cotton crops slowly stretching towards the sky, and then came the magical bloom of the pink and cream flowers and the ripening of the boll, which signalled that the cotton – *mudonje* as it was called – was on its way. By harvest time, we had over three hundred people working with us on the farm, day and night, picking cotton by hand.

After weeks of work, the last of the giant bales had finally been packed onto a truck headed for the gin in Bindura at midnight. It was our first cotton crop and we felt triumphant when the truck rolled down the gravel driveway.

We were a little sad to bid farewell to Rhodesia. Our ten months had been a time of great happiness and even though the landscape could be harsh, the people were wonderful and the simple lifestyle was a breath of fresh air. I'd miss the warmth, the cloudless skies and the sweet scent of frangipanis drifting through our bedroom window in the morning. Africa had stolen my heart, and I returned to Germany with memories that warmed my soul during the chilly winter.

Later I would realise that Friedrich left part of his heart in Africa. He came home with dust and desert in his blood, in love with the physical and mental challenges and the overwhelming triumph of bringing life to the harshest earth. Rhodesia had planted a seed of confidence in him that had fully taken root by the time our plane touched down in Frankfurt.

Just a few seconds after I turned on the tap, the hot water gushed out and ran down my back, instantly soothing my spine and muscles – oh the joy of hot running water for the first time in almost a year! I stood under the shower for what felt like an eternity, the warm steam softening my bones. We were home and the creature comforts we'd taken for granted before our trip were now very much appreciated.

Our return coincided with Fritz's fourth birthday, so a special celebration was in order. It gave me such joy to snip the last of the late-summer sunflowers from the garden. I filled big vases of the brilliant yellow blooms, which instantly brought a 'welcome home' cheer to the house.

As a special treat for Fritz and Margret, I always made them a traditional German tree cake, *Baumkuchen*, for their birthdays. For the grand occasion of Fritz's birthday, I added a few extra layers of the fine sponge and was particularly proud of how toweringly tall it sat on the cake stand waiting to be devoured.

Cooking always gave me a great deal of pleasure, and I was thrilled to be back in my kitchen with a pantry full to the brim and a stove you could turn on with the flick of a knob. After the dinner plates were whisked away, my ginger-blond firecracker blew the candles out on his birthday cake, then promptly fell asleep!

Friedrich carried him upstairs and I tucked him into bed. *'Alles Gute zum Geburtstag, Fritz. Ich liebe dich,'* I whispered as I kissed him on the forehead – happy birthday, Fritz. I love you.

He was feeling warmer than normal but after a long day getting reacquainted with the farm, he'd run himself ragged and needed to rest. I went into Margret's room and kissed her goodnight, and she felt a little warmer than normal too.

The children both had temperatures and during the night Margret coughed persistently. I reasoned that with the long flight and the excitement of arriving home the children were probably coming down with colds, and tomorrow they would need to rest.

Both children woke up irritable and niggly, and by the afternoon a dotty red rash had appeared across Margret's face.

'Fritz, lift up your shirt,' I said, beginning to sense that this was more than a cold. 'Is your tummy sore?' I asked. He nodded, and I could see a fine red rash developing; I knew what this meant. We raced into town to our family doctor, who confirmed my hunch that Fritz and Margret had rubella.

Other than giving them oatmeal baths to soothe their skin and paracetamol to ease their pain, there was very little we could do to help them until the virus passed. Both children were to be confined to bed for a week until the rash had gone and they were feeling well again. We kept our fingers and toes crossed that the virus hadn't been passed on to anyone else, but only time would tell.

Although I didn't have any of the symptoms, the doctor had taken a precautionary blood sample from me too. He called three days later with the news that I had rubella as well.

But I was also eight weeks pregnant. My heart sank.

Rubella is one of the most serious complications pregnant women can have. The doctor told me there was a strong chance it would lead to a stillbirth or miscarriage, and potentially terrible defects for the baby. The earlier the infection in pregnancy, the higher the risk. At just eight weeks along, I was in the most dangerous range.

The standard medical response at the time was to end the pregnancy. This was incredibly confronting for Friedrich and me, but we both knew in our hearts that this pregnancy could not go ahead. I cried myself to sleep that night because we desperately wanted another child.

After the termination, test results showed the tiny foetus was seriously unwell too. Although the experience had been harrowing, we'd made the right decision.

We licked our wounds and when everyone was fully recovered and rubella long gone, we resumed trying, believing that God would bless us with a new baby when the time was right.

Chapter 3

With all he'd learnt in Africa, Friedrich was excited about the potential of the crops we could sow now we were back in Germany. He was also energised by the prospect of international partnerships.

The Duke of Schleswig-Holstein was passionate about this too and invited a group of German farmers, including Friedrich, to get together to talk about expanding their businesses. They began to take regular familiarisation tours – or 'famils' as they're known – to study the methods used on other farms, and their successes and failures. I didn't begrudge Friedrich's time away at all, because it was a wonderful means of companionship for men who often worked in isolation.

After only a few months back home from Rhodesia, I could tell Friedrich was getting restless; he had a head full of ideas and he wanted to challenge himself. He often spoke about setting up a farm in another part of the world and tossed up the idea of heading back to Africa.

Despite the distance from home and the dangers of the simmering civil war, he was convinced of the untapped potential of the subtropical region.

He became quite obsessed by his desire to expand our business and would reminisce fondly about Shamva. I loved Friedrich's passion and enthusiasm, but I wasn't keen to pack up and go again. I'm not a tree that's easily replanted. My desire was to build a home and a family of my own, to establish roots and fill the enormous void of family love I was denied as a child. As much as I'd enjoyed our time in Africa, I had no desire to ever leave home again.

In late 1975, the Flensburg council approached us because the town was expanding and they needed more land for a housing development, a university and a bypass road. As we bordered the edge of the town, they hoped we'd agree to sell some of our land.

The price they offered us was very generous and we happily signed the contracts. Although this land was part of the Bolten family property, Father Bolten had given it to us.

With extra cash in the bank, Friedrich was eager to invest in a new property, one that was ours alone. Much to my chagrin, he decided to travel to South Africa to look at potential farms. However, one of our dear friends, a farmer named Peter Schmidtsdorf, offered to go on a trip to Johannesburg to take a look at property and report back on what sort of land was available. We trusted Peter's opinion, and this arrangement was preferable to Friedrich heading off on a whim. We paid for Peter's trip and his flight insurance

Peter's Lufthansa flight from Frankfurt to Johannesburg stopped to refuel in Nairobi. An hour later, the Boeing 747 rolled back down the runway headed for Johannesburg – but passengers very quickly sensed something was wrong. They recalled a feeling of lurching soon after the engines began thrusting, and the plane didn't feel like it was going fast enough to take off.

Reassuringly, near the end of the runway the nose began to lift, followed by the front wheels, but then the jumbo began to shudder violently. Inside the cabin, luggage flew from the overhead lockers, glasses smashed in the galley and passengers screamed in panic.

Unable to lift off properly, the plane skimmed a concrete barrier and crashed to the ground at 250 kilometres per hour. The plane tore apart, one wing shearing through the side of it like a can opener, spilling fuel all over the strewn wreckage. Instantly, it exploded into flames.

News of the accident swept through Germany; this was a great tragedy for our beloved national carrier. Miraculously, there were survivors among the 157 people on board and Friedrich reassured me: 'He'll be fine, Frauke.' Sadly, he wasn't. Our friend Peter, a father of three young children, was killed.

We were gutted by the news and Friedrich took it very badly. He was terribly shaken by the loss of his friend, and the thought that this could've been him weighed on us both.

Immediately after the accident, Friedrich took out life insurance. He was distressed at the thought of Peter's wife being left to raise children with no support.

For now, Africa would have to wait, but Friedrich never gave up believing that there was something bigger and better on the horizon and that our future was far away from Germany.

With the windfall from the sale of our land, we purchased a new property in Seedorf, which is about a two-and-a-half-hour drive south of Flensburg, near the city of Lübeck. On more than 300 hectares, we began to build our own home and developed a very productive farm with impressive crops of wheat, barley, sugar beets and canola. We rented a house nearby while our own home was being built and began a new life.

We were so lucky to have lived on the family farm; it gave us an opportunity to establish ourselves and I'll always be grateful to the Boltens, but having our own farm was something very special and I felt this was a new beginning for our family.

I longed to have more children, and we had been trying, but my body wasn't making it easy.

I fell pregnant again after being given the all clear from the doctors following the rubella. The telltale nausea and tiredness were an immediate giveaway that another Bolten was on the way.

For a week before Christmas, I was busy every day, filling the house with the smell of gingerbread and spice biscuits and plum pudding. I fell into bed one night feeling tired but so happy with myself that I'd wrapped all the presents and decorated a fir tree Friedrich had freshly cut from the woods near the farm. We were organised.

During the night I didn't sleep well; I tossed and turned and gently rubbed my belly, failing to settle the niggles that were becoming more like a cramping sensation across my stomach and back. When I turned in bed, a sharp stabbing pain went through me. Friedrich made hot water bottles to comfort me, but nothing seemed to ease the pain.

Just before dawn, a great rush of fluid gushed down my legs – it was blood and I was bleeding heavily.

Friedrich called an ambulance and I was rushed to the hospital. By the time we arrived, I was haemorrhaging badly and I knew I'd lost the baby. I was sixteen weeks along and we were devastated.

I spent the next two weeks in hospital over Christmas and was released just after New Year. I tried my best to put on a brave face and be as cheery as I could for the children but my heart was broken; I wondered if we'd ever have another child.

It was a very long two years before I fell pregnant again. Just after celebrating the New Year in 1979, the telltale morning sickness began. Knowing how nervous I was about this pregnancy, my doctor kept a very close eye on me, checking me every week.

Everything was going well and I was taking things very easily around the house, until the fifteen-week mark, when I began to get contractions – not Braxton Hicks, but real contractions. I was rushed to hospital and given medication to stop the onset of labour. For almost a month I stayed there resting completely until the doctors thought I was stable enough to head home, but only on the promise of complete bed rest.

If I had to stay in bed for the rest of my life I would do it. I would've done anything to make sure this baby was delivered safely.

Being stuck in bed wasn't much fun but Friedrich did his best to help me and thankfully we had several home economics apprentices helping us, just as I had done with the Boltens. Friedrich always brought me a newspaper when he came in for his lunch, and I looked forward to him popping in. I devoured every conversation or snippet of news from outside the house and the bedroom where I was patiently growing our baby.

This particular day, he rushed in quite excitedly with the newspapers under his arm. 'Frauke, you must hear this, you will not believe it, it's the great escape!'

Friedrich cuddled up on the bed next to me and began reading the front page story aloud. 'In the middle of the night two East German families, flying a homemade hot air balloon, crossed the border into West Germany and landed safely in a field.'

Our farm was near Zarrentin, only 5 kilometres from the border between East and West Germany, so the tragedy and fear of the divided Germany was very close to home. It was rare that anyone escaped East Germany alive.

Eager to find out how, Friedrich read on. The two wives had made a patchwork balloon from bed sheets, shower curtains and old raincoats while the husbands, both aircraft mechanics, put together a makeshift gondola right under the noses of the Stasi. When the wind was just right, they grabbed their children and took off with just minutes to make their escape.

There's no doubt they would've been shot if they'd been seen. I thought of the women cowering in the bottom of the basket, covering their children and praying they wouldn't be gunned down, such bravery for a taste of freedom. By the time the balloon rose above the nearby forest where they'd found a small clearing, they were virtually out of reach of border patrol guards and their guns. Their safe landing on the other side of the border was nothing short of a miracle.

These families graced the front cover of newspapers and magazines all over the West and Walt Disney made a movie about their ordeal. The division of our homeland was heart-breaking for all Germans, and Friedrich and I both felt very strongly about it. Friedrich refused to acknowledge the separation and always wrote 'Germany' on his correspondence, not 'West Germany'. This story warmed our hearts.

Less than a month later, the next big adventure in our lives began to unfold when I went into labour. With the fear of miscarriage haunting us, this time my baby would be delivered in hospital. We'd fought hard for this little one's arrival, so we were leaving nothing to chance. The birth was complicated: the baby was posterior, facing into my stomach instead of my back. It was a long and painful delivery but every ounce of pain was forgotten the moment the midwife lifted the hungry, crying bundle into my arms.

'It's a boy!' she exclaimed, and with an impressive cry, Peter Heinrich Bolten let the world know he had arrived. We named Peter after Peter Schmidtsdorf and our uncle Peter-Hartwig Petersen. I was besotted and spent hours staring at my little Peter, counting his fingers and toes, re-counting his fingers and toes. He was absolutely perfect and my world felt complete.

Chapter 4

Peter instantly stole our hearts and blended into family life without a hitch; he was a very settled baby and, other than a cheerful gurgle every now and then, we barely heard a peep from him. Fritz, at ten years old, was growing into a fine young man, the spitting image of his father. Eight-year-old Margret, with her mass of curls, mirrored me. Peter was a good blend of us both. He had Friedrich's fine blond hair and blue eyes and my smile.

Fritz and Margret adored him as much as we did. I'd often find Fritz crouched beside the cot, 'shaking hands' with Peter, the baby's tiny fingers wrapped around Fritz's big thumb. Margret was a natural mother, offering to change his nappy and dress him at every opportunity.

Our miracle baby was hardly ever alone; there was always someone cuddling him or trying to catch his attention in the crib. It was very easy to while away the hours, completely besotted by his big toothless smile.

After years of planning and smoothing out niggling hurdles with the local council, the new home we'd been building on our farm in Seedorf was finally ready for us to move into. I'd dreamt of this day for a very long time and I heaved an enormous sigh of relief when we carried the last box into our new house.

Our new farm was about 300 hectares surrounded by thick forest. The house was a modern wood building with rich timber fittings inside, Canadian red cedar shingles covering the outside and enormous windows offering lovely views of the fields and forest. From the living room we quite often saw red deer, wild pigs and pheasants foraging for food.

It was the most wonderful place to raise our children, and they enjoyed the same freedom I'd had as a child when I played with Dorte and the boys from the neighbouring farm.

I sent my children off in the morning and as long as they were home by 6pm, sitting up straight at the table, hands washed, ready to eat, they were relatively free to explore the neighbourhood.

Margret had two ponies, Ilka and Tipsy, which she rode all day. She'd ride to the farm next door and play with the girls who lived there; they'd saddle up their ponies and canter off together.

Fritz was his father's son: he was happiest when he was shadowing Friedrich tinkering around the farm, or exploring the world around him. When he wasn't doing that, he would go fishing or hunting, and sometimes camp out in a tent we'd put up for him in the fields. Every day was a Boy's Own adventure for Fritz, and his fearless streak sometimes led to trouble.

I knew he and Margret had wonderful adventures but sometimes I didn't know what they'd done until after the event, which was probably lucky!

Margret sometimes did gymnastics after school and one particular afternoon, running late and with a flat tyre on her bike, she asked Fritz if she could take his.

'No,' was the typically blunt big-brother response.

'But Fritz, you're not riding it and I'm late,' she begged.

'No,' came the answer again. 'Nick off.'

So Margret did what any self-respecting younger sister would do. She bolted out the front door, scooped up her brother's bike and took off, pedalling furiously down the driveway.

She'd ridden about 300 metres from the house when she heard a shot ring out. Suddenly she felt a stinging, burning sensation in her leg and blood began to soak through her jeans. The bike and Margret both came to a crashing halt.

Fritz had shot her with his air rifle! He'd been aiming to shoot the tyre so she couldn't ride the bike, but had missed.

Luckily, she was fine, but both of them knew I would be furious, so a deal was made to keep it secret. That didn't last long.

'Margret, what happened to your leg?' I asked over breakfast the next morning, running my hand over the enormous purple bruise that popped out below her pretty gingham dress.

I smelt a rat. The stunned silence that greeted me gave a clear hint I needed to do a little more investigating.

'Okay, which one of you is going to tell me what happened, because the one who doesn't will be the one in trouble.'

'Fritz shot me!' Margret blurted out.

'It was an accident, Mutti, I swear, I swear,' Fritz begged.

They both gave their versions of the event, talking over the top of one another so quickly I could barely understand a word they said, but I heard enough to get the gist. Our house was normally very calm and I rarely yelled at my children, but I was a raging bull and Fritz copped an earful that could've been heard in China. He was grounded and the air rifle confiscated. The adventures of Huckleberry Bolten had come to an abrupt end.

The farm was very run-down when we bought it, and Friedrich set to work immediately to make it productive but there was still much to do. Even though we were now living on site and it was just a short walk to the sheds, Friedrich left home long before dawn every day to dig the soil, prepare the fields for crops, grade and separate rows for sowing. He ploughed hundreds of hectares, and settled on alternating crops of wheat, barley and canola depending on the seasons.

Friedrich never slept in. From sun-up to sunset he worked his fingers to the bone. I made his favourite *Milch* soup, like a porridge, for breakfast and he came home for a hot lunch every day to keep his energy up. Most days, I made lunch for all of the farm workers, and I enjoyed my role cooking for the hungry men. Happy workers meant a healthy farm, and it gave me a strong purpose each day and the feeling that I was playing a valuable role.

Farm life became increasingly busy and so, we took on a young home economics apprentice permanently, just as Mrs Bolten had done with me. Steffi lived with us and quickly became part of the family; she was a wonderful help to me, and the children adored her. I was always grateful for her extra pair of hands.

Living at the farm, there was no such thing as popping to the shops or running to the supermarket. Ratzeburg and Moelln, both ten minutes' drive away, were our nearest towns, and when we did go shopping there, it was for the little luxuries we couldn't make ourselves like special cheeses and coffee. Otherwise we lived by the rule that if we didn't grow it or we couldn't make it, we didn't have it. We killed our own game and had a thriving garden.

It didn't take long for us to really hit our stride, and after a few years of hard work the farm was financially thriving. We had a new home and a new car. We had created the life that I'd always dreamt of and longed for, and I was blissfully happy. But Friedrich still had itchy feet.

He longed for the warmth and wonder of Zimbabwe, especially during the subzero winter mornings in Germany when we had to scrape the snow away from the door to get out.

When he was invited to join a famil to Australia with a renowned European farming company, Velcourt, he jumped at the chance. They were visiting Perth with German agriculture academic Dr Herman Effland to look at cropping techniques and ways to improve yields. Friedrich was an admirer of Dr Effland's work and he was proud to have been asked along.

He asked me to come too but I had no interest in a trip to Australia and there was no way I was going to leave the children for four weeks, especially Peter, who was still a baby. I was happy to stay home and keep an eye on the farm while Friedrich had a break.

'The sun, Frauke!' he enthused when he called to say they'd arrived in Perth. 'It never ends!'

He was clearly enjoying himself and soaking up this country that was so foreign to Germans. I was very happy for him; some sunshine on his bones would help ready him for the long winter when he returned.

While he was in Perth, Friedrich was introduced to Harry Perkins, a very successful Western Australian farmer. Harry talked about crops and yields and wheat with the same passion and ferocity as Friedrich, and the two of them got along like a house on fire.

In the rare moments we got to speak on the phone, Friedrich peppered his conversations with anecdotes about this visionary man who'd set up the Three Tonne Club, a group of farmers working towards the goal of being able to harvest 3 tonnes of wheat off 300 millimetres of rain. These sorts of yields were unheard of at that time, farmers wouldn't have dared dream of such a result. Harry sounded part visionary, part renegade – no wonder they got along so well.

Over dinner and a few glasses of wine at a Perth restaurant, the farmers from opposite sides of the world got chatting about the magnificent Ord River irrigation scheme on the northern tip of Western Australia, a stone's throw from the border with the Northern Territory. Crocodile country, thousands of kilometres away.

'It's turned desert in a virtual no man's land into rich farming land,' Harry boasted. 'It's a bloody miracle!'

Friedrich booked a flight to this oasis the very next day. He flew from Perth to Kununurra, back to Perth then home to Germany via Malaysia. Quite a detour.

Fritz and Margret raced with arms stretched out wide to embrace Friedrich when he emerged from the pack of weary travellers at Hamburg airport. His creamy skin was slightly pink from sunburn but he looked more relaxed than I'd ever seen him.

We had arrived early to meet his flight, because we all got such a thrill from visiting this very cosmopolitan, bustling place. Fritz and Margret loved watching the enormous Lufthansa jets take off and land, and hearing the noise of the giant engines humming.

I expected Friedrich to be tired after his flight but during the hour-long trip home he barely took a breath, telling us about all of the things he'd seen.

'The sun and the soil are so rich, Frauke, they can grow anything,' he enthused. He told me how much bigger Australian watermelons grew, spreading his hands out wide to show me the size.

He regaled us with stories of his adventure, of the enormous crocodiles that stared him down from the waters of the Ord River, of the dusty pink horizon like 'nothing you could ever imagine', and the taste of the exotic mangoes and their sweet juice dripping down his chin, 'the most amazing thing I've ever eaten'.

Something other than mosquitoes had bitten Friedrich during this trip; he had fallen in love with this wild faraway place and couldn't shake it out of his mind. When he laid out a map of the Kimberley on our kitchen table and pulled out a dusty packet of pictures for us to see, I soon learnt this was far more than a sentimental longing.

He grabbed my hands and held them tight in his and, looking at me with wide eyes, he said, 'I have some exciting news, Frauke. I've found a house and a farm in Kununurra. I want us to move to Australia.'

I couldn't even get my tongue around the word Kun-un-urr-a, let alone get my head around where this place was. At first, I thought he was joking, testing the waters to see what I'd say. But when he called the children into his office, sat them down and explained that we were moving to Australia, I knew this was no joke. Later, I discovered that the moment

Friedrich arrived in Kununurra he had made up his mind that this was where our future would be.

With Harry's help, he had looked at farms and land, found a property and begun the necessary paperwork. By the time his plane landed back in Germany, visa documentation was already on its way to us.

Friedrich had chosen 1000 hectares on the fertile flood-plain of the Ord River – an oasis, so he said. All we needed to do was sign loan documents with the bank in Germany and arrange the transfer of the money.

There was no lovemaking that night – not even a friendly peck on the cheek goodnight – even though my husband had been away for a month. I could barely look at him.

We were turning our backs on everything we had worked for – and worse, borrowing money to fund it. We'd never borrowed a dollar in our lives prior to this; now we would be in debt.

That night, I rolled away from him, tucked the sheets in tight around me and cried myself to sleep. For the first time, Friedrich and I fought, really fought, when we'd never even really argued before. We fought for weeks. How could he do this? Australia was such a long way from our home and our family, from all we'd worked to build, and I did not want to move there. I wasn't interested one little bit; but he'd made up his mind and I was left with no choice.

When we said our wedding vows, I accepted my role in the marriage. Friedrich was the decision maker and that's how things were to be. But even still we always spoke about things, so I was deeply hurt that he'd made such a big decision without consulting me.

Uprooting us again to move to the opposite side of the world had no appeal to me at all.

Friedrich cleverly worked his charm on the children, building an unwavering alliance to help win me over. He whipped them into a frenzy of excitement, telling Fritz stories of crazy adventures he could have in the outback, and painting images of swimming in warm-water springs and enjoying endless sunshine, which delighted Margret.

He could've told them they were going to the moon and they would have followed him. He was so passionate and excited about this big adventure, and they adored their father – they fell into step effortlessly.

Frauke may mean 'little lady' but this little lady was no pushover, and he needed to mount a better offensive to win me over.

Not surprisingly, he had a plan. His battle tactics changed markedly: rather than continue talking in terms of a fait accompli, which riled me, he began talking about the business of farming and the opportunity for us to cement a future our forefathers could only have dreamt of.

This was an opportunity for us to prove what we could achieve with rich soil and endless water. We would create farms that Germans would envy. Then he launched his final attack, guerrilla warfare on my heartstrings, my weak spot: the children. The rivers, the lakes, the adventure and the endless sunshine would be perfect for the family, he reasoned. No more cold winters and illness, no more fear of a Germany divided into east and west by a wall. Our children would thrive, they would be strong and independent, in a peaceful country, a land of freedom.

His decision took our marriage to the brink, but I would never have left him. That just wasn't an option.

Then came an olive branch that sealed the deal: we would go to Australia for two years and two years only, and Friedrich would arrange a visa for Steffi to come too so I had help.

After two years we would return home to the farm. It would be just like Zimbabwe.

A peace deal had been brokered and the warring territories were reunited.

We put away most of our clothes in the attic and packed only a few suitcases of the lightest clothes we had. We left our furniture, wedding presents and most of our belongings in the house and locked the doors behind us; friends would move in to look after the farm and our home while we were gone.

After saying our farewells to family at the airport, we boarded the plane and got settled for our very long flight. Fritz was excited, but by this time Margret was inconsolable because she'd had to say goodbye to her ponies.

We had brought Peter's favourite soft toy, a puppy dog, on board with us. But rather than Peter being soothed by the toy, it was Margret who cuddled it up tight under her arm and cried into it. That was until the ever-resourceful Fritz worked out that he could make his little sister smile with an endless supply of Coca-Cola from the generous air hostess. My children never drank soft drinks unless it was a very special occasion, so they guzzled them down like it was Christmas the whole way. Each sugary glass seemed to help wash away Margret's sadness.

Peter was quite restless on the flight; he was teething and I reasoned that the air pressure was probably playing havoc with his ears too. Steffi and I took turns walking up and down the aisle trying to rock him to sleep. It was a godsend having an extra pair of hands to comfort him.

Twenty-four very long hours later, with a stop in Malaysia, we finally made it to Australia. We were to spend the first few days in Perth, in the southwest corner of

Western Australia, a state seven times the size of Germany. Then we would head to Kununurra, 3200 kilometres away at the very top of Western Australia, near the border with the Northern Territory.

As soon as we touched down I could see why Friedrich had fallen in love with Australia: Perth was a beautiful city on the edge of a river, with the Indian Ocean lapping at its edges. A handful of high-rise buildings dotted the skyline but otherwise it was like a big country town, half the size of Hamburg, with acres of open space and parklands, and glorious sunshine.

As we came through the customs gates, a tall, sun-kissed man stretched out his hand towards Friedrich and they embraced warmly.

I'd heard a lot about the mysterious Harry Perkins. When Friedrich introduced us, I didn't know whether to punch him or kiss him! It was Harry who'd invited the European farmers to the Kimberley, introducing Friedrich to 'paradise'. It was Harry who had helped Friedrich buy our new home; this man I'd never met had seen my new home before I did.

It was 29 degrees the day we arrived; our lightest German shirts would be too warm for this weather. The next morning after breakfast, Margret and I headed off to the shops to find some more suitable clothes.

Boans, the major department store in Perth, was a quaint place steeped in history, with brass plaques by the door indicating it was a significant historical building, and lovely old wooden floorboards that squeaked when you stepped on them. We went up a marble staircase to the next level, but other than sunhats and a few cotton shirts, there wasn't much that appealed to me. I figured that I would wait until we got into our new house and see what else we needed, then purchase it in this place Kununurra, or via mail order like we did in Germany. I loved the thick glossy catalogues from Quelle and Neckermann arriving in the mailbox each month. We could order beautiful clothes and food – anything the heart desired – and it was delivered within a matter of days.

Peter continued to be unsettled and after he'd had several sleepless nights and a mild fever, I noticed a rash appearing on his tummy. From the moment I saw the angry red spots I knew that he had measles. We took him to a nearby clinic the next morning and the doctor confirmed the diagnosis. By that afternoon the poor little thing was covered in the most dreadful red rash and there was very little we could do to settle him. Thankfully we'd had him immunised in Germany, otherwise I'd hate to think of how serious it could have been.

Friedrich, Steffi and I took turns nursing him, which was the only thing that would keep him calm. The doctors warned us that the bright sunlight could blind him, and with his sensitive baby eyes we would need to keep him in a darkened room for a week until the rash and the virus had gone. So that's exactly what we did.

During the day, I sent Fritz and Margret out to play at a nearby park; they went off exploring and had a wonderful time, while we stayed inside in the dark, nursing Peter with cool baths and calamine lotion. What a welcome to Australia! Many, many times, I wanted to pack our bags and board the first available flight back to Germany.

In the nick of time, Peter's rash settled and the doctor gave us the all clear to fly to Kununurra. I was so relieved, I wanted to see our new home and get settled in to this paradise Friedrich raved about.

With Peter smothered in lotion to help stop the itch and dosed up with paracetamol to help soothe any potential earache, the Boltens finally began the last leg of a very long journey.

We boarded a Fokker Fellowship and for six hours we bobbed up and down between the clouds, catching glimpses of sandy desert and golden fields, a patchwork of arid colours below us. Fritz and Margret were glued to the windows, soaking up a landscape that was totally foreign to the lush green rolling hills of Northern Germany.

After a quick stop in Derby, the landscape began to change. The tapestry of brown, beige, cream and white salty desert morphed into pops of rusty red rocks and scorched orange earth with occasional tinges of green scrub.

As we began our descent, Friedrich pointed out the Ord River that snaked through huge rock escarpments and the desolate valley. It only just resembled the images in the dog-eared photographs he'd shown us.

He saw an oasis in the desert; I saw dirt, dust and bulldust, the odd stick-thin tree with a green cotton-ball canopy to break the sun's fall to the earth and strange bloated-looking boab trees dotting the scrub. Every now and then the sun would catch the top of a shed's roof and the corrugated iron would sparkle in the distance, but buildings were few and far between.

The plane banked around to prepare for landing and the airstrip came into view. I squeezed Friedrich's arm tight. How on earth would the pilot land this plane on a scratch in the earth that stopped dead in the middle of a field of rough cane grass?

The wheels of the plane were locked in place, ready for landing. Bright blue cloudless sky met the red dusty landscape at the horizon. No matter where you looked, dirt and sky were all that was to be seen. The airport was a lofty corrugated iron shed. I cuddled Peter up close as we bounced along the tarmac and pulled up in front of the tiny airport.

Fritz and Margret, dressed in their finest clothes, with shoes polished to perfection, were glued to the window with smiles from ear to ear.

When the flight attendant opened the door, we got our first true taste of the Kimberley. Intense heat rushed through the plane like a furnace, sucking the air from our lungs, and sticky black flies swarmed us. I thought we'd arrived in hell.

I hoisted Peter up onto my hip while Fritz reached for our bags from the overhead locker. By the time we gathered our things and got to the door, the metal handrail on the steps was so hot your fingers had to skip along it so they didn't get burned.

We hurried across the tarmac to the shed as the plane's turbines whizzed down to a slow humming stop. Sticky, melting tar stretched out like lengths of chewing gum under our feet and glued to our good shoes as we walked. 'No intelligent soul could live here,' I muttered under my breath.

We'd only been out in the heat for a few minutes but I was already sweating. And then the heavens began rumbling and suddenly opened up, dumping rain down on us, completely out of the blue.

No dark skies, no black warning clouds.

I've come to learn that these spontaneous downpours are common during the wet season. Dry one minute, bucketing the next.

Our brand-new expensive leather suitcases were soaked.

Welcome to Kununurra indeed.

At almost the same time on that very day, on the opposite side of the world, an almighty blast propelled NASA's first-ever space shuttle into orbit.

Two astronauts piloting the shuttle *Columbia* were rocketed into the future, crossing an unknown frontier, touching the stars and the heavens.

We too had arrived at an unknown frontier, surrounded by dust and dirt. But far from the future, we seemed to have taken one hellish leap back in time.

We were all so far from home.

Chapter 5

The storm left as quickly as it had arrived and the sky almost immediately returned to the brilliant cloudless blue that had greeted us when we stepped off the plane; what a strange place this was.

As we gathered up our belongings, a battered old white ute, its sides covered in thick red mud, swept around to the front of the hangar. 'G'day,' the driver said, unfolding his long limbs from behind the wheel. He stretched out a weathered brown hand and said, 'You must be Frauke. I'm Les. Welcome to Kununurra.' Les Jackson was a local farmer whom Friedrich had met when he visited, and I could tell right away that he was a knockabout kind of bloke who took great delight in welcoming newcomers to this faraway land.

By this time, I was desperate to get to our new home, wash the day away with a long soapy shower and begin to get settled in, as were the three wet and hungry children beside me. Hopefully God would've looked after us with some dry clothes tucked away in the middle of our otherwise sodden suitcases.

Friedrich loaded our bags onto the back of two utes; we rode with Les Jackson in the first one while the children and Steffi followed behind. We turned onto the Victoria Highway and began heading towards town in convoy.

Red dust 'and thick clumps of wiry-looking cane grass lined the roads to the left of us; on the right were the swollen bellies and spindly ghostlike arms of boab trees popping up through dry scrub. We were in the heart of a wide, flat valley framed by rocky outcrops and blood-orange-coloured stone like nothing I'd ever seen before.

A pretty blue lake appeared on our right – Lake Kununurra, Les explained. Huge green lily pads floated on the calm waters; I didn't dare imagine what might've been lurking underneath.

As the town appeared ahead of us, Les delivered a bombshell.

'Now, there's been a bit of a problem with the house,' he said with an air of confidence, not wanting to alarm us. 'The previous owners haven't quite finished moving out yet, but no need to worry, we've booked you into a nice motel and you can get settled in and stay there until you can move in. It'll be right as rain.'

My heart sank. We had a contract of sale and the owners were supposed to have moved out a week ago. They knew we were coming from Germany and I felt quite let down that our house wasn't ready, but Les didn't seem to be too bothered. Kununurra, I would find out, moves to its own beat, and Kununurra time means things might happen today or tomorrow or the day after – 'no worries, mate', all in good time.

Les pulled up to a brown brick motel on the side of the Victoria Highway, the main road in and out of town. Our 'nice' motel, The Swagman Inn, was pretty much the only accommodation in town other than the caravan park. It was a home away from home for interstate truck drivers doing the long stretches between isolated outback towns and cities thousands of kilometres away. Their huge B-double trucks lined the road and the car park.

I was just happy we'd have somewhere to rest our heads, and the motel had a pool so the kids were happy. Friedrich and I dropped our bags and dug out dry clothes, then hopped back into Les's ute for a tour of the town while Steffi took the kids for a swim to cool off.

'Town' was a fairly generous description of Kununurra and our tour didn't take long. It was a pretty little place, but there wasn't much of it. The main shopping strip was a few streets from the motel: one bank, a bakery, two grocery stores, a farm supplies shop and, of course, a pub. Friedrich's words – 'You can get everything you need in Kununurra, Frauke' – as we sat around the kitchen table in Germany a few weeks earlier were ringing in my ears.

The shopping strip was flanked by streets named after trees: Coolibah, Bauhinia, Rosewood. A handful of homes lined each street, all sitting high on stilts, with corrugated tin roofs that looked strange to my eyes because they didn't have gutters.

'That's because the rain in the wet season can be so fero-cious it would rip the spouting right off. One downpour and she'd be gone,' Les explained. He pointed out Kelly's Knob, a pretty rock escarpment that overlooked the town.

Kununurra was relatively new, he told us, then gave us a potted history. It was built to accommodate the men working on the Ord River dam diversion and was formally gazetted as a town in 1961. It should've been gazetted long before that but debate had raged about an appropriate name. The names Arawi and Ord were originally suggested, but the author Dame Mary Durack, whose family were pioneers of the Kimberley, suggested the land be named Cununurra, which meant 'black soil' and was the native name for the Ord River.

There was general agreement among the politicians that this was a good choice, but the postmaster general refused, arguing that it was too similar to Cunnamulla in Queensland and people would be confused. Resourceful Mary quickly put pen to paper again, changed the first letter, and so Kununurra was born.

Kununurra was surrounded by vast agricultural holdings, some of Australia's biggest cattle stations which spanned hundreds of thousands of inhospitable acres and held 40,000 or even 50,000 head of cattle, which thrived on the scrubby Mitchell grass. The scale of these farms was beyond our wildest imaginations and I could see why Friedrich was drawn here. He was enthusiastic about the potential for farming in this region, which he believed could be developed into a major global food producer.

But I couldn't shake the feeling that we were so far from home. This tiny village ten hours' drive from the nearest city – Darwin, in the Northern Territory – and half a world away from our family and friends was not my idea of paradise.

Farmers are naturally early risers but you have to be up pretty early to beat the sun in the Kimberley. By 6am, the brilliant pink sky is alive and the birdsong fills the air.

I woke to the sound of truck drivers grinding the gears of their huge road trains into action, rolling out for another day's driving. Some of these men would drive all day and not see a single soul or come across another town. It was already hot and I'd slept with just a sheet over me, sticky from the humidity.

Friedrich knew I was cross that we couldn't move into our house, so to take my mind off it, he planned a few days of adventures to show us around the area. He wanted us to see what he fell in love with. Our first excursion was to Lake Argyle, about an hour's drive from Kununurra. A freshwater dam, it is about twenty times the size of Sydney Harbour.

The clear blue water stretched as far as our eyes could see. It was like glass, flat and perfectly mirroring the steep red rock that formed the dam walls. It was a magical place.

'Let's swim,' Friedrich shouted, stripping his clothes off. He sprinted down the red dust bank and plunged into the water, Fritz and Margret racing behind to catch up. They squealed with delight as they hit the blue water, while I kicked my shoes off and buried my toes in the warm red dusty sand.

At home, we loved to swim in the Baltic Sea, which was a bit chillier than the tropical waters of the Kimberley.

We spent the whole day at the lake, swimming, lying on the banks with the sun soaking our bones, sleeping, and more swimming. I'd never heard Friedrich so chatty; he could barely contain his joy and I think it was one of the happiest days of our lives.

Over the next few days we took farm tours to meet other families and see how things were done here, hiked up Kelly's Knob to soak in the view, and explored other scenic sights like the Ivanhoe Crossing and the Hidden Valley.

I was coming to realise that this was a majestic place.

Friedrich had bought our new house off the promise of a few pictures and a real estate agent's glowing description.

As unhappy as I was about what he'd done, I agreed that it sounded wonderful: a brick home only a few years old, with hectares of green grass to one side, the other looking out onto the Ord River.

When word came that the previous owners had moved and we were good to go, we packed up the motel without a minute to waste and headed for our new home. The drive to Riverfarm Road took only a few minutes. We passed through town and as we headed towards the Ord River, rows of towering crops lined the road.

We turned off the main road and onto a long dirt track, swept around a bend past two other gates that led off to other houses along the riverbank, and arrived at our home.

'Well, here we are,' Friedrich said, grinning. 'Frauke, you take the keys, you do the honours.'

A musty dampness greeted us as I opened the door. We were told the owners had just moved out, but the house smelt like it had been locked up for some time. I walked across the living room to open the curtains and let some light in. I shouldn't have.

The curtains were covered in dust and daddy-long-legs spiders.

The children came running in behind me, with Steffi following, and went straight into exploring mode, searching out their rooms, opening cupboards and getting familiar with the place. I was still reeling from the state of the curtains when I heard a bloodcurdling scream from the passage.

It seemed not all of the home's residents had moved out. Steffi had been greeted by a slimy gecko, clearly unhappy his peace had been interrupted. He reared back his head and raced straight for her, letting out a hiss to tell us he didn't want our company. Steffi ran outside, but Fritz thought it was marvellous and began chasing the little lizard around the house.

The gecko had plenty of company. As we moved from room to room we found dozens of dead frogs, dead geckos and dirt. As I peeled the curtains open in each room, more and more horrors emerged. In some rooms the curtains were gummed together with spider webs.

Steffi was beside herself and I did what any self-respecting woman would do: I wilted to the floor and cried. How could anyone live here?

'It just needs a woman's touch,' Friedrich said, desperately trying to reassure me. 'Once you work your magic, Frauke, it will be wonderful. You made that house in Shamva a home. We will do the same again; Steffi will help.'

It was little consolation, but short of heading to the airport and flying back to Germany, I had little choice other than to roll up my sleeves and get to work. This was Friedrich's big idea, but we were in this together.

That night, hot, hungry and covered in grime, all of us slept on the lounge-room floor. I couldn't let the children sleep in those bedrooms. At least we weren't cold.

The next morning as soon as the sun was up, so were we. The gargantuan task of making our home began. Steffi and I unhooked every curtain in every room, vacuumed the cobwebs off and then soaked and scrubbed them until they were spotless. Thank goodness for the hot sun so that we could lay them out to dry.

We went room by room, washing and wiping, vacuuming, cleaning windows. I offered Fritz twenty cents' pocket money for every gecko he caught; he had a ball.

Beds and mattresses had been ordered in Perth and they would arrive within the next week; in the meantime, the bedrooms were clean enough that the children could camp out in them until then.

Then we conquered the kitchen.

We swept and sucked out every skerrick of dirt from every corner and cupboard, then attacked the oven. We washed and rubbed, and scrubbed and washed again.

After a lot of love – and elbow grease – the oven shone. I felt such a sense of triumph when the black enamel looked glossy again. The vent above the stove was gummed together with thick grease that had formed a beeswax-like texture; we had to work hard to clean it, but eventually it sparkled.

The cupboards and benchtops, which had been covered in a layer of fine, sand-like Kimberley dust, were back to laminate and ready to be stocked.

We quickly learnt that frogs had made a wonderful home at the back of the oven. I shuddered at the sight of dead frogs' legs poking out and lost count of how many we discovered.

Exhausted but proud of what we had achieved, I slept soundly on our camp bed, hopeful there were no more surprises in store and satisfied our house would pass even my mother-in-law's white-glove standards.

However, I was soon to learn a very big lesson: that no matter how often you cleaned and scrubbed, in Kununurra, red dust and little critters reappeared again like magic.

Chapter 6

With the house clean and some basic furniture en route from Perth, the next step was to head into town to do the first big shop and stock our bare cupboards.

Friedrich had bought a second-hand car so we could get around, an older-model Kingswood. I got dressed up in a nice cotton shirt and skirt and made an effort to look presentable. I was looking forward to getting out on my own and having some time around people in town.

I loved shopping back home; it was such a treat. We were a forty-five-minute drive from Hamburg, which was a very cosmopolitan city and had everything my heart ever desired. Sometimes I would rug up in a thick winter coat and head into the city to go window shopping. Hamburg was especially beautiful in winter when the lights in the shops would sparkle and a fine layer of snow would dampen my hair. I loved wandering through the perfumed cosmetics halls of the department store Karstadt, just to soak up the beautiful surroundings. I didn't buy things very often but I spoiled myself looking.

By 8am in Kununurra, it was blisteringly hot and the humidity was stifling.

Since we had arrived seven days ago it had been 40 degrees or more every day and not a cloud in the sky. The sun burnt our winter-white skin to a crisp and the humidity sucked the energy from our bones. In the quick walk from the house to the car, beads of sweat had already formed on my forehead.

The summer clothes we had brought with us were not suited to this weather at all. We had suitcases of thick T-shirts and sleeveless tops when we needed light cotton garments with long sleeves that covered our arms to protect us from the sun and allow the skin to breathe.

I underlined 'new clothes' on my shopping list.

There was no air conditioning in the car and as I passed farm after farm, the sweat was soaking through my clothes. Deep irrigation channels wove through fields of fruit orchards.

The drive into town only took about seven minutes and the one main street constituted 'the high street', but that didn't dampen my enthusiasm. I wedged the Kingswood in among a line-up of dusty white utes; a dear old blue kelpie popped his head up from the back of the ute parked beside me and greeted me with a lazy growl before lying back down on his makeshift hessian bed.

Kununurra had two grocery stores opposite one another on the main street and both were very small. Friedrich was right that we could get everything we needed, but it didn't take long to work out that everything we *wanted* was another matter.

The first little shop had a funny curtain of beaded plastic strips hanging in the doorway; apparently these were to keep the flies out and I soon noticed them on every shop door.

Inside, it was at best described as rustic. It had weathered linoleum floors, old wooden shelving that was filled with tinned food, and a handful of wooden baskets of vegetables on the floor near the counter.

I scanned the shelves, trying to understand the English labels and what the contents of the packets and tins were. They were all brands I'd never heard of and I couldn't really read the labels. I picked up a large can and asked the shop-keeper, 'What is this?' Over the top of his glasses, he gave me a curious look and said, 'Dog food.'

'Ah, danke,' I said, putting it back.

He pointed me in the direction of the human groceries, towards the back of the store, but nothing familiar appeared there either. There was more pet food than human food.

There was a small freezer at the back of the store that initially offered some hope, but when I slid the glass door back, I found the contents were powdered milk and frozen packaged white bread. I slid the door closed as quickly as I'd opened it.

The butter had gone rancid in the heat and there were few other dairy products – some cheese but no yoghurt – and only salted dried meat. We'd come from an area of lush green farmland, fresh creamy milk straight from the cows and wonderful cheeses, cured meats and gourmet food. This was so disheartening, but I tried to remain optimistic. Perhaps people ordered things by catalogue, like we did in Germany?

Large sacks of flour and rice lined the walls of the store, big bulky bags too heavy for me to carry.

'During the wet season, love, the roads could get cut off,' the shopkeeper said. 'There'll be nothing coming into town, so you want to make sure you've got plenty of supplies to get you through.'

Thank goodness we'll only be here for two wet seasons, I thought.

Fruit was dehydrated or tinned, and the small range of vegetables on offer had gone limp in the heat, which I sympathised with because by then I was feeling a bit wilted too.

I bought a few basic things I needed and the shopkeeper helped me load up the car, then I wandered across the road to the other grocery store, hoping there might be more on offer. Disappointingly, it was pretty much the same; however, they did have a real butcher inside the store, so at least we had some meat to keep us going until we could butcher our own.

Clearly the fridge-freezer we had would not be enough: we needed to be better prepared and better able to store food if we were to survive.

Friedrich had asked me to pick up a jerrycan while I was in town. The man at the counter of the hardware store was very patient as I struggled to find the words in English to explain what I was looking for.

'Tin,' I said, drawing a rectangle in the air with my fingers then making a pouring motion. He nodded and raced away to the back of the store, then came back a few moments later with a teapot in his hands. I shook my head, 'Nein, nein,' and started again, virtually miming my way through a description in a hybrid English–German.

He still looked puzzled, so I grabbed a pen off his counter and drew a picture and eventually he worked out what I was trying to say. I thought my English was pretty good but I struggled with the language of the bush, and clearly the bush struggled with me.

The last item to tick off the list was clothes, but this was a lost cause.

There was a small gift shop with bits and pieces for tourists, not what I needed.

I drove back home with my ramshackle supplies, feeling somewhat deflated and disappointed, but still determined to overcome the limitations of the outback.

The cupboards were now stocked as well as could be with enough flour, rice, potatoes, powdered milk and dehydrated fruit to last us a little while, so I decided to make us a special dinner to mark our arrival and help us all feel a little more settled.

I grabbed my apron and got to work in my kitchen, glad to be doing something useful. To begin with, a cake for afternoon tea would help put us all in a happier mood.

The flour came in giant thick brown paper sacks that were tricky to handle. I opened up the bag and carefully filled my measuring jug, tipping the flour into a bowl through the sifter. When I tried to turn the handle, the flour gummed in the top of the sifter and wouldn't go through. I looked closer and could see the flour was moving. It was full of little grey weevils. It was the tipping point and I burst into tears.

'Steffi!' I yelled. 'Look at this! Look at this!'

I threw my apron off and, energised by my rage, dragged the huge bag back into the car, and flew back into town. The shopkeeper could see I'd been crying.

'Sorry, love, but that's just how it is,' he said. 'The flour comes up by container ship from Perth. Sometimes it takes months for supplies to arrive and by the time the flour gets here, it's got weevils. Nothing we can do about it. Every bag'll be the same and everyone else in town has 'em too. Sorry love, it's the best we can do.'

I lugged our bag of flour back to the car and slunk down into the driver's seat, disgusted. This godforsaken place.

With Steffi's help, I sifted the flour, and sifted it again, and again, and again until all of the weevils were gone. We soon found that the dried apples, plums and apricots I'd bought were full of weevils too, but we either had to learn to make do or starve.

It was clear the Kimberley was going to challenge me in ways I'd never imagined. Every day I prayed to God to give me the strength I needed to survive.

The children loved the tropical climate and couldn't wait to get outside each day. My funny little Peter would strip his clothes off as soon as he felt grass under his toes, and eventually Steffi and I gave up chasing him around trying to get him dressed again; we just let him go, because he was happy.

The back of the house faced the Ord River, overlooking a pontoon the previous owners had built. The Ord was filled with water that came from the heart of the outback, off sunburnt plains flowing through scorched earth banks, it eventually ran out to Cambridge Gulf – but not before it ran past our house and not before the Bolten children bathed in it to their hearts' content. They spent hours swimming in the river, dangling their legs off the pontoon, diving in and out of the water, pale little swans shedding their winter feathers.

One afternoon not long after we arrived, the children were down having a swim, so I made myself a cup of tea and sat out on the back porch looking over the river. I could hear Fritz barking instructions at Margret, as Steffi held Peter and dipped his toes in and out of the water at the river's edge. I took some comfort that despite the challenges of this place, the children were settling in very easily.

As I lifted the teacup to my lips, I saw movement out of the corner of my right eye.

I turned my head in time to catch a glimpse of a crocodile on the riverbank opposite, sliding its thick-scaled body into the water. I dropped my teacup and ran down the grass as fast as I could, screaming to Steffi and the children, *'Geh raus, geh raus!'* – Get out, get out! My heart was racing as the croc glided towards them. I yelled and yelled while sprinting down the bank. Fritz dragged Margret out and Steffi scooped Peter up and held him tightly.

I pointed out the huge beast to them. We could just see its eyes and knobbly back skimming the top of the water, and the tail moving from side to side like a giant rudder propelling it through the water. It swam past the pontoon and down the river before disappearing under the surface, quite oblivious to us and the fuss. I gathered the children up and took them inside, my heart racing a hundred miles an hour.

'You'll get used to them, you just have to keep an eye out,' Friedrich said remarkably calmly after he heard about it.

The next day, without a worry in the world, the kids wanted to go straight back into the river again. I was reluctant, but they loved the water. I followed them down and sat anxiously on the riverbank, my eyes racing backwards and forwards, scouring every ripple.

Only today, I had Friedrich's shotgun beside me, within arm's reach.

Early one morning not long after we'd moved into the house, I saw a trail of dust coming down the driveway. A ute pulled up and a tall Italian-looking man got out, took off his hat and knocked on the door.

'G'day,' he said, 'I'm John Caratti. I live two doors up. We heard we had new neighbours, so I thought I'd come to say hello and welcome you to the neighbourhood. My wife Judy and I were wondering if you'd like to join us for dinn —'

'Yes! Yes, that would be wonderful,' I said, before the poor man had even finished his sentence. I was so excited to have some adult company!

When Friedrich got home from our farm, which was a few kilometres away, I told him to get in the shower quickly and find some nice clothes; we were going out for dinner.

The Carattis lived two properties away down Riverfarm Road, but our gates were only about 100 metres apart. We wove along a dirt track to find a lovely house sitting up high on the riverbank like ours.

John and Judy had also invited a Scottish couple who were new to town and faced similar challenges getting used to outback life. The Carattis had arrived in Kununurra long before us, but they'd lived in town. A few months earlier they had moved to Riverfarm Road and had done the hard yards of settling in. Judy had laid out a beautiful table and prepared a wonderful dinner for us. She and I hit it off straightaway, as did Friedrich and John.

After a few glasses of wine, I heard Friedrich laughing. It was the first time he'd really relaxed since we'd arrived in

Australia. He was telling jokes and seemed to be enjoying himself and enjoying company. It had been a stressful time for us all, packing up our lives and moving to the opposite side of the planet. At last we were in our new home and we could begin to settle. This was just what the doctor ordered for us both.

With the others happily telling tales around the dining table, Judy called me into the kitchen to help clean up – or so I thought. She took me through the laundry door and outside to a lovely little nook overlooking the river, then pulled a packet of cigarettes out of her pocket. 'Would you like one?' she asked.

'Oh, would I what!' I said, lighting up with glee.

I didn't smoke very often – Friedrich absolutely hated it, so it was only ever a sneaky cigarette on the odd special occasion. I hadn't had a cigarette since long before we left Germany and I savoured this one. What Friedrich didn't know wouldn't hurt him.

I slowly inhaled the smoke, my shoulders easing with every breath. Judy and I didn't speak, but in the shared silence, I instantly knew this was a woman I could rely on. As we bade one another farewell at the end of the evening, she took my hand and made me promise I would keep in touch or call her if ever I needed anything; she was a ray of light.

81

Chapter 7

Each morning when I woke, I crossed my fingers and toes that when I peeled back the curtains, there'd be a dark storm rumbling on the horizon. Inevitably, I was greeted by bright sun smiling back at me, translucent blue skies and not a cloud as far as the eye could see. Exactly as it had been the day before, and the day before that.

This was, of course, one of the reasons we had come to Kununurra. It was just as Friedrich had promised: 'Sunshine, Frauke, like you've never seen before, endless sunshine.'

He was dead right. It was never-ending!

Even though I absolutely love warmth, I longed for variety, to feel a brisk cold wind on my skin or a winter chill in the air, a dark autumn day that would inspire us to light a fire or reach for a jumper – something to break the monotony.

Locals promised me that the rains would come and warned that when they did, I'd need to batten down the hatches; the wet season would be like nothing I'd ever seen. I could hardly wait.

This big adventure to Australia was Friedrich's dream, a chance to make his own name in farming, and he had a head full of plans and ideas he was itching to get started on. So when we had first laid eyes on our new farm, we were terribly disappointed. The 'dream farm' we'd purchased with our life savings was made up of long, flat paddocks of rock-hard earth, unrelenting tumbleweeds of saltbush scrub and thick tussocky grass, rusty sheds and broken fences as far as the eye could see.

I wouldn't have argued if Friedrich said we were packing up and heading home right there and then.

Getting this farm functioning was going to be a much bigger task than we'd imagined and we needed to borrow more money. This sat uncomfortably with me, but as the saying goes, 'in for a penny, in for a pound'.

Before anything could be planted, the weeds had to be completely removed. This was a terrible job and although we had a tractor to help, the root systems on some of the scrub needed to be hand dug to be properly removed or sometimes burnt to make sure they wouldn't reshoot.

The bulldust then had to be ploughed up, because crops can't grow on concrete-hard earth. The soil needed to be turned and broken up so the seeds could penetrate and germinate. It would take about six weeks to plough up all of the fields in readiness for planting.

Friedrich never shied away from the task. He walked every paddock, corner to corner, covering 1000 hectares and he got rid of every wretched weed. It was backbreaking work, especially in the heat, but I could see the satisfaction on his face when the last weed was lifted and the ploughing could begin.

Giving in was never Friedrich's way; he relished being out in the open and found joy in seeing a seed spring to life. He was focused on this farm with single-minded determination.

'The first harvest will be even sweeter,' he said.

Most days, long before dawn, he would wake me with a kiss. I always got up and made him a cup of tea and some breakfast, and packed a little hamper of food for him to take to the farm. By the time the sun turned the ranges pink each morning, Friedrich had done half a day's work. Even at that hour of the morning it was steaming hot. He came home for lunch and a rest in the middle of the day because it was too hot to be out in the fields by then.

He'd return to the farm, staying until sunset. Some afternoons I went back out with him; I'd walk along behind the tractor to check the plough was carving straight seed beds. We'd move through the paddocks at a snail's pace, Friedrich on the tractor, me walking behind.

One evening, after a couple of hours of this, he suddenly stopped. As dusk was rolling into darkness he turned off the tractor and its lights, which were the only illumination we had. Jumping down, he called me over. He put his arm around my shoulder as we leaned against one of the huge rubber tyres. 'Frauke, look up,' he said. I lifted my eyes to see the night sky awakening above us. Millions of tiny stars began to sparkle in the darkness – so many stars I didn't know where to start looking. I'd never seen anything so beautiful.

The twinkling stopped at the horizon, where the sky met the shadowy black of the ranges. There was no noise, no cars, no lights off in the distance, no voices, not a sound.

Just the earth and sky together in silence, and the two of us in the middle of it.

For a moment we felt like we were the only people on earth, and for a moment I thought, *Maybe there are diamonds in this dust after all*. We packed up and went home, and fell into bed exhausted, but when I woke the next morning Friedrich was already gone again. He'd barely had two hours' sleep.

Even before the first crop was planted, Friedrich had decided on a name: Oasis Farms. It was obvious that in the middle of outback Australia, my German farmer truly felt at home.

Schooling in outback Australia was quite unlike anything we'd known. Some kids living on vast cattle stations or remote Aboriginal communities were so isolated they had to learn by School of the Air, a uniquely Australian system of giving lessons via two-way radio to kids who were hundreds, even thousands, of kilometres away. The Kimberley School of the Air, based in Derby, covered 450,000 square kilometres. There were others servicing even bigger areas in the Northern Territory, Queensland and South Australia.

We were fortunate that a primary school had been built in Kununurra, originally to accommodate the families of the men working on the Ord River Irrigation Scheme. The school had grown as mines opened up nearby and farms were developed. Margret and Fritz spoke very basic English – enough to get by. Being immersed in the local school would be a great chance to pick up the language and make some friends.

Fritz, with his mop of blond curls and big blue eyes was the spit of his father, and a farm boy too – he would've happily followed Friedrich around the paddocks all day or whiled the hours away fossicking in the shed in between adventures, but he was quite happy to go to school. Margret was very worried that she didn't know the language well enough to understand what was going on.

On their first morning, I packed their lunches, kissed them goodbye and sent them off to meet the bus at our gate.

When they came home, they told me their teachers were very welcoming and made quite a lovely fuss of the new children 'all the way from Germany'. It had the effect of making Fritz and Margret feel very special, but this sort of attention isn't always welcomed by the other kids and some of them didn't take too kindly to it.

There is a law to the schoolyard jungle, a pecking order, and new kids start at the bottom. They have to earn respect and earn their place, and the initiation can be brutal.

On her first day, Margret, with her brunette curls tucked up in a neat ponytail and shoes given an extra polish, found herself seated in between two boys. She pulled out her nice new notepad and pens and laid everything out on the table in readiness for class. She was a diligent girl, always taking great pride in everything she did.

She turned to the boy on the left. 'Hello, I'm Margret,' she said, with her funny European accent.

'Heil Hitler,' he responded. Some of the children giggled.

She turned to the boy on the other side and said again, 'Hello, I'm Margret.' He too greeted her with 'Heil Hitler.' The children thought it was a great joke. In fairness, they were just kids; they couldn't understand how hurtful this was.

Margret ignored the comments but they continued. Kids know how to get a rise and these boys knew the right buttons to press to get a reaction from her. About a week after they'd started at school, after recess one day Margret came in to find 'Heil Hitler' written on the beautiful new notepad she had proudly taken to her new school.

She burst into tears and ran out of the classroom.

In Germany we were ashamed and saddened by this dark period of our history. It was the most horrible thing you could say to someone, especially an innocent little girl. I spoke with Margret's teacher, who was wonderfully compassionate and sorted the situation out very quickly.

Things settled down and after a week or so she came running to me after school one afternoon saying, *'Mutti, Mutti, die Schule ist nicht schlecht'* – school isn't so bad.

Friedrich was working very hard, but thankfully he'd struck up quite a friendship with our neighbour John Caratti and they often got together for a late afternoon drink. I think

John's Italian background helped him understand our strong European accents, but also Friedrich's quirky sense of humour.

Friedrich wasn't your stereotypical German: he wasn't a beer drinker, preferring a more sophisticated glass of wine, and he wasn't loud; he was quite a serious man and went about life fairly quietly, but when he let his guard down you could be almost guaranteed of good-natured mischief.

One particular afternoon, fed up with cane grass and salt-bush, he tucked a bottle of wine under his arm and wandered over to Judy and John's for a pre-dinner drink.

John always made Friedrich laugh and the pair enjoyed a drink on Judy's back porch, entertaining themselves with tales of farming and hunting, which often became more colourful and dramatic as the glasses emptied and the after-noon wore on.

Friedrich loved hunting in Germany, it was quite a family tradition, and it turned out John did too.

'Pour yourself another drink Friedrich, let's have a bit of fun,' John said as he disappeared into the garage, emerging moments later with a shotgun in his hand. 'We'll do some target practice.'

Judy's back porch faced onto the Ord, the same as ours, so the tipsy men thought they'd try their luck targeting any unsuspecting crocodile unlucky enough to glide past at the wrong time. After a few random shots that skimmed the bark from a nearby tree and knocked the heads off water lilies, it was pretty clear that the marksmen were off their game and the crocodiles were in no danger, but they were undeterred.

'This is what we need,' Friedrich said as he grabbed a handful of Judy's good cushions from her brand new outdoor setting and piled them up high on the coffee table in front of them.

Friedrich built up a cushion parapet with his elbows resting on the cushions, gun cocked on his shoulder, determined that this was going to be the shot that landed a bounty, even though there wasn't a crocodile to be seen. He rested his head on the stock, eyes on the sight line and fired.

From inside the kitchen Judy heard another ungodly bang. This time though, it was followed by an unnerving silence. She looked out the window and saw a cloud of smoke, and ran outside to find the two ashen-faced men on the ground.

'Good God, John! What's going on?' she yelled, as the silence was suddenly broken by their laughter. They weren't injured. Friedrich had somehow misfired and shot up Judy's lovely new cushions. The outback odd couple were covered in a mess of feathers and foam, but without a scratch on them. Wisely, Judy called time on the shenanigans and took the gun from the hapless hunters. Friedrich was sent on a sobering walk home.

We continued to speak German at home because I didn't want the children to lose their language, and it was important that when we went home to Seedorf they could continue their schooling and not be disadvantaged. Deep down it also helped me feel a connection to home. I missed my family terribly and felt a sense of sadness sitting below the surface that wouldn't budge. Because Friedrich was very focused on the farm, he spent very little time at home, so I'd lost my family and friends in Germany and at times I felt I'd lost my husband too. I reminded myself constantly that this was just for two years, but two years is a long time. We were so far from the rest of the world, surrounded by nothing but open space, and yet I felt utterly suffocated.

John became an invaluable friend to Friedrich, and Judy was my lifeline. She popped in for coffee every few days to see how I was going; I think she sensed that I was finding life difficult. Judy had joined the Kununurra tennis club and played regularly. She suggested I come along with her one day and have a game. I loved tennis and played back home, and wouldn't dream of knocking back the chance to get out and meet some new people.

It was quite a transient club. Many of the players worked in nearby mines, so they may only be in town for a few months at most, but they were a lovely bunch, very welcoming, and there were a few other expats like me who were finding their way in a foreign landscape.

One afternoon when Judy came to pick me up for tennis she found me in tears at the kitchen bench. Frozen bread had tipped me over the edge. I could not stand eating the Kununurra bread for one more day; it was just horrible. I longed for some thick dark rye bread from home and I'd been trying to bake it, but something wasn't right with my oven and every loaf turned out like a brick. Friedrich laughed when I showed him   we could've used the black loaves as doorstops if we needed to – but this frustration added to my anxiety.

I wanted a taste of home to soothe me, and every rock of rye bread I baked made me feel like a total failure. When Judy walked into the kitchen I was hunched over another disastrous batch of the bread.

'I think something's burning, Frauke,' she said with a confused look as I sat in my tennis clothes with an apron on, wiping away tears.

'I can't stand it, Judy. This stupid oven won't work,' I said, dropping the rock-hard loaf into the bin.

'Don't worry, Frauke, just bring your dough to our house and we'll cook it there until you get the oven worked out.'

And so I did. The next day, with a renewed sense of purpose and determination, I made up the traditional dough. The recipe says you need to find a warm place to let it rise and proof. We had no trouble finding somewhere warm for it to sit – we couldn't find anywhere cold.

When the dark dough had doubled in size I wrapped the bowl in a tea towel and headed over to Judy's. An hour later, we had edible rye bread – the joy! Judy was wonderful; she said I could use her oven whenever I needed to, as long as I cooked a loaf for her too.

The deal was done and none of us had to eat frozen bread ever again.

Chapter 8

We'd been in Kununurra for almost six months, but I missed home more than ever. I longed for a familiar voice to calm my fragile nerves. Although we had a phone at the house, we couldn't just pick up the receiver and dial a number. It was connected to a remote telephone exchange in Wyndham, a town smaller than Kununurra, 100 kilometres away. To make a long-distance call we had to book in advance through the exchange. The tiny exchange looked after all of the calls for the entire Kimberley region and they had a window of two hours each day when long-distance calls could be made.

If we were lucky enough to secure a booking, we were allowed only a three-minute call, and if they could connect you, that three minutes cost $50. Three minutes every now and then was my only lifeline to the world outside Kununurra, where loneliness and frustration came free with the plane ticket. I treasured each precious second.

Some days, I instinctively went to pick up the phone and call my sister or Tante Banta to share the stories of our long-distance life. When I realised I couldn't, the weight of loneliness descended, to the extent that the pain became physical, like my heart might burst. To fill in the gaps between calls I poured my heart out in long letters home and savoured those that came in return.

The fact I couldn't just pick up the phone and call Germany whenever I wanted had a huge impact on me emotionally. When I had managed to book a call, I would barely have time to get the 'Hello, how are you?' in before a strange voice from the exchange would come on the line and say, 'One minute.' When the time was up, the plug was pulled, often mid-sentence. Even still, just hearing the voices of loved ones gave me a spring in my step that would last for several days.

Thoughts of home consumed my mind; sometimes it was all I could focus on. I'd be in the middle of something and find myself momentarily paralysed by thoughts of distant friends and family; a smell, a picture, a memory would take me back home. I'd be transported to the stables feeding Margret's pony or to my kitchen table with farm workers lapping up soup at lunchtime on a winter's day.

The feeling of loneliness was something I'd never experienced before. In Zimbabwe, we were only an hour's drive from

Harare and we lived on the farm like we did in Germany, so Friedrich would pop in and out and we were in the middle of a busy, bustling environment.

In Australia, the farm was a few kilometres away from the house, and although town was barely a ten-minute drive in the other direction, we visited it only for essential supplies, not socialising.

Friedrich and Steffi sensed what was going on. Sometimes Steffi would catch me wiping away tears; other days I was just quiet and a little bit melancholy, reflective perhaps.

The children and their relentless energy and adventures helped keep me sane. They loved Kununurra more than I ever imagined, and I tried my best to soak up their enthusiasm and put on a cheery face for them, even though I was secretly counting down the months until we could return home.

Out of the blue one afternoon in late October, as we ate lunch together, Friedrich gently tossed up the idea of the two of us taking a quick trip back to Germany; my heart almost skipped a beat. 'Can we do that?' I asked. There seemed to be so much work to do at the farm, I never imagined we could take a break, let alone fly back to Germany.

The dry season had just come to an end and the true wet season was a little way off on the horizon, so Friedrich reasoned that there was an opportunity during the lull between seasons to make a quick visit home. We would pick up a few bits and pieces that might make Kununurra feel homelier and see our family, and Friedrich could see our bankers and check on our finances. He didn't say as much to me then, but I suspected we needed to borrow some more money. I didn't care why we were going; I was so happy at the thought, it was almost like a second honeymoon.

Steffi would look after the children for us. Fritz and Margret were well settled into their school routine and she only had Peter home during the day, which was quite manageable. Steffi was very much part of our family, and I don't know how I would've coped over those first few months without her. She only had a twelve-month visa to Australia, which was due to expire in the New Year, when she would have to return to Germany. If we were going to make a visit home, it was now or never.

Friedrich had barely finished his sentence before my mind began to race: I'd visit Hamburg and do the Christmas shopping so we had nice things for everybody; we'd have dinner with Tante Banta and my brother and sister, lunch with my father at his favourite restaurant; I could go to the hair salon and get my hair done; and for a few blissful days I would smell of my favourite perfume, not insect repellent.

In early November, we kissed everyone goodbye at the Kununurra airport. We would miss the children, but Steffi was very mature and very capable of looking after them. We flew to Darwin to catch a flight to Singapore, where we boarded an Aeroflot flight to East Berlin. Our trip home would be short – eight days all up – but I could hardly wait.

From the moment we stepped off the plane in East Berlin, we felt as if we were being watched. It was well known that East Germans didn't like Westerners; we were a threat to their socialist regime. We were in no doubt that some of the airport staff, police, security guards and passport control were members of the Stasi.

At the passport control desk, the official pushed the plastic tip of his black peaked cap up ever so slightly above his eyes so he could study our faces. His dark uniform was menacing and he was in no mood for pleasantries. 'Where are you going? What is your business here?' he said.

We explained we were just passing through on our way to West Germany from Australia, which seemed to prick his attention. Friedrich explained that we now lived in Australia; we would be picking up some things from our old home, visiting family and returning to Australia.

'Do not lie to me,' he snapped.

Then he demanded our visas. But we didn't have any, because we were in transit, not staying. That didn't ease the tension of the situation. Apparently, we hadn't lodged the right paperwork to get us through East German passport control, and we both began to worry. The guard was deeply suspicious of us and asked us to gather our bags and follow him to be questioned further. My heart was racing. We'd heard terrible stories of people going missing in East Germany, being locked up in jail for doing virtually nothing wrong.

We were taken to a small room, with an imposing picture of the East German leader Erich Honecker staring down at us, where the guard told us he would waive the need for a visa, on the condition we paid a fee directly to him, in Deutschmarks – a bribe.

We didn't have any German money on us, only a small amount of Australian dollars.

The tiny airless room suddenly seemed very stuffy and suffocating.

In a desperate attempt to break the impasse, Friedrich took my bag, opened it up and emptied out every last thing in it, including my wallet, to give him our Australian dollars. But the official wasn't interested.

He wanted cold hard Deutschmarks, which were very valuable in the East, in contrast to their failing East German marks, which were virtually worthless.

A 'fee' from a tourist desperate to get past a checkpoint could be worth more than a month's salary. But we literally didn't have a Deutschmark to give him.

After realising we had nothing to offer and were therefore useless to him, he reluctantly stamped our papers and let us go, on strict instructions we were to leave East Germany immediately. We were more than happy to fulfil his orders and jumped in the first bus we could find to get us to the border.

Our friends Fritz and Marion were waiting for us on the other side and drove us back to their house in West Berlin. It was a typical German winter – grey, cloudy and bitterly cold, with a light sprinkling of rain to dampen our hair. It was wonderful and I couldn't have been happier. Their smooth German voices were so easy to understand by comparison to the Australian accent, which I sometimes found difficult.

When we arrived at the farm the next day, everything was exactly as it was when we left. Our beds were made, our coats and clothes hung in the cupboard, the shoes were clean and polished on the racks where we'd left them.

After a long hot shower, I fell into my bed, resting my head on crisp cool cotton sheets. I tucked myself up under the covers and fell into the deepest, most wonderful sleep, waking to the first snow of the season on the fields outside. It was heaven and I was back where I belonged, my withering tree momentarily taking root again. *'Ich bin zuhause, Friedrich'* – I am home.

Our days were filled with long coffee catch-ups – a half a year of conversation to catch up on in just a few days. Our family could not believe some of the stories we told them. My sister Dorte recoiled in horror at the thought of the children swimming with crocodiles, and my father physically bristled when we told him about the state of the house when we moved in.

Tante Banta thought it all sounded wonderful!

Friedrich arranged a hunting trip with his old farming friends. They spent the whole day scoping the forest and came home in the darkness, soaking wet, head to toe in mud, almost frozen to the bone, but blissfully happy.

Our time was short but wonderful and we said our goodbyes again on the promise that everyone would come to visit. I made sure that before we left we had a schedule planned. Friedrich's father would soon come, followed by Tante Banta and Dorte. It gave me so much to look forward to, and I flew back to Australia feeling that I would survive this after all.

~

I guess the one blessing of our lack of phone service at the house in Kununurra was that bad news travels slowly. From the other side of the world, we were blissfully unaware of a drama unfolding at home.

'Peter, Peter, come for afternoon tea,' Steffi had called through the kitchen door one day.

Peter had been outside running around in the nude, as he always did, while Steffi was getting afternoon tea ready in the kitchen for Fritz and Margret when they arrived home from school.

She called and called him, and although he didn't come, she wasn't too bothered. The children had a cat called Midnight and a little dachshund named Barbarossa, who shadowed Peter everywhere he went. When Peter was playing, especially if Barbarossa was nipping at his heels, he was often oblivious to anyone or anything around him. At the grand age of two, he was quite a competent adventurer: he had found little nooks and crannies that he could play in, and trees to climb; he'd wander around the garden getting up to all sorts of fun. Sometimes when we called him, he wouldn't come straightaway, but eventually he'd amble his way back, especially when he was hungry.

CHAPTER 8

Most afternoons he'd head down our long dirt driveway and wait at the gate for Fritz and Margret to come along on the school bus. Steffi figured the three of them would wander in any minute. The familiar thump of schoolbags dumped at the back door signalled they were home, but only Fritz and Margret came inside.

'Where's Peter?' Steffi asked. They both shrugged; they hadn't seen him.

Steffi rushed down to the river, fearing he'd taken the dog for a swim or snuck out onto the pontoon.

But when she got down to the riverbank there was no sign of Peter. She raced back to the house. 'Fritz, Margret, I need your help, I can't find Peter,' she called out.

The three of them broke up and headed in different directions to search but couldn't find him. It wasn't the first time he'd gone missing; he had a track record of wandering off. There was tall cane grass along the road that wound past the handful of riverbank homes; few cars ever came along here and it was quite safe for the children to ride their bikes or play. Peter could often be found playing in the grass, but this time was different. He wasn't to be found in any of his usual hiding spots.

Distraught, Steffi rang Judy and John, who rallied a small army of people, including our neighbours on the other side.

They came to scour the property; they looked behind every bush and inside every shed; they walked the length of the riverbank, through the orchards, then spread the search through neighbouring properties. They walked up and down the roads calling his name. He was nowhere to be found.

Steffi was grief stricken, convinced he'd drowned in the river or been taken by a crocodile. Judy helped comfort Steffi, while the search escalated. One of the neighbours grabbed his ute and with Fritz on the back calling out for Peter, they slowly went along the surrounding roads one by one. After two hours of searching, as dusk began to set in, Peter was found, several kilometres from home, happily playing in the warm gooey mud of an irrigation channel.

The channel was empty because it was the end of the dry season, leaving just a lovely pool of gushy thick mud that Peter and his buddy Barbarossa were thoroughly enjoying.

The cane grass on the side of the road was so high they couldn't have seen him without standing on the back of the ute. Fritz scooped him up in his arms and hugged him tight.

'We've been looking for you, buddy,' he said.

Peter arrived home, hungry but oblivious to what all of the fuss was about. In his eyes, he hadn't been lost; he knew exactly where he was, and he was having a lovely time. He only got upset at the thought of having to soak in a bath to wash off all of that mud.

Everyone was astonished at how this little boy could've walked so far. Steffi picked him up and squeezed him tight, then promptly burst into tears. Judy made coffee for everyone and after a nip or two of Bacardi, the relieved searchers retreated home. This was a lucky day, which no one cared to repeat.

A week or so later, with Peter's sun-bleached curls in front of us safe and sound, Steffi trembled as she recalled what had happened. It had obviously been a nightmare and she didn't take her eyes off Peter for another second until we arrived back in Kununurra.

Chapter 9

Slowly, I was becoming accustomed to frogs under the fridge and geckos skating across the cork-tile floor, even crocs in the river; if we didn't bother them, they didn't bother us.

But I was absolutely terrified of snakes.

It sent a chill up my spine when locals told tales of finding snakes in their houses, curled up in the base of a damp shower or coiled around the inside of the porcelain 'dunny'.

Our house in Germany had thick sliding glass doors, so it was very well sealed from Mother Nature's creepy-crawlies, but our house in Kununurra had French doors that the children always left swinging open. Little lizards and geckos managed to find their way in without too much bother.

Friedrich reassured me with an Australian old wives' tale that where there are lizards, there are no snakes. The myth goes that they don't like one another's company, so as much as I hated having lizards around, it was of some comfort that they would keep the snakes away.

Even still, if I needed to go to the bathroom at night I'd wake Friedrich and make him come with me to check there were no snakes popping up out of the toilet. Barbarossa was a fierce little sausage dog and very territorial. He barked at everything that moved; if there was a lizard or a stray bird on the lawn, I knew well in advance. It was quite a sight to watch him wind up his tiny legs and race around chasing creatures away.

With Christmas on the horizon, most days I was either in the kitchen cooking or preparing the house. We'd come to learn that no sooner had you finished cleaning in Kununurra, than a fine layer of red Kimberley dust would reappear in every nook and cranny, even on the towels in the cupboards. Steffi helped me to wash and re-wash linen and napkins for the Christmas table, then I'd seal them in plastic to keep them fresh for Christmas Eve, which is when Germans traditionally celebrate.

One day, we'd beaten a well-worn path between the kitchen and laundry when I saw Friedrich's ute pull up; he was home for lunch. The house smelt wonderful, the heady mix of spices and biscuits cooling on trays.

The children's cat, Midnight, was annoying me; she was heavily pregnant and constantly wanted attention. We sat down and tried to have lunch, but she sat at the door hissing and growling and carrying on. The arrival of kittens was the last thing I needed today.

I called her over but she wouldn't budge. Instead, she arched her back, tail bolt upright in the air, and made a deep, guttural growl like I'd never heard before.

I walked over to the passage to see what was going on and could very quickly see why the cat was upset. The long, shiny tail of an enormous king brown snake was visible against the passage wall; its brown body was almost camouflaged by the caramel-coloured carpet. It stretched along the wall and around the corner into the laundry, where another good half-metre of the fat reptile was curled up around Barbarossa's water bowl.

My heart stopped. *'Friedrich, Friedrich! Da ist eine Schlange!'*

The snake clearly didn't like the cat and the cat didn't like the snake, and this was a stand-off that wouldn't end well for one of them. The king brown snake is one of the most venomous snakes in Australia.

Steffi screamed and the children, who'd been playing outside, came rushing in to see what all the fuss was about. They were running around in circles squealing their lungs out and busting to get a glimpse of the creature.

'Grab the children and take them into the kitchen,' Friedrich said very calmly.

Then he did what any self-respecting bushman would do: in a split second he grabbed the snake by the tail, dragged it outside onto the lawn and shot it dead.

'Good shot, Dad!' said Fritz.

The noise was deafening and although the snake was well and truly dead, it took quite a while before it stopped moving. The children and I were aghast watching the headless reptile writhing around on the grass.

Thankfully Mother Nature eventually took over.

My whole body was numb. Steffi and I had walked in and out of the laundry all morning and up and down this passage a thousand times, and we hadn't seen it. Had it been there the whole time? I shuddered at the thought.

While Friedrich and Fritz bravely searched the house for any other creatures and moved the dead snake's remains well out of my sight, I poured myself a cup of tea to settle my nerves. It was some days before I could bring myself to go into the laundry again.

It took months of work to get the ground ready to plant and the farm functioning fully, so we had a great sense of triumph when Friedrich was finally ready to plant the first crop. He'd chosen mung beans, a fast-growing legume that needed very little water and fertiliser. There was a strong market for mung beans and the crop could be turned around quickly to bring in some much-needed income. It would also give us a good understanding of the soil and how things grew here.

Some German friends came and pitched in to help Friedrich and me get the crop sown, but Friedrich still did the bulk of the work. He was out at the farm by 6am every day walking the paddocks. Some days it was so hot that by the time he got back to the sheds half an hour later he had blisters all over his feet. He never complained, and on Christmas Eve 1981 the seeds were all sown and ready to grow.

This was a huge relief and meant we could celebrate Christmas together and have some time to relax. I always had a big gathering with friends and neighbours and family. This time it would be just us.

Christmas in Australia felt so strange. In Germany it often snowed, but it was deathly hot here, relentless days of 38 to 40 degrees, and I found it very difficult to adjust.

We had our own forest at the farm in Seedorf, and a few weeks before Christmas, Friedrich and I would rug ourselves and the children up in thick coats and snow shoes and go out together to choose a special tree.

In the days leading up to Christmas Eve, Friedrich would cut it down and bring it to the house. Most often the tree would be 5 metres tall, reaching to the top of our high ceiling – a thick, lush green fir or spruce tree that would perfume the house with a rich pine smell.

On Christmas Eve the children spent the day decorating the tree while I prepared food for an evening banquet. Our tree always had real candles, made from a red wax that would slowly drip onto the branches below, and we'd hang Christmas cookies as decorations; needless to say, there were always a few little morsels that never made it to the tree.

The house was cleaned top to toe, windows washed, floors washed, linens starched and ironed – everything was spotless so by the time dinner arrived we could sit back and enjoy one another's company.

We had carp for dinner – a much finer fish than the Australian carp – and horseradish and salad. Then dessert, always fruit salad and German cakes, plates of iced gingerbread biscuits and Kipferl biscuits the children had decorated with chocolate and hundreds and thousands. The children would get a small glass of stout as a treat and I'd have a glass of champagne. Friedrich wasn't a champagne drinker, but he'd have a glass of wine.

When I was a child we often went to church before dinner on Christmas Eve. Friedrich wasn't much of a churchgoer, so we didn't continue that tradition; instead we opened our presents. During our last Christmas at home, knowing we were headed for Australia, a friend played Father Christmas and visited just in time to give out the gifts; it was very special, a beautiful time for everyone.

The morning of our first Christmas Eve in Kununurra, we woke early and began preparing food and getting the house ready. I could never get the house to the standard of cleanliness that we had in Germany because you'd barely put your duster away and fine red speckles would cover everything again. It was terribly humid. The flywire on the windows and doors worked hard to keep the flies and mosquitoes away from the kitchen, but it didn't stop the little midges finding their way in; we learnt to live with the tiny black insects that dive-bombed into your drink the moment you took a sip.

Preparing for Christmas in the heat was a reminder of how far away from home we were. I was terribly homesick, and the more sweat that gathered on my skin, the more I longed to be in the middle of a thick winter snow.

I drove to the mailbox twice that day, desperately hoping for a big bag of letters and cards from Germany, any correspondence I could immerse myself in to take my mind home and away from this heat. Each time, the letterbox was empty. We couldn't schedule phone calls because the exchange was so busy. The only thing I could do to ease the feeling of sadness in my heart was to prepare as many German delights as I could think of – like my mother-in-law's traditional rum balls, which were always gobbled up – and celebrate with German gusto.

As the afternoon wore on, an enormous thunderhead began rumbling awake over the ranges. The clouds were black and merciless, and the sky electric; bolts of lightning lit up the horizon. It was a spectacular sky show and our first real taste of the wet season.

I was excited that there were dark clouds on the horizon. Maybe God would deliver me a German Christmas after all.

As the storm moved over us, the angry clouds released their contents, and down she came.

The rain was torrential. It fell in sheets, not drops; thick, wide walls of water with extraordinary force. Les Jackson hadn't been exaggerating: if the houses in Kununurra had gutters, they would indeed be ripped from the roofs.

We stood in the living room, all of us lined up at the windows, eyes glued to this spectacular sight; we'd never seen rain like it.

Since we'd moved in, we'd been confident that our house was high enough from the river that if it rose, flooding wouldn't dampen our toes. What we hadn't anticipated was that water would gush through the doors on its way down to the river, and pour down through the roof. It was raining inside our house, and soon the living room was filled with water centimetres deep.

Steffi grabbed the mop and Friedrich raced for a broom and towels, and we did our best to try to sweep the water away, but as we pushed a wave of water out, a new tide would follow.

The storm lasted several hours and it was devastating. The cork-tile flooring buckled and curled up; it was ruined. The Christmas presents were soaked and the house was a wet, sticky mess.

Steffi and I mopped and washed, while Friedrich went out to the farm to survey the damage. It was worse than we imagined. Around the area, roads had quickly flooded as irrigation channels overflowed. The earth, baked during the dry season, was so hard the rain couldn't soak in; it washed the soil away.

Our freshly planted mung-bean crop was all but destroyed. The paddocks were flooded, and any seed beds that weren't washed away were sitting under inches of water. The seeds would never break through.

Friedrich came home utterly deflated, an exhausted shell of a man. Farming life is hard but this was a cruel turn of events. He had worked so hard and we were relying on the money from that crop to start paying back the bank.

We managed to salvage some food and scrape together enough for everyone to eat – it wasn't quite the dinner we'd planned.

The next morning, Christmas Day, Friedrich got up and went back to the farm and began preparing to sow every single seed again. Others came to help him. We would not be defeated.

Chapter 10

That Christmas downpour heralded the beginning of the true wet season. The days were always cloudless and hot, with humidity that would snatch the air from our lungs. Often in the afternoon a swelling thunderhead would rumble across the heavens and dump its contents down upon us. Or we might get a warm shower, a torrential downpour or the stinging tail end of a coastal cyclone.

Thankfully we had enough of a break between heavy rains to allow the second mung-bean crop to take root and germinate. We were so relieved to see a lovely green tinge sprout across the brown paddocks. Fingers, toes and anything flexible were crossed in the hope that the crop would survive further rains.

As Friedrich had predicted, the rich red landscape was wonderful for growing; but as good as it was for growing mung beans, it was equally fertile for growing weeds. The loamy soil and abundant water proved to be the perfect conditions for capeweed and Mitchell grass. It was a full-time job trying to keep the weeds at bay so the crop could thrive.

Friedrich also battled pests we'd never previously encountered: birds. The wetlands that developed around the Kimberley in the wet season were home to huge colonies of bustards (although that's not what we called them!), magpie geese and cockatoos. These birds devoured everything in sight.

The aptly named magpie geese with their black-and-white plumage could use their bills to dig deep down into the soil and completely uproot plants; they could destroy a crop virtually overnight. Remarkably, their wiry necks were also strong enough to knock heavy green fruit right off trees.

One year wildlife rangers estimated there was a flock of 80,000 magpie geese, forcing the closure of the Kununurra airport at sunrise and sunset because it was too dangerous for aeroplanes to take off or land. The worst kind of pests we'd had to deal with in Germany were deer nibbling the heads off crops, and wild boars; a skilled hunter could manage both relatively easily. However, in Kununurra shooting the birds was ineffective because the flocks were so huge. The best approach Friedrich could take was to sit in the field with his shotgun and fire randomly into the sky: the deafening noise of the gunshots was enough to send the cloud of feathers back to the heavens. It was only a temporary fix though.

Friedrich did his best to nurture that crop. Day and night he was at the farm, like a first-time parent with a newborn baby; he didn't take his eyes off those paddocks. But he faced an uphill battle. When we finally harvested several months later, it was a disappointing yield. The weeds had infiltrated much of the mung-bean crop and what was left was worth very little, certainly not enough to pay back what we owed the bank.

As promised, Friedrich's father, Fritz Bolten Snr, arrived in June to visit for a few weeks. It was his first visit to Australia and the furthest he'd ever travelled.

Excitedly, we all lined up at Kununurra airport, dressed in our Sunday best, hair done and hands washed, waiting for the arrival of the midday flight from Perth. Anyone would've thought the king was coming to town; as far as we were concerned, he was.

I caught the first glimpse of the shiny Ansett wings on the horizon and we watched as the plane came in to land with a thud in the dust.

The children raced onto the tarmac as soon as the cabin door opened, beating the standard Kununurra greeting party – a cloud of sticky black flies – to their beloved Opa.

He scooped them up in his thinning arms, and Margret squealed with delight, 'Opa! Opa!'

He hugged us all, then looked at Friedrich and said, laughing, *'Guter Gott, Friedrich, wo bin ich?'* – Good God, Friedrich, where am I?

Then he shook Fritz's hand and said, *'Du bist jetzt ein Mann!'* – You are a man now! Lovingly he pulled Fritz to him and kissed him on the head.

As Friedrich and his father walked side by side to the car, the similarity of their mannerisms struck me: eyes down and brows furrowed, concentrating. With both of their heads bowed, I could see their once-thick strawberry-blond curls thinning ever so slightly around the crown. Fritz Jnr had the same blue eyes and fine features as his father and grandfather. The resemblance between the three of them was striking. Age was catching up with my father-in-law, though; he'd lost weight since I'd last seen him. But the advancing years could never diminish the proud marching posture he unconsciously adopted as he walked, the result of years serving in the army in Russia.

It'd been a long journey for the 71-year-old. We gave him a quick tour of the town and took him home to rest, but instead of heading for an afternoon nap, he surprised the children with a huge bag of gifts that my mother-in-law had put together.

Among the gifts for the children was a beautifully wrapped box for me. I gently peeled back the gold ribbon and lifted the lid.

'*Wunderbar!*' I cried, clapping my hands with delight. '*Danke, Vater, danke.*' It was a box of Katjes, my favourite German licorice, which I'd longed for. It was a little taste of home. The rich salty aniseed smell wafted through the kitchen as soon as I opened the bag. I had a tiny piece, enough to savour the taste, then wrapped it carefully and put it away, hoping to make it last as long as possible.

Our special welcome afternoon tea had become an impromptu, very belated Christmas celebration. In the spirit of the mood, Friedrich poured a beer for his father and wine for himself, and I brought out coffee and cake for us all as we spent the next few hours catching up on all of the news from home.

With the alcohol warming their hearts and loosening their lips, the men moved out onto the back veranda overlooking the river, and although Friedrich and his father had never been big talkers, they chatted and laughed well into the night.

Every now and then Friedrich would see or hear a movement in the river below and he'd yell, '*Vater, Krokodil!*'

It was good-hearted teasing, because the poor man could barely see 10 feet in front of him after losing an eye during the war. Not to be outdone, the wily old man turned his head and popped his glass eye out for the children to see. It was an old trick, one we'd seen many times before, but Fritz and Margret never tired of it. They adored their Opa and thought he was hilarious.

I finally got all of them, children and grown men, to bed quite late, promising Vater we would take him out to the farm first thing. He was eager to get out into the fields and see this 'oasis' Friedrich had talked about. Despite the long flight and the revelry that followed, old habits die hard and Fritz Snr was up before sunrise, just like his son. A perfect dawn, the sky swirling pink and orange, greeted them as they set off down Riverfarm Road.

It was wonderful to have some company from home and it meant the world to Friedrich that his father made the effort to come all this way. Neither of our families could understand why we left Germany for Australia. My father virtually cut me off because he was so upset that we were leaving, and at first Friedrich's family were very hostile about his decision. They just couldn't imagine why he would leave a very successful farm to go to Kununurra. After we'd taken Fritz Snr for a swim in Lake Argyle, a picnic lunch in the sprawling Hidden Valley and fishing on the Ord, he loved it too.

Fritz Snr particularly fell in love with the hot weather. No matter how hot it was, we'd find him sitting out in the sun, jacket off. He took himself on long walks around the property, along the river and through the orchards next door to us, which eventually led to Judy and John's. He was endlessly taking photos to show Friedrich's mother, Margarethe. Being a farmer too, he was intrigued by the different plants and vegetation that grew here.

Some days he'd wander around for a good few hours taking in the scenery, come in for lunch or afternoon tea, then wander off again, regaling us that night with stories of things he'd seen. I was always telling him to drink more water, worried that he would get dehydrated, but he seemed to have the constitution of an ox.

One afternoon he decided to go for a bike ride after lunch. He was gone for some time in the heat of the day, which wasn't unusual, but he always returned home in time for afternoon tea with the children when the school bus arrived. The kids came in and dumped their bags in the laundry but Opa was nowhere to be seen. I assumed he'd found a farmer or a neighbour to chat with on his travels, but by the time I began preparing dinner he still wasn't home and I was beginning to get worried.

I called Judy and John; they hadn't seen him. I sent Fritz and Margret out to search around for him and they came back half an hour later with no sign of Opa either.

I called John again and he jumped in the car and went out to the farm to raise Friedrich, while I bundled the kids into our car and drove along Riverfarm Road. Still no sign of Opa.

By this time, he'd been gone several hours. The worst thoughts flashed through my head: he could've been taken by a crocodile or bitten by a snake.

A search party of neighbours and friends was rallied and groups went separate ways, scouring the edge of the river and the surrounding roads. They poked through 2-metre-high cane grass, walked the banks of irrigation channels and searched through fields.

The search team reconvened at our place and Friedrich called the local police. Once word had spread that an elderly man was missing, dozens of people – some we'd never met – showed up offering to help. That was Kununurra. The sun was setting and darkness quickly descending; our stomachs were churning with the thought of what might have happened.

As the search groups prepared to head out again, a local water company worker, on his way to our place to join the search, spotted what looked like a man hunched over on the side of the road. He thought his eyes were playing tricks in the dark, but sure enough, it was Opa, more than 20 kilometres from home.

Fritz Snr had been having a lovely afternoon ride around the nearby farms when he took a wrong turn and lost his bearings. Along the way, his bike got a flat tyre, so he ditched it on the side of the road and tried to walk home. All of the roads and farms pretty much look the same around here and he couldn't find his way back. He'd been walking around in circles for hours.

We were so relieved to see the ute pull up with Vater in the front seat.

While he soothed his blistered feet in a cool bath, Friedrich decided a celebration was in order. He emptied the fridge of our beer stocks, and we put on an impromptu barbecue to thank everyone who'd come to help; a cheer went up when Opa eventually joined us all for a 'tinnie' on our back veranda.

Despite some sunburn and a little dehydration, Opa wasn't too bothered by his ordeal and came through it relatively unscathed. I think it took us longer to recover from the fright he'd given us. We never did find his bike.

We farewelled Fritz Snr and our wonderful nanny Steffi the following week. Sadly Steffi's visa had expired and it was time for her to go home. She had been part of our family for a long time and we had become very close over the years. Steffi had been with us through some of the biggest events of our lives. The children adored her and I was especially grateful for her support settling into this place. I was sad to see her go, but she promised to return when she finished her studies. We arranged for them to fly back together. I was sad to see Opa go too. We loved having visitors – that little touch of home kept us going.

With our money running out fast, Friedrich had one last roll of the dice. In May he went to work ploughing the fields again; this time he'd plant peanuts, a dry season crop and a much hardier plant. It was backbreaking work getting the weeds out again and the soil turned over in readiness.

One afternoon after we'd finished lunch, Friedrich asked me to come out to the farm with him. He wanted me to see how far things had progressed. We drove through paddock after paddock of freshly ploughed soil, deep furrows carved to precision, ready to be planted. But as we drove along, I could sense something was troubling him.

'Frauke, we've run out of money,' he said bluntly. 'We need to sell the farm in Germany.'

I was overcome with a wave of nausea. I wound down the window, gasping for air. An ache washed over me, from my heart to the pit of my stomach.

'This farm has enormous potential,' he went on. 'We can grow things here in a way we could never grow them in

Germany. The sun, the water – I feel like I'm only beginning to see what we can achieve. It is the right thing to do.'

We had mounting debts and the bank wouldn't loan us any more until we paid them down, he explained. The farm in Seedorf was our best asset. We could've packed up and moved back home, but Friedrich was too proud for that.

My silence said everything. But Friedrich wasn't so much asking for my permission – he was softening the blow of a decision he'd already made. Friedrich arranged the sale of the farm, and the signed papers arrived a month later.

My home was gone. Everything we had worked for. Sometimes in the early hours of the morning, when I should've been sleeping, I wondered whether Friedrich had planned this all along. Did he know we would be selling when we took that trip back home? Was that what the trip was really all about?

For weeks, I felt a knot in my stomach. I could barely look at food, and the feeling of exhaustion was overwhelming. I put it down to the stress of what had happened and the desperate sadness I felt. Waves of dark depression clouded my soul.

Friedrich insisted I see the doctor at the Kununurra medical centre, which was a tiny one-room clinic. The doctor called me in and took my blood pressure and my temperature, then felt the glands in my neck and prodded my tummy.

'I'd like you to do a urine test please, Frauke,' he said, so off I went, dutifully returning with my sample a few minutes later. That was when the next bombshell was delivered: 'Congratulations, Frauke, you are expecting a baby!'

Chapter 11

I had longed for another child and with the sadness of the Seedorf farm being sold, this baby came at the right time to warm my heart. It gave us all something to look forward to and any tensions were quickly dissolved amid the joy.

Germans like to announce things in grand style: we had a lovely card printed that we posted to all our friends and relatives, heralding the pregnancy and sharing the news that we'd sold the farm. It's fair to say it was met with a mixed reaction.

Tante Banta was very happy for us and immediately booked a flight. Friedrich's parents were sad that we'd sold up, but having visited us, his father now understood why Friedrich loved this place. They booked tickets to come over after the baby's arrival, bringing with them Maren, a new au pair to help us.

My father, however, didn't take the news well. He wrote me a long letter expressing bitterness and great disappointment. There was 'no point in me benefiting from his efforts

My mother and father with my brother Juergen and sister, Dorte. I am about six months old.

The Bolten family home in Suenderuphof, where I began my apprenticeship and met my husband.

Just married, my wedding day to Friedrich.

Like father, like son, Friedrich and Mr Bolten Snr.

Zimbabwe, the roads around Shamva.

Workers on the farm in Zimbabwe
during the cotton harvest.

Our new home in Seedorf, Germany.

Margret and her pony Ilka at our new farm in Germany.

Peter on Friedrich's knee.

Friedrich surveying the vast expanse of the Kimberley.

Before – the farm in Kununurra when we arrived, we were so disappointed.

After – Friedrich worked tirelessly ploughing the concrete earth getting it ready to sow.

Maria and Julia Caratti with a croc in the backyard at Judy's.

Margarethe and Mr Bolten Snr
at the Knx races on their trip to
Australia, 1983.

Tante Banta during a visit to
Australia, she relished the heat.

My wedding to Robert.

establishing our family in Germany', he wrote. Therefore, my share would be distributed to others in the family. In other words, I was disinherited.

His reaction broke my heart. It wasn't the money – I couldn't have cared less about that. It was that my father, of all people, should've understood the bond between a husband and wife, and the vow 'for better or for worse'. It was Friedrich's decision to sell the farm, not mine, and I had little choice but to stay and support him and make my marriage work. The weight of his words sat heavily on me, so I slipped the letter back into its envelope and placed it out of sight, never to be opened again.

The farm in Seedorf had been a security blanket for me; I had in the back of my mind that we could pack up and head home at any time if things didn't work out in Australia. That sense of comfort was now gone and I had to accept we would never go back to Germany to live. This baby, though, was a sign from God that everything was happening for the right reason. Now I had to plant my roots here and allow the branches of my heart to flourish.

We organised family and friends to pack up our things. Some furniture was given away, some sold, while the rest of our precious belongings went into relatives' attics. I had been very sad the day the thick envelope of signed sale documents arrived in the mail, but not long after, a big parcel of precious baby clothes, blankets and toys that I'd had for Fritz, Margret and Peter was delivered. This new little one would be swaddled in precious heirlooms from home. I was so touched to think that people we loved had carefully washed, wrapped and packed these things for my new bub, who was already in their hearts and minds. It was a wonderful surprise. A few months before I found out I was having another baby, Judy and John announced they were expecting their first child. I was so excited for them and it was wonderful to have someone to share this special time with. Judy and I compared our growing tummies and how we coped with morning sickness (which lasts all day) in the relentless heat and humidity.

Julia Caratti was delivered safely on 2 January 1983. Judy and John were besotted with their little girl. Her playmate arrived exactly three months later, on 3 April.

That morning I woke with a niggle in my belly – not enough of a contraction to cause alarm, but a familiar discomfort that signalled this baby was on the way. It was Easter Sunday and we were off to church because Julia was being christened.

Not wanting to cause any fuss, I did my best to keep the simmering contractions under my hat. I hoped the congregation would mistake my wriggling for the usual irritation of sitting on wooden church pews. Afterwards we all went back to Judy's for lunch, but we weren't there long before I whispered to Friedrich, 'We need to go to the hospital – now!'

Tante Banta had arrived a few weeks earlier to help out. While some German visitors couldn't stand the intense heat, this sprightly eighty-year-old relished the outback sun. She suffered terrible emphysema and the harsh European winters played havoc with her health, but out here the hot air seemed to soothe her lungs and bring her fragile frame to life. That was fortunate because she'd need every ounce of energy to keep an eye on my adventurous little Peter while I was in hospital.

When we got to the car, I said to Friedrich, 'Please hurry, this baby is on its way!' By then the contractions were coming hard and fast, and in the confines of the car I could happily let go of the cries I'd been stifling for the past hour. Friedrich hot-footed it into town, while doing his best to be helpful. 'Breathe, Frauke, breathe,' he said. 'We are nearly there.' I wanted to punch him!

The Kununurra hospital, with white paint peeling off the fibro walls and blowflies swarming over the flywire door, was a far cry from the modern German hospital where Peter was born. Yet despite the dilapidated exterior, many miracles had been performed in this little bush clinic.

Kununurra women didn't have the luxury of a team of gynaecologists or obstetricians on hand, but thankfully we had Dr Fred, who'd delivered just about every baby ever born in the Kimberley. Dr Fred had overseen the safe arrival of babies on remote cattle stations, in the midst of cyclonic wet-season storms, even on a bumpy plane ride to Derby, so I was confident I would be in good hands. The nurse helped Friedrich get me inside and raced off to phone the doctor.

'The good news is, Doctor is on his way,' she said when she returned to put clean sheets on the bed. 'But the bad news is, we can't find the matron. She's apparently gone fishing.'

Matron or not, this baby wasn't going to wait.

Dr Fred's car pulled up about ten minutes later. Clearly, he'd taken the nurse's advice to come post-haste, because he arrived in the emergency room in farm shorts, an old T-shirt and bare feet.

The baby's head was crowning by the time he'd scrubbed up; one last big push was all that was needed. 'Congratulations, Frauke,' Dr Fred said. 'You have a beautiful baby girl.' There were cheers all around when she gave her first squeal. Ten fingers, ten toes, one good set of lungs. The nurse wrapped up my little bundle and handed her to Friedrich.

Judy was shocked when Fritz and Margret ran down her driveway a few hours later, proudly announcing, 'We've got a new baby sister!' That afternoon when she visited me in hospital she said, 'I thought you looked a bit uncomfortable at church!'

Dorte Maria Bolten – or Maria, as we called her – was a very easy baby. Fritz and Margret adored her; she looked so tiny cradled in the arms of Fritz, who was now thirteen years old. But it was three-year-old Peter who took a real shine to her, and she to him. Almost instantly the two of them seemed to have their own language and communicated in their own way. They were inseparable.

With Maria's arrival we really needed to make some changes to the house, and after Friedrich sold the farm he had promised me a renovation at Riverfarm Road to soften the blow.

The kitchen would be gutted and redesigned to be open plan, with more space to move around, and with a bigger stove and oven so I could cater for large numbers of guests. The brown kitchen walls would be replastered and the matching brown Marimekko curtains would be replaced with some curtains I'd bought at IKEA in Germany; modern and lighter, they would give the room a more open feeling.

My non-negotiable, though, was a built-in coolroom. Regular fridges didn't have enough space for us to store food long-term, which was vital over the wet season when roads in and out of Kununurra were often cut off by floods for several weeks. We designed a large walk-in coolroom with a freezer – enough space that we could store our own kills, giving us access to good-quality meat, which we could source from surrounding cattle stations, all year round.

The final step in the transformation was to build a swimming pool out by the veranda. The government had made it illegal to kill crocodiles and their numbers were increasing rapidly. It was no longer safe for the kids to swim in the river, and with the heat and humidity all year round they needed somewhere to cool off.

Virtually all of the building materials had to be shipped in from Darwin and Perth, so I made a plan that once the demolition of the kitchen began, I would pack up the children and drive to Darwin for a week. From there I would arrange delivery of the last of the bits and pieces, like tiles and furnishings, and at least we would have hot water and flushing toilets. Friedrich, who was staying behind to run the farm and keep an eye on things, would have to do without those luxuries once the work began.

Maria was just ten weeks old when I loaded up the car and took off for the ten-hour drive up the Victoria Highway. I'd need to stop and feed her somewhere along the way, so I'd made a booking at a motel in Katherine for the night; we would head off again the next morning fresh for the last leg to Darwin.

The Victoria Highway was dual-lane bitumen. I couldn't imagine what it must have been like trying to navigate this stretch of road a few years before, when it was still gravel and largely used only by enormous cattle trucks taking stock from remote stations to the port of Darwin for export. A cattle train could stretch 100 metres, with two or three trailers carrying hundreds of rowdy steers and freshly mustered Brahmans.

The first time I saw one of these long, rattling trucks appear in the rear-view mirror I felt butterflies in my tummy. I'd never encountered anything like it. Out on the open road, hundreds of miles from nowhere, it was a formidable beast bearing down on our little car. It was daunting watching the dusty steel workhorses get closer and closer.

I knew these trucks reach great speeds, and this one was like a beef-laden bullet ploughing up the highway. I ummed and ahhed for a few seconds about what to do. I could plant my foot and try to accelerate away, but I soon decided I couldn't compete with his size or speed, so I pulled off the road and let him past. By the time we'd travelled a few hours, I had become quite confident at negotiating the road with these trucks. I had the utmost respect for the truckies behind the wheel and thought the best option was to keep well out of their way.

The cattle trains weren't the only danger I had been warned about. Kangaroos were common, particularly at night, and car headlights startled them. They could dart across the road in a split second. While majestic to look at, they are powerful and can grow to some size, so a kangaroo could wipe out your car or cause you to veer off the road. So as dusk descended, I gripped the steering wheel, my eyes searching all around me for any flicker of movement.

I breathed an enormous sigh of relief as the lights of Katherine appeared before us and we could put our heads on a pillow and get some rest.

We all enjoyed our week in Darwin, then drove home to our newly renovated house. I took great delight filling our coolroom. Even more exciting, though, was the news that we would soon have STD phone access and a new satellite that would give us television reception.

Television had arrived in Kununurra only a few months before us, and there was just one TV channel, the ABC.

To be able to ring our friends and family whenever we liked and watch something other than the ABC news on television would be a godsend. I was looking forward to watching shows I'd only ever read about, *A Country Practice* and *Hey Hey It's Saturday*.

Kununurra was coming into the modern age.

Chapter 12

The realisation that we were staying in Australia threw up an unexpected dilemma: we had to make decisions about schooling for Fritz and Margret, who were now fourteen and thirteen years old. Although they could stay at school in Kununurra, many local kids went to boarding school for their teenage years. In Germany, children were only ever sent to boarding school if they had problems or their parents were divorcing. We had to accept that life was different in outback Australia and sending your kids to boarding school was quite the norm.

Realistically, boarding school offered Fritz and Margret a more rounded education and greater opportunities – but the thought of being separated from them, especially at these delicate teen years, was unbearable. I wanted to wrap my children up tight and never let them leave me; I didn't want them to feel the absence of a mother for a minute. Friedrich adored the children and he loved the hum of a busy household: Fritz was his right-hand man and Margret his little princess. Maybe we were more worried about how *we'd* cope than how Fritz and Margret would cope.

Over many cups of tea, Friedrich and I agonised over what to do. Every decision we'd ever made was with the children's best interests at heart, and we both knew deep down we really had no choice: they had to go to boarding school.

I took comfort in my staunch belief that when you give birth to a child, part of you is with them forever. They are always in your heart and head. The love between a mother and child never wavers, no matter whether you are together or apart.

Next we had to choose between boarding schools in Darwin, a ten-hour drive away, or Perth, which was much further away, a four-hour flight.

Darwin was a relatively small place, more of a big country town, and it was still rebuilding after the devastation of Cyclone Tracy in 1974. Perth was more advanced and had a German consulate, and the children were familiar with it from the time we spent there on our arrival in Australia. We felt they would settle more easily there.

Fritz was accepted into Wesley College in Perth, a wonderful school renowned for its nurturing of boarders. He would finish the year at school in Kununurra, then head off to Germany to spend Christmas and the summer holidays with family before beginning at Wesley in 1985. Margret would start at St Mary's Anglican Girls' School, which had a reputation for its gentle spirit and extra care of country girls, straight away. Both would have the chance to make friends from very similar backgrounds, children from remote farms and cattle stations. Though we had heavy hearts, we felt that enrolling them in these schools was the right thing to do.

Peter would turn five that year and was not yet off to kindergarten, and although just a baby, Maria had already developed quite a personality. Friedrich and I were confident that with these little adventurers at home our house would never be quiet.

Margret settled in well, though the discipline of boarding school was a world away from the carefree life in Kununurra. We missed her terribly. I'd sometimes go to call out for her and suddenly realise she wasn't there. Trying to call her at the boarding house was tough: I'd have to ring very early in the morning before school to get through. I'm sure all of the girls knew when the phone rang early that it was Margret's mum.

Each week I bundled up a package of special treats from home and posted it down to her: cookies, photos, notes and cards from us all.

Friedrich missed his Little Lise, as he called her. Often after we spoke to her, he became very quiet and withdrawn, so for his birthday in July, I secretly organised to fly Margret home to surprise him.

I told him I was heading into town to do some shopping; instead I raced to the airport to meet the afternoon flight from Perth. Margret and I had so much to catch up on, and the words poured out in the car on the way home. When we reached our gate, she ducked down in the front seat so he couldn't see her, then quietly followed me inside.

I think Friedrich thought he'd seen a ghost when this tall teenage girl appeared from behind me. 'Hello Vater, happy birthday!' she said, beaming.

'Margret Liselotte Bolten!'

He was ecstatic, wiping away tears as he hugged her. He declared it was the best birthday he'd ever had, and I made us a special birthday dinner with our traditional *Baumkuchen* cake to celebrate.

The farm was still struggling and each crop experiment we tried failed dismally. Our cash reserves were dwindling and with the added expenses of boarding school, money was tight.

Friedrich felt that more land was what we needed to make the farm profitable. One thousand hectares wasn't enough to get the best yields. He reasoned that additional land would give us economies of scale, and we could diversify the crop and by planting on rotation would always have an income-producing crop in the field.

It was a lot of money to spend, but I had to have faith in Friedrich's vision and his ability to look after us. Farming in Kununurra had been a steep learning curve. We'd already conquered unpredictable mountains trying to tame this fragile and temperamental land, and Friedrich was eternally optimistic that God would eventually reward us for all of our sacrifices; we just had to be patient and work harder.

The biggest lesson we'd learnt so far was that everything we knew about farming in Germany was pretty much useless here. We were starting from scratch. Every new crop taught us something; every failure did too. Wisely, Friedrich tried to find a farm manager to come and work with us, someone with a depth of local experience that could teach him the nuances of this land, but we struggled to find the right person. And so we battled on, very much alone.

With the extra 700 hectares to look after, Friedrich decided a gyrocopter would be a valuable asset to the farm. Some nearby cattle stations were using helicopters or gyrocopters to help in mustering, with great success. Friedrich reasoned he could fly over the crops and check large expanses of the fields in just a few minutes, rather than slogging on foot, furrow by furrow, which took hours in the debilitating heat. It would save us time and money.

The day it was delivered we all went out to the farm, terribly excited to see this magnificent flying machine. For our $12,000 investment, we'd bought what I thought looked like a lawn mower with wings, with a tiny amount of space for the pilot, and the razor-sharp rotor blades sat uncomfortably close above your head.

With the motor off and wheels firmly tethered to the ground, we each took turns sitting in it, and Peter and Maria sat on Friedrich's knee, playing around with the joystick. Fritz was busting to fly in it, but there was no room for passengers – it only accommodated a pilot – so he would have to wait.

Friedrich had taken some lessons in South Australia and although he'd completed formal training, his certificate hadn't arrived. I was nervous about him flying it without paperwork, but he was confident enough to take it on a little test flight around the farm. 'One quick lap of the paddock to see she's working,' he promised. 'It'll be fine.'

Secretly, I knew, he was keen to show his new flying skills off to the children.

With great fanfare, he instructed us all to step back under the protective cover of a shed, then he strapped himself in to the little buzz box. With all of us eagerly watching on, he took control of the joystick and started the motor. Within about thirty seconds the long, thin blades were whipping around furiously, cutting through the air, and the gyro was ready for take-off.

As the tiny craft began to lift off we all cheered with delight. Friedrich was airborne, and you couldn't wipe the smile off his face. He was loving every moment, like a child with a new toy. Up and up he went, higher and higher, then with the slightest nudge of the joystick, the little craft tilted and off he zoomed. We clapped with joy; the children were so proud of their dad. He did a lap of the paddock closest to the shed and the soya-bean crop, then buzzed past us, flying dare-devilishly close to the shed.

'Wave to Daddy,' I said to the kids. Maria, who was on my hip, was oblivious to the fuss, but Peter was clapping his hands with delight. One last lap clearly wasn't enough, and Friedrich indicated he'd go around again.

This time, though, as he veered around to head over the paddock, he banked a little too hard and the hot north wind seemed to catch the blades the wrong way. The gyro tilted hard to one side and bounced around in the air, losing balance. With limited skill, Friedrich couldn't right it. We watched in horror as our very expensive toy spun out of control and crashed on the banks of the irrigation channel about 100 metres from the sheds. Fritz and I raced over to Friedrich, who, thankfully, was absolutely fine except for a bruised ego. One of the rotor blades hadn't fared so well though. It was just bent enough that the gyrocopter couldn't be flown again until it was fixed. It would have to be transported to Darwin for repairs.

'*Scheisse!*' Friedrich cursed, throwing his helmet down hard into the mud, furious with himself. '*Blöd Dummkopf!*'

Fritz burst out laughing at his father swearing at himself, and soon we all had the giggles.

'I'm sorry, Frauke,' he said. All I could do was shake my head at him and smile, relieved he hadn't hurt himself.

The tiny craft was so light that with the help of a few neighbouring farmers and the tractor we could lift it out of the ditch and onto the back of a trailer. It was towed back into our sheds, where it would stay awaiting repair. No one dared mention it again.

Soon enough it was time to farewell Fritz. We would miss him at Christmas but the experience of being at the Boltens' farm would be invaluable for the farmer-in-waiting. Friedrich worked even longer hours after Fritz went to Germany. I guess he felt that he wasn't needed at home as much now and could dedicate more time to the farm. With the extra hectares came more work too, and he'd spend hours tinkering on machinery in the sheds or walking the paddocks until the last of the dusk light, checking the crops. He'd come home for a few winks of sleep and be gone again before sunrise. There was always something to do. One morning I caught a glimpse of him in the shower and wondered how on earth his willowy European frame could keep going each day. He'd always been a very lean man – not an ounce of fat on him – but his lithe body was thinner than normal and I worried he would easily dehydrate in the perishing heat. The tropical heat sucks every drop of moisture from you and at times your sanity too. He grew a beard to protect his fine skin and he always wore a cotton hat, but long days working in the sun eventually take a toll.

At times I put my foot down, because I could see him getting very tired and it was dangerous for him to be driving heavy tractors and headers in that state. Using every womanly charm I could muster, I sometimes managed to persuade him to take some time off, but he'd get up in the night and pace around the house. His mind ran at a frenetic pace, churning over new ideas.

With Fritz and Margret both away I entertained as often as I could, inviting friends and guests regularly for barbecues and special dinners. I'd invite friends from the tennis club and newcomers to the town, to welcome them as Judy and John had done with us, as well as nearby farming families.

I used any excuse to have people around for dinner; every birthday, anniversary or special day, we celebrated. I needed noise and activity and company around the house. Cooking and entertaining gave me a purpose, and it gave us something to look forward to.

Working on a farm can be very isolating and the company of other men, particularly other farmers, was important for them; mateship is a quintessential part of Australia, and I felt it was important for Friedrich to socialise with other men too. Friedrich wasn't a big drinker, but on nights when we had guests, I'd encourage him to have a social glass of wine, because after a good meal and with the help of a little vino I could coax him into a rare and much-needed full night's sleep.

He could be wonderful company and he rose to the occasion when we had people around. It was good to see the old Friedrich appear, but as the alcohol and the false bravado wore off, a shadow appeared again, a lingering melancholy I couldn't put my finger on.

Under the guise of a general health check-up, I made an appointment for Friedrich to go and see the local doctor.

He had been our GP since we arrived and had become a good friend, often sharing a meal with us. I told him I was worried about Friedrich.

Friedrich told me later that he spoke about issues at home and the farm, the doctor nodding in sympathy and peppering him with a few questions along the way. 'Does Frauke feel homesick for Germany?' Yes, of course! 'Does she miss the children?' Terribly.

Apparently, Friedrich said very little about himself and he certainly didn't express any worries, he just nodded in acknowledgement to the questions being asked about me. When the doctor asked how he was feeling, Friedrich answered, 'I'm fine.' That was it, end of discussion.

At the end of the consultation the doctor prescribed Valium – for me.

There was no treatment for Friedrich, nothing but to soldier on.

When Christmas was on the horizon, Friedrich was working doubly hard at the farm preparing the paddocks for the next crop.

He weeded, ploughed, weeded again, then fertilised. The deep, straight furrows of red earth were an impressive sight and would be perfect for the latest crop we were trying: soya beans. There was no doubt Friedrich was a perfectionist.

I'd done my Christmas shopping months before, on a visit to Perth, so I was quite organised but there was always baking to do.

We would have our traditional celebration on Christmas Eve, as always. It would be a big affair this year, with neighbours and newcomers to the community invited to celebrate with us. Fritz was the only one missing; he'd be spending Christmas with his grandparents. It was such a wonderful adventure for a boy his age, and I knew the Boltens would take great delight in spoiling their grandson.

I looked forward to Christmas every year, and especially to the days I'd spend beforehand with Margret, baking a feast of delicious traditional German cakes and treats.

In mid-December she flew home on school holidays. Friedrich insisted on being at the airport to meet her. He hugged her tight when she stepped onto the tarmac, and he whispered, 'I'm so happy you are home, I really need you here right now.'

We had no idea of the true meaning of what Friedrich had just said, because we were blissfully caught up in the joy of welcoming Margret home. But his words would soon take on a tragic significance.

Chapter 13

In addition to our traditional Christmas Eve celebrations, I'd also invited the entire Kununurra Tennis Club over for an end-of-season dinner on a Friday night ten days before Christmas. It would take a few days to get everything ready, so on the Wednesday I began preparing for a sumptuous hot and cold buffet.

By that evening most of the menu was organised and some food already prepared, wrapped and stored in the coolroom. Margret, Maren and I would do the final tasks, including polishing up the glassware, the next morning. Friedrich's job was to get the barbecue ready for me. Otherwise, we were organised. I fell into bed exhausted but happy.

Friedrich had gone to bed earlier, very frustrated because one of the crops had been planted too deep to germinate and he would need to re-sow the paddock. Things just weren't going to plan.

It wasn't unusual to wake in the middle of the night and find myself alone. I'd stretch an arm out and the coolness of the sheets meant there was no one beside me, no warm skin resting on mine. I'd become so used to it, I'd just roll over and go back to sleep. Often I'd brush up against Friedrich's leg a few hours later when he'd crawled back under the covers at some ungodly hour of the morning.

I'm not really sure what woke me that morning, but I knew instinctively that Friedrich wasn't in the bed with me before I flicked the light on. I checked the time, 3am. Sometimes I could hear him in the office or see the glow of the light in the passage and knew he was at his desk studying farming books or journals, but this morning all I saw was darkness.

'Friedrich?' I called gently, trying not to wake the children. There was no response, so I turned the light off and went back to sleep. Surely he hadn't gone out to the farm at this hour?

At 5am, the sun was beginning to poke through the curtains, but still Friedrich hadn't climbed back into bed. I got up to see where he was.

I poked my head into Fritz's room, mentally taking everything in. He wasn't in Fritz's bed, and the three guns we kept mounted on the wall in Fritz's room were still in place. I breathed a sigh of relief.

Peter and Maria were fast asleep. Margret was sleeping soundly, happy to be home in her own bed.

I walked into the kitchen and could see Friedrich's car through the window. He was home, but where on earth was he? The back door was slightly ajar. I half expected to open it and find him sitting on the porch pulling his work boots on, but he was nowhere to be seen.

The air outside was cool on my face and slivers of the pink dawn smiling from the horizon caught my eye. The sunrise was spectacular and the rich colours were reflected on the river, making it swirl orangey pink.

I wandered down the damp grass towards the river, captivated by the stillness. It was a beautiful morning, not a breath of wind, not a sound, not a ripple on the water.

And then I found him.

I saw his feet first; he was lying peacefully like he'd fallen asleep on the lawn. But he hadn't and I knew. A gun was resting alongside him; he must've had one hidden away at the farm somewhere.

Being an experienced hunter, he'd carefully positioned himself so that when he pulled the trigger he fell onto the side of the wound, masking the horror from our vulnerable eyes.

Always a perfectionist.

I sat down on the dewy grass alongside him and gently stroked his legs. 'Oh Friedrich,' I cried. There was nothing I could do, he was dead. I prayed and held his hand. I cursed him, then told him how much I loved him. I sat with him for a long time, talking to him, crying for him, but the children would be up soon and I didn't want them to find their father the way I had.

The first person I rang was the doctor. 'Friedrich's dead, I don't blame you for it, but he's dead.' He arranged for the police and ambulance to come. Judy arrived soon after.

By the time the children were awake, our house was full of strangers and I was sinking into a deep shock.

My body felt numb and cold, and images flicked backwards and forwards in my mind so quickly I couldn't grasp hold of anything to focus on, and things became quite a blur.

Someone had placed a sheet over Friedrich's body. I had no idea who, but I was grateful.

'Mutti, what's going on?' Margret asked, wiping the sleep from her eyes. 'Where's Vater?'

Chapter 14

The sense of loss hit me immediately. Part of me was gone. An emptiness settled in my bones and there was a pain in my chest that was physical, like a hand had reached into my ribs and was slowly forming a fist around my heart, squeezing me breathless minute by minute. My muscles ached and I was so very tired.

Yet even though I was overwhelmed with grief, I caught myself automatically turning my head to speak with Friedrich, then reality would hit that he was dead. Friedrich was dead.

His body was still resting on the lawn at the side of the house. Thankfully, from the back window we couldn't see him – but even so, I couldn't look out. Time seemed to be standing still and I was getting agitated that my husband was not being taken care of. I hated the thought of him being out there alone. Finally, once the police had finished taking photographs of the scene, the ambulance took his body to the hospital, where an autopsy would be done.

The police had written pages of notes in their books, and then once Friedrich was gone, they came inside to question me. They were very polite and respectful. They wanted to know what time I found Friedrich, had there been anyone else in the house, did Friedrich have any enemies, where did he get the gun, did I hear a shot? I answered everything as best I could, but my mind was in quite a foggy state by then. Judy was wonderful; she brought me tea and sat with me quietly while I tried to make sense of it all and offer the police some sort of coherent response. On their way out, the local constable gave me his card and told me not to hesitate calling the station if there was anything I needed; he said they would handle the formalities and file a report with the coroner.

It was early morning in Germany, but I had to tell Friedrich's parents. Dialling their number was terribly hard; I had a knot in my stomach. But when the phone rang, they'd already braced for bad news; it's never good news when the phone rings at 4am.

At first, Friedrich's father was very angry with him. 'How could he do such a terrible thing – leave a wife and children?' he muttered. I could hear the shame in his voice. What would they tell people?

Anger and frustration towards Friedrich were an under-standable emotional shield at that stage. It was only later that the sadness and despair bubbling just below the surface would inevitably rise.

Friedrich's mother took the news very badly. She couldn't fathom that Friedrich died by his own hand. 'It must've been an accident, Frauke, a terrible accident,' she declared. 'He would not do something like this.'

She howled down the phone – enormous guttural, chest-heaving sobs that came from a place I completely understood: mothers and their children have a special bond; a child is a part of you. No matter what age our children are, they will always be our babies. It's not the natural order for a child to die before his mother, and when it's by his own hand it's a pain worse than any other, especially for a proud German family. This was considered an insulting and dishonoura-ble way to die. Margarethe would never get to hold her son again, and the very thought of it was unbearable to her. She was a mother minus her child; part of her was lost and she felt her heart would never recover.

They offered to break the news to Fritz when he woke up, which I appreciated because I wanted someone to be with him.

Word spread quickly around the district that there'd been a terrible tragedy. Friends, neighbours and people from the tennis club began to arrive to comfort us and offer sympathies.

There is an unwritten and unbreakable community spirit that is without doubt the backbone of the Australian outback. Bush people are selfless and will drop whatever they are doing to help someone in need; the kindness shown to us by complete strangers was overwhelming and wonderful. People dropped off food and flowers, the house seemed to be full of people and the kettle was permanently boiling. I think I drank a thousand cups of tea and coffee that day. There was always someone on hand to sit with me and comfort me or distract the children, which I appreciated, but despite this, I'd never felt more alone.

I was in a strange state of limbo and felt very confused about how I should be reacting and what I should be doing. There's no handbook on what to do when someone you love dies unexpectedly. One part of me wanted to politely shoo everyone out of the house and get on with life, soldier on as if nothing had happened.

The other part of me was absolutely terrified. I wanted to lock myself in my bedroom and cry until there was nothing left to come out. I was thirty-seven years old and alone in the outback with four children, a world away from home and my family.

What on earth would become of us?

I put on a brave face, smiled and tried my best to be present – but it was an eggshell-thin veneer that could crack apart at any time.

After accompanying Friedrich's body to the hospital, the doctor returned to check on me. He was worried I'd shoot myself too. How could he even think I would contemplate such a thing? I knew what it was like to grow up without a parent: my absolute focus was the children and making sure they were okay. I wouldn't leave them alone for a moment, let alone kill myself too.

He offered me some tablets to help me sleep, but I wasn't interested. I was absolutely paranoid about what would happen to the children if I got sick. In my mind, it suddenly seemed urgent that I have a tetanus shot, because I couldn't take any chances. He could see I wasn't taking no for an answer. I agreed to accept the sleeping tablets if he would give me the shot. If giving me a tetanus shot helped calm and reassure me, then that's what he would do – but he also arranged for one of the nurses to come and stay overnight to keep an eye on me. This was not negotiable, he told me. Otherwise he would admit me to the hospital and keep me under observation.

Judy stayed with us too, she and Maren were my salvation.

That night the children slept in my bed with me, all of us cuddled up together. I needed them and they needed me. For most of the night I lay awake, churning questions over in my head: did I hear a shot in the night? Could I have done anything to stop him? What would become of us?

During the night as my mind raced, I prayed to God. I didn't go to church very often, but I never lost my faith, and as I lay in the darkness with my precious children tucked in my arms, I held tight to the belief that God would help me. He would show me the way.

When I woke the next morning, I felt the warmth of a body next to me, and momentarily breathed a sigh of relief. Friedrich was right here beside me. But he wasn't, it was Margret cuddled up close, with Peter and Maria next to her. Maren was asleep on a mattress on the floor. My precious children had lost their father and it broke my heart.

I needed to hear Fritz's voice, so I called him first thing in the morning. When he came on the line I broke down and cried. That was the first time I really cried.

Fritz told me that the night before last, he'd had a bad dream that Friedrich was dead. He'd woken up relieved that it was just a nightmare. A day later, Opa broke the news.

'Opa said it was an accident, but how, Mutti? I don't understand,' Fritz said. He was a wise boy for his fifteen years, who was very close to his father and knew farming life well. It didn't make sense to him that his father, who was a seasoned hunter and very careful with guns, died in a shooting accident. He kept probing for further details: 'But which gun was it, Mutti? And why was he out so early in the morning?'

The only time I'd ever seen Friedrich get very angry was some years before we'd left Germany, when he caught Fritz playing with one of his guns. Fritz was around nine or ten years old and the gun was hidden under our bed. Friedrich gave Fritz a hiding and threatened to kick his backside from Seedorf to Switzerland if he ever saw him touching the gun again. Fritz got the message loud and clear.

'Was he cleaning the gun, Mutti?' he asked.

'Fritz, I need to speak with your Opa, can you please put him on? I'll call you again later and we can talk more,' I said, stewing over his need for the truth and my need to protect him from it.

The hospital asked what was to be done with Friedrich's body after the autopsy. My first thought was that he would be buried here on the banks overlooking the Ord, the river he loved so much, but Western Australian laws wouldn't allow a coffin to be buried near a residence.

He would need to be buried in a cemetery or cremated. There was a cemetery in Kununurra, a lovely little resting place at the entrance to the Hidden Valley. A giant boab tree gave a little shade to historic gravestones, the final resting place of the pioneers of this land, but it didn't feel right to bury Friedrich there. His heart was here at Riverfarm Road and I wanted him near us.

Friedrich's family wanted him returned to Germany, which I understood too. I had long discussions about it with our children, Fritz Snr and Friedrich's brother, Hartwig. These were difficult conversations to have when the emotion was so raw. Together we decided that the best outcome was to cremate his body, bury some of his ashes at Riverfarm Road, and return the rest to Germany. Cremation posed a unique problem, though. There was no one in the Kimberley who did cremations, so Friedrich's body would have to be flown to Perth. I got in touch with the German consulate there. Friedrich was still a German citizen and I needed their help to sort through all of this. The consulate got in touch with funeral homes and airlines for me and began the process, which was a weight off my shoulders.

I was living on adrenalin at that point, fuelled by a need to get things organised and have some control over my life. I also hated the thought of Friedrich's body lying cold in the morgue; I needed to get him home.

In the midst of all of this, I was due to have the entire tennis club and their families for dinner that very evening. I obviously had to cancel, but I had a coolroom full of food ready to entertain everyone. Judy was wonderful; she organised for the food to be distributed around town so no one went hungry and the food didn't go to waste.

I went back and forth with the consulate on the phone the whole day. The good news was that it could be done: they found a lovely funeral home that was sympathetic to our unique circumstances and would happily help. Ansett would fly Friedrich's body to Perth, he would be cremated there, and his ashes would be flown back to us. This was terribly expensive – it cost more to fly his body in a coffin than a living passenger – but it was the right thing to do and I felt he was in good hands.

A couple of days after he died I had a dream about Friedrich. He came to me in my sleep and reassured me he was fine. He looked strong and happy, and he had a black dog with him, the beloved dog that he'd raised in Germany before he met me. That strange dream gave me comfort.

~

A lot of what happened during those first few days after Friedrich's death remains a blur. I mostly have memories of people being around and lots of activity and noise. But two distinct moments are etched in my memory with crystal clarity, because they became turning points in my life.

My conscience struggled with what we'd told Fritz about his father. It was a lie. I completely understood why Friedrich's parents wanted to protect Fritz from such horrible news, but in my heart I felt it was better for him to know the truth, and he needed to hear it from me.

Telling Fritz that his father committed suicide was the most difficult phone call I've ever had to make, but it was the right thing to do. Deep down he was suspicious about what he'd been told; his instincts told him something didn't add up.

We spoke for as long as we could, and I told Fritz everything about how I'd found his father and what had happened. He knew that Friedrich had been under a lot of pressure, and he'd sensed a change in his mood and behaviour over the previous months; we all had. He could see that Dad wasn't quite right. It was a very frank conversation.

As we hung up the phone he said to me, 'Thank you, Mutti, for telling me the truth, otherwise I would never have trusted you again.' Fritz had always been a very resilient child but I felt a shift, a sudden progression, within him that day: my boy became a man.

The second moment that would have a long-lasting impact on my life was when I called a German expat called Doris Brinkhaus, who lived in Perth with her husband Karl. When they'd first arrived in Perth for a holiday, the consulate introduced us and we suggested they visit us in the Kimberley. We welcomed any visitors but especially loved having Germans come to stay.

Doris and Karl had stayed with us for a few days and we instantly hit it off. They loved Australia so much they decided to stay, and they opened a jewellery store in Perth. When I visited Perth to pick up Margret from boarding school, Doris returned the favour and I stayed with them at their house in Claremont.

We weren't great friends by any stretch – we were acquaintances – but right now I needed all the help I could get, and I had a task that would've tested the best of relationships.

I phoned Doris and told her the news about Friedrich. She was very sad and offered her sympathies.

'Doris, I have a favour to ask – a big favour, and I completely understand if you say no,' I said.

'Okay,' she said warily. 'Go on.'

'Would you meet Friedrich's body at the airport and accompany him to the funeral home?'

'Of course, Frauke, of course,' she said without hesitation.

I breathed a sigh of relief. It gave me enormous comfort knowing that Friedrich wouldn't be alone on his final journey.

Two days later we went to the Kununurra airport to say goodbye to him. The airline was worried that passengers might feel uncomfortable knowing there was a body on board, so his coffin was discreetly loaded onto the plane inside a hangar before the plane taxied to the tarmac to take on the passengers. We quietly stood in a line at the edge of the tarmac as the plane took off.

In Perth, Doris was waiting at the airport to receive our most precious cargo. She took flowers with her and placed them on the white coffin as it was unloaded from the plane. It was a lovely gesture and meant the world to me. That day cemented a friendship that has lasted a lifetime.

Chapter 15

The German consul general, Kurt Kayser, brought Friedrich's ashes back home to Kununurra. Friedrich had met Kurt the very first time he came to Australia for the Valcourt farming famil – the journey that led us here – and Kurt had been instrumental in helping us settle. He stayed on for a few days for the small funeral service I had arranged on the lawn of our home on 23 December, ten days after Friedrich died.

Friedrich's parents decided not to come. It was too big a journey for them, physically and emotionally. We all felt it best Fritz remain with them and come home as we had planned at the end of January.

The service began early in the morning to avoid the debilitating humidity of the wet season, and to give us the best chance that we wouldn't be washed out by an unexpected thunderstorm. By 9am, it was already 31 degrees.

I dispensed with the formality of a traditional German funeral but insisted we have as many flowers as we could muster. There was no florist in Kununurra, so I couldn't order wreaths or bouquets. I had to make do with what we could find in the garden, and I asked each of the guests to bring flowers with them too.

A nice white tablecloth was draped over a small coffee table as a makeshift altar. The lacquered wooden box containing Friedrich's ashes rested in the centre, next to my favourite picture of him. Around these we laid all of the flowers. Friends had gathered together big beautiful blooms of bougainvillea – the bright pink gave a lovely splash of colour – and frangipanis, which were in abundance around the area. Their heady sweet scent perfumed the air.

We had dug out every chair we could find and placed them around the garden, so no one had to stand in the heat. All the mourners had been asked to dress in white. The river flowed along serenely in the background, framing a lovely backdrop, and I felt confident this was what Friedrich would've wanted.

The head of the local Agriculture Department office spoke. Then I said the Lord's Prayer in German. Others said a few kind words about Friedrich.

When the eulogy and prayers were over, one of my neighbours took a small shovel and dug a hole at the spot where I'd found Friedrich's body. It was there that we buried his ashes. A second urn of ashes was packed away to return to Germany.

When the last of the earth was patted down, I walked up with a cross we'd made from frangipani blooms. A beautiful towering gum offered some shade as I knelt down to place the cross on the grave. With one hand in the red dirt to balance myself, I said a prayer for Friedrich, then whispered, 'Goodbye, my darling.'

Almost instantly, the raw grief of the past ten days rushed to the surface and I could no longer hold my emotions back. I buried my head in my hands and broke down, bereft. My tired bones didn't have any strength to carry me any more. The one who comforted me was Peter.

Up until this point, Peter had been very quiet about his father's death. He had taken it all in but hadn't shown too much emotion, but as I wiped away the tears, he gently touched my arm and said, 'Don't worry, Mum, Dad is fine now.' It was subtle reassurance I'd expect from someone much more than five years old, and let me know that Peter had been thinking deeply about his father's death.

That evening, Peter insisted he brush his teeth with his father's toothbrush. Strange as it seemed, I let him. We all had our ways of finding comfort; I was in no state to argue.

The following day was Christmas Eve, but no one was in the mood for our traditional celebration. It happened more by habit than intent.

I'd done all of the Christmas shopping weeks before, and Maren wrapped all of the presents for me. Someone brought in a tree – to this day I don't know who – and we pulled together a meal. We lit candles for the loved ones we'd lost and said a special prayer for Friedrich. Lighting the candles was an important ritual we did each year, and at this time my thoughts always turned to my mother. Maybe she and Friedrich were in heaven together.

John and Judy and some other friends who'd travelled for the funeral joined us. Over dinner, someone asked: 'Frauke, when do you think you will head home to Germany?'

The question caught me off guard. 'Return to Germany? Well, I haven't given much thought to that yet,' I answered.

It was a little white lie. Every waking minute since Friedrich's death had been spent worrying about our future and what would become of us. It would've been easy to pack our bags and head back, but something in my heart was telling me that wasn't the answer just yet. I needed time to sort through Friedrich's affairs, and time to think about what was best for us.

After Christmas, Friedrich's brother, Hartwig, and cousin Soeren flew in to see us and take the second urn of Friedrich's ashes back to Germany. The Bolten family had arranged a memorial service and Friedrich's ashes would be interred alongside his grandparents in the family plot. We drove Hartwig and Soeren to the airport with the box tucked in the boot, carefully packed and wrapped, then placed inside a thick cardboard box to be stowed in Hartwig's luggage.

Saying goodbye was sad. It meant the world that they'd made the effort to come, when no other family members had. We all hugged before they walked across the steamy tarmac to board a flight to Perth and then one to Frankfurt. As sad as I was, it was comforting to think that on Friedrich's final journey to his homeland he was accompanied by people he loved.

The pilots knew they were carrying special cargo that day, and after take-off we watched as they banked back around and flew one last lap over the town and the Ord and up through the valley for Friedrich, before heading up into the clouds. Tears poured down my cheeks and my eyes were fixed to the sky until the last shiny speck of the aeroplane's tail was long gone. It was a beautiful tribute, and I felt Friedrich had now truly said goodbye to us all and his spirit was soaring free.

'God bless you, Friedrich,' I whispered.

Grief doesn't put food on the table and I very quickly realised I didn't have time for tears. I had to get a grasp on our financial situation. There was also the looming issue of crops that would soon need to be harvested.

My first conversation with our bank manager didn't go well.

Although sympathetic to my situation, he bluntly told me that he wouldn't extend a line of credit to a widow with four children.

Eventually, Friedrich's life insurance would help pay down what we owed, but our assets would be frozen until his estate was settled. I couldn't access our joint bank accounts.

After we sold the farm in Germany, we'd purchased a couple of shops in Kununurra as an investment, predicting the town would expand and grow and more businesses would develop. Mercifully, they were purchased in my name and they had long-term tenants, a hairdresser and a gift shop. Although the rental income was fairly small, the trickle of cash would help us survive.

There were papers scattered among the farming books and journals in Friedrich's office. I spent many hours sorting documents, insurance papers, invoices and ledgers into some sort of reasonable shape so I could begin working through it all.

In the process, I discovered that Friedrich hadn't updated his will. It included a farm we no longer owned and made no mention of the new assets we'd purchased in Australia. Technically this meant he had no valid will.

This was a major setback.

I needed to prove what assets we had purchased, in whose names, what we had sold and when. That meant I had to sort out not only the documentation relating to our assets in Kununurra but also in Schleswig-Holstein. It would be difficult enough if I was in Germany, but being on the opposite side of the world made sorting it out a nightmare.

To complicate matters, many of the receipts and other documents I needed had been packed into boxes by our friends and family when we sold the farm. I had no idea which boxes to begin looking in.

And worse, I couldn't sell so much as a nail without having approval from the bank and accountant until we went through probate.

Not knowing where to begin, I rang Kurt Kayser. He recommended a German lawyer who'd been living in Australia and knew both legal systems well enough that he could help me unravel the mess. Untangling the will, along with looking after four bereaved children, left very little time to get the farm books up to date. The bank wanted the books urgently, otherwise they were threatening foreclosure.

I knew just the right person who could help me: a woman named Helga Weiss, whom Friedrich and I had met through the German consulate. Helga was a livewire, an avid traveller with an adventurous spirit and an appetite to see the world. Kurt Kayser had introduced us and suggested she pay us a visit on her travels, and sure enough, one afternoon a big semi came barrelling down Riverfarm Road and stopped at our front gate, tooting furiously. I raced out to see what on earth was going on, and out jumped Helga. She'd hitchhiked all the way from Perth to Kununurra. We welcomed her with open arms and over a few nights and many long dinners, she regaled us with stories of her crazy adventures around the world. Friedrich enjoyed Helga's company as much as I did. She was smart, well educated and a one-woman dynamo.

Since that visit, she had been running the office of a global manufacturing firm in Perth. But her boss had been giving her a hard time, so she'd quit. She phoned to say she was coming up to see me after Friedrich's death and planned to stay for six weeks. On the spot I offered her a job getting our books up to scratch. I couldn't offer her much money, but I could offer a room for her to stay in and decent food.

Two days later, Helga was on our doorstep and got straight to work. God was smiling down on me.

The future of the farm kept me awake at night. It was a huge liability, because I owed a great deal of money on it. I reasoned that if Friedrich couldn't make it work, how could I, with four children on my own? I had no hope.

Once the estate was settled, I could sell, but in the meantime I had to somehow maintain the farm with no money, so that there was something left to sell. The soya-bean crop that Friedrich planted before he died was also ready to be harvested.

Before he left, Hartwig had advised me to plough the plants in. 'Forget about them, Frauke,' he said. But every ounce of Friedrich's blood and sweat had gone into the farm; the best way to honour him was to finish what he started. If I could bring in the crop and send it to market, I could pay back some money to the bank to keep them off my back.

But harvesting the soya crop would be a huge undertaking, physically and emotionally. I couldn't do it alone.

Fritz arrived home at the end of January, just before he headed to school. He'd learnt a lot during his time in Germany and had a greater sense of confidence around the farm. Fritz was determined to honour his father's legacy too and he worked Friedrich's fields with enormous pride. I brought in casual farm workers, and other local farmers like John Caratti and Richard Titmarsh pitched in. The farming community in Kununurra was close-knit. We'd come to know other farmers including Richard and his wife Cynthia well. Friedrich had great respect for Richard, and Richard was one of the first to offer help when Friedrich died: 'Whatever you need, Frauke, just call,' he promised. He was as good as his word.

We all worked from sun-up to sunset. I could never repay my friends enough for what they did to help me, but I could feed them.

The soya beans turned out to be very good quality, and the market was strong. Ironically, this crop was one of the best Friedrich ever planted.

After the harvest I had no choice but to make tough decisions. I had no means of continuing to pay the workers at the farm, so I had to sack them. It was a horrible day.

Not long before Friedrich's death we'd managed to employ a foreman. He wasn't easy to get along with, and he seemed to think he was the boss now. He kept bringing me documents that needed to be signed and invoices that needed to be paid. One morning, when he came in with an envelope full of invoices, I said to him, 'Please tell me what these bills are for.'

He snapped at me: 'I am the manager, I don't need to tell you anything.'

'Well, if I have to pay it, I have to know about it, and if that's your attitude, you are fired, immediately,' I shot back. From that moment, I was alone on the farm – no workers, no foreman. I can only assume my sacked foreman went straight to the Kununurra pub to tell the entire town what a disaster Oasis Farms was, because a few days later, a well-known local farmer who liked to get his news over a pot or two of Foster's popped in for an impromptu visit.

I knew him well enough to say hello to him around town, but that was about the extent of the relationship, so it was a surprise to see him at my door. He asked if he could come in and talk business.

He explained that he'd heard around the traps that I was in a pretty desperate situation, so he was making an offer to help me out: he wanted to buy part of the farm – 330 hectares of land – and our house, for a grand sum of $100,000.

It was insulting on so many levels. Our home alone was worth much more than that amount, let alone a house and a huge chunk of land. The fact that he thought I was so naive was deeply hurtful. I told him to get out of my house and never come back.

People assumed I had absolutely no idea. They thought I was just the little German housewife who cooked for people on the farm. They underestimated me.

Chapter 16

The one thing the bank and I happily agreed on without the need for any discussion was the immediate sale of Friedrich's gyrocopter.

Over dinner with the children, I broke the news. No one seemed surprised and Margret recalled Friedrich's flight of fancy with great delight. The discussion prompted the children to share other funny stories about their father and what ensued was a lovely evening telling wild tales of Friedrich's adventures, and reliving happy family memories. It was a fitting way to farewell the grounded buzz bird.

I sold the gyro a few weeks later for $7000, enough to keep the bank manager happy.

~

February marked the beginning of the school year, and the time had come for Margret and Fritz to head to Perth. I dreaded the thought of them leaving home, but in my heart I knew it was the best thing for them both. I hoped that being away from Kununurra would take their minds off Friedrich's death.

With Maren and Helga at home, I was comfortable leaving Peter and Maria so I could fly down with them. A quick trip to Perth also gave me the chance to pick up some paperwork from the consulate and visit the lawyer to check on the progress of unravelling Friedrich's will. Doris offered me a bed for a few nights, which I gratefully accepted.

Fritz was beginning Year 11 at his new school, Wesley College, and Margret was returning to St Mary's for Year 9. Margret's principal was one of the first people who contacted me after Friedrich's death, offering to support me in any way she could.

On Margret's first day, I took her to the boarding house then met with the principal, who was very compassionate as I explained that although we had the money to pay the fees, the accounts were all frozen for the time being. She understood and insisted we take some help, offering to waive the school fees as long as we could cover Margret's board. This was a huge relief.

The boarding house-mother assured me that they would take special care of Margret, and I knew they would, but even still I could barely let go of my precious girl when it was time to leave. That last hug had to carry me until she was home again in four months, and we both sobbed.

The following day it was Fritz's turn. I met with his headmaster to discuss our situation, and he was also incredibly kind and offered to postpone the fees until I was back on my feet. Fritz was with me during the meeting, and as we chatted afterwards, the principal put his hand on Fritz's shoulder and said, 'You should always be proud of your father.'

Those words warmed my heart and I could see Fritz's chest lift upon hearing them. It's hard enough when a parent dies, but there's a stigma attached to suicide – a mistaken belief that it's somehow a cop-out.

Being so far from my children, especially during such a difficult time, was in many ways the toughest thing I had to deal with after Friedrich's death. My heart and my head had wrestled with sending them away. I wanted to wrap them up in cotton wool and protect them from the cruelties of the world, but that's not how life works.

Fritz adjusted reasonably well but he missed the farm terribly. He was an outdoor boy who needed space and freedom. Being cooped up in a boarding house, constrained by the daily discipline and routine of boarding-school life, wasn't his ideal. He would much rather spend his days on the river, but he toughed it out and made the best of it.

It was harder for Margret. Teenage girls can be cruel. On her first night some of the girls gathered around her bed and asked, 'So, how was your holiday?' They knew full well that her father had died. The only words she could muster were, 'Oh, not very good.' Then they mined her for further information: 'Why not? What happened?' The poor girl was sobbing her heart out on her bed as the young vultures picked at morsels of information from her emotional carcass.

Margret has always had a beautiful heart and generous spirit. She didn't say a bad word about those girls; she kept her own counsel and grieved in private. She lay her head on her pillow each night, dreaming of her precious ponies and friends back home. I was furious and so sad when she told me what had happened, but equally so proud that she had the courage and grace to rise above it and carry on.

The question of our future had been weighing heavily on my mind and I thought of little else as I flew back to Kununurra. Friedrich's family were very keen to see us move back to Seedorf, as was my family. My father had phoned telling me he was going to buy the house next door for us to move into. I was aghast at the thought. 'Thank you, Father, but I won't be making any decisions just yet,' I said, politely declining an offer that would inevitably make me beholden to him.

The Boltens had offered a house at their farm, which was also very generous but would put me morally in debt to them. While it was of great comfort to know that we had support, and I knew both families genuinely had our best interests at heart, with either option I would spend my life indebted to others for their generosity. That was the last thing I wanted, and I know Friedrich would have turned in his grave at the thought.

The pressure to return was immense, and a delegation of family members was on its way to convince me to come back. Friedrich's father had given clear instructions to Hartwig and Soeren to fly to Australia again and bring us home.

My brother, Juergen, and his wife, Ingrid, had been wanting to visit so I asked them to come at the same time. Juergen was an accountant and his advice on some tricky financial matters would be very welcome, but I also felt I needed him there to support me. Juergen would never push me into doing something I didn't want to do.

Everyone would be arriving a week after I returned from Perth. I'd barely had a night without guests since Friedrich died, and I always loved the buzz of lots of people around. I was looking forward to seeing them, but I was also acutely aware that they were all on a mission to foster our return to Germany.

As my plane descended into the valley, I couldn't help but feel a sense of happiness that I was coming back to River-farm Road – it was an easiness, a feeling of being home. The spindly limbs of the lonely boab tree at the end of the tarmac seemed to reach out and greet me like an old friend.

Friedrich and I had invested an enormous amount into our life here; not just financially but emotionally. We had worked together to build a dream from scratch. His blood and sweat had gone into this place, as had mine, but he'd given his life for it. Although it was very much his idea to come here, I understood his dream and I knew the backbreaking effort it had taken to build Oasis Farms. His soul was here and part of mine was too.

Over the previous days in Perth, I'd spoken at length with Fritz and Margret about the future. They were unanimous in their wish: they wanted to stay. The children had made friends and settled in well. They loved the lifestyle and both felt an enormous sense of connection to this place.

The evening I arrived back, Judy came around to say hello and see how I was going. Helga poured wine and we all sat out on the back porch talking as the pink sun set over the river. The warm air and a rare cigarette soothed our lungs, and I laughed for the first time in months. I wondered if Friedrich was watching over me from the tall gum where we'd buried his ashes. What would he make of me drinking and smoking!

Kununurra was a place of such contradictions: barren and hot, wet and humid, harsh and yet so beautifully fragile. It was a long way from the rest of the world, but at times felt like it was the centre of the earth. Life here is complex and some days are bloody hard, and yet it can also be so wonderfully simple.

I thought of my little boy, Peter, who loved nothing more than running around the farm stark naked, blissfully bathing in warm mud. I thought of my precious baby, Maria, a miracle we created in this place; of Margret's adventures riding her bike through mango fields with her friends; and Fritz hauling in bag after bag of barramundi while fishing in our backyard.

In our time here, I'd come to know that the riches of the outback aren't material. It's not in the money made mustering cattle or pioneering vast frontiers of inhospitable land. Money comes and goes quicker than a wet-season storm. The true wealth of this place comes from the rich character and unbreakable spirit of its people. Those who can find the silver lining in any wretched storm.

In Kununurra we were the masters of our own destiny; if we worked hard, we would prosper. Friedrich believed that and so did I. In Germany, I would be at the mercy of others, always someone's daughter or daughter-in-law, always a widow.

By the time the family delegation all converged on Kununurra, my mind was made up. I cooked us all a special dinner, and we ate, drank wine and enjoyed one another's company. Then, over my mango cheesecake, which was a proven favourite, I dropped 'By the way, I've decided to stay in Kununurra' almost nonchalantly into the conversation.

'The best way to honour Friedrich is to finish what he started,' I went on. 'This is what he wanted, so this is what we'll do.' You could've cut the air with a knife.

Hartwig and Soeren exchanged annoyed looks, and Ingrid's eyebrows arched upwards, but no one said a word.

'Anyone for seconds?' I asked, breaking the awkward silence. 'We should make a toast to Friedrich and to new beginnings.'

'Very good idea, Frauke,' Helga said. 'To Friedrich!'

'To Friedrich,' we said in unison, glasses clinking in his honour.

Now I was very much on my own – a widow, alone with four children and no money, a failing farm and debt you couldn't climb over. In hindsight, I can see why they all thought I'd gone quite mad. And I was absolutely terrified – yet for some reason, the decision felt so right.

Chapter 17

Juergen and I went over the farm's books together with a fine-tooth comb. Ultimately, his advice was to lease it out. I spoke with Richard Titmarsh, who I felt understood farming in the Kimberley better than anyone. He said leasing the farm wasn't just the best option – it was the only option, at least for the short term, given that I was in no position to hire staff or borrow more capital to get the farm going again.

With Richard's contacts, I was able to lease it quickly for just enough to cover the water and shire rates, not a dollar extra. It was quite a load off my mind to know that the farm would be looked after and I had some more income, albeit small, to keep us going until everything was sorted.

The lawyers and banks also gave me permission to sell three very good new tractors that Friedrich had shipped up from Melbourne just before he died. Thankfully the dealer who sold them to us was sympathetic of my changed circumstances and happy to take them back on consignment. I had them loaded onto trucks, and off they went back down the Victoria Highway for the long journey to Ferntree Gully.

Piece by piece, I was tying up loose ends, but I couldn't settle the will or receive Friedrich's life insurance payout until I received the formal report from the coroner. This giant jigsaw puzzle was coming together, but the process was frustratingly slow.

Maybe it was the German stiff upper lip, or maybe it was the spirit of the outback that had quickly seeped into my bones, but I was very much in survival mode. I battled on each day as best I could. During the day I was so busy keeping everything together I didn't have time to grieve, but at night, alone in my bed I cried often, the cold sheets a reminder I was very much alone. Of course, there were some days when it all became too much and I needed to let my grief out. I was very honest and open with the children about how I was feeling, and I wasn't ashamed that they saw me cry. I was sad and they were too.

One morning I hopped in the car to head into town, and my feet couldn't quite reach the pedal. Someone had been driving the car and moved the seat. I reached underneath to pull the lever and felt something rough in my hands. It was the old towelling hat Friedrich wore to the farm. I held that hat close to my heart and sobbed.

Helga was a godsend. Without me ever asking her, I'd often find her in the kitchen doing the dishes, or playing with the kids, or hanging out washing. She was a workhorse and never sat still. Moreover, she was gregarious and fun and brought much-needed laughter to our sombre home.

For weeks she tried to get me to have a night out with her in Kununurra. The sports club ran a disco on Friday nights and she thought time out of the house would do us both good. 'Sporties', as it was known, was the preferred place for miners, station hands, farmers and truck drivers to go when they converged on town for the weekend.

I was reluctant, to say the least. It had been years since I'd been to discos, and I wasn't too fond of them then, so I couldn't fathom the thought of one now. Also, in the back of my mind I worried that everyone in town knew what had happened, and I didn't want people thinking the merry widow was out to pick up a new husband.

Helga kept gently prodding and by the end of March I caved in. She cleverly pricked my conscience by reminding me that she'd been working very hard; she deserved a night out and wanted a chaperone. 'A good friend would come to look after me,' she said, ever so gently twisting my arm.

I did my hair and put on some nice red pants and a blouse that I kept for special occasions. Helga was right, making an effort to get dressed up and get out of the house did make me feel better about myself – but from the moment we walked through the door of Sporties, I knew I'd made a mistake.

We could just make out the bar through a thick curtain of cigarette smoke and the crush of bodies bobbing up and down on the dance floor. Everyone was a good decade younger than us. We were a couple of old birds out on the town, and I was cringing at the thought of it.

Helga wasn't embarrassed at all. Summoning her trademark chutzpah, she pushed her shoulders back and confidently squeezed through the crowd until we found a pocket of air at the bar.

'Two glasses of wine please,' she said, her warm German lilt floating across the Strine hum.

From the comfort of the bar, we watched the passing parade – young station hands dressed in their best mole-skins, miners in jeans and T-shirts, a few young jillaroos in freshly pressed chambray shirts, R.M. Williams boots on everyone.

Helga was enjoying herself, but I felt so out of place. Some of these people were only a few years older than Fritz. Several times we were asked to dance, which was nice and very flat-tering, but after a few drinks I convinced Helga we needed to go home. We'd had fun, but this just wasn't my scene.

As we were driving home, I thought back to a conversation Friedrich and I had very early on in our marriage. Over dinner one evening we were chatting about what each of us would do if the other died. The conversation was light-hearted and a bit tongue in cheek, but when Friedrich said, 'Frauke, if you were to die, I'd look for someone the day after the funeral,' I knew he wasn't joking. Maybe he knew all along that he wasn't going to have a long life. I tossed Friedrich's words around in my mind that night. I was still a young woman with a lot of life to live. I didn't want to be someone's widow for the rest of my life, and I didn't want to raise my kids alone.

From the grave, Friedrich had given me permission to love again. I knew he would want me to be happy and although I wasn't in any hurry, I hoped that one day I'd find someone new. However, I probably wouldn't find him at Sporties.

The one thing that really struck me about our night out was the huge number of young people now living and working around the Kimberley. Opportunities for an entire community to come together were rare, and we didn't often get to see the huge workforce that was scattered around the valleys, gorges and plains that made up the vast Kimberley.

It wasn't uncommon to go for days, even a week without seeing another soul and even on the days when you headed into town to do the shopping, you'd perhaps only see a small handful of people. And yet, out there in the desert, beyond the ochre hills were many others living, functioning and building lives and businesses, all of us working together, in isolation.

Clearly there was a good number of people seizing new opportunities in the Kimberley; our sleepy region was slowly coming to life and the work of one woman was behind much of this.

In 1976, geologist Maureen Muggeridge had been prospecting on the floodplain of a small creek that fed into Lake Argyle, about 100 kilometres out of Kununurra, when she discovered minerals that indicated the presence of diamonds. Her discovery would change many lives, including mine.

Maureen was a pioneer of the Kimberley, arriving in Perth from the United Kingdom in 1972 with ten pounds in her purse, no job and nowhere to stay. She spent her first night in Australia sleeping under a tree in Kings Park, but within a fortnight, the mining company Tanganyika Holdings had offered her a job looking for diamonds in the top western pocket of Australia. At first, she thought it was a joke because Australia was famous for gold and iron ore, not diamonds, but she accepted the role and found herself on her way to the Kimberley.

It took Maureen less than a year of prospecting to find a diamond sample at Pteropus Creek. When news spread of her discovery, an influx of explorers packed their bags and headed to the region, prompting Maureen to work day and night under the luminous Kimberley moon to beat her rivals to four successful claims.

Maureen fell in love with the Kimberley, then fell in love with handsome mining heir John Towie, the son of Ashton mining magnate Rees Towie. They continued prospecting and in 1979, when Maureen was six months pregnant with the couple's first child, she discovered diamonds in an alluvial claypan, which she traced back to the headwaters of Smoke Creek.

Maureen had uncovered a tranche estimated to contain as many diamonds as were then known to exist in the rest of the world. It became known as the Argyle pipeline.

De Beers had previously spent more than £10 million exploring the Kimberley region but had come up with nothing. This one-woman dynamo was finding up to fifteen diamonds in her pan each time she sieved gravel from the bed of the creek. She'd trumped the world's biggest diamond company, using cheap aluminium pans and sweat.

Maureen found such a significant volume of diamonds that Tanganyika Holdings partnered with Rio Tinto and immediately began developing plans for an open-cut mine, the largest in the world.

In 1983, the Western Australian government granted the consortium permission to develop the mine, and capital funding of $450 million was invested into the project. By 1985, the mine was open and the first diamonds unearthed. The first commercial sale of diamonds made the front page of the *New York Times*, and our little town was suddenly on the world map.

This was wonderful news for Kununurra: a huge workforce began to arrive, and the mining companies bought dozens of homes to accommodate workers and invested a lot of money into the town. It sparked a boom, with the need for new shops and new facilities, and of course the very welcome arrival of new faces. It was a time of new beginnings for us all.

In the early days after Friedrich's death, Richard had given me a sage piece of advice: 'Frauke, never lend your machinery to anyone. You'll never get it back!'

Around late April, I got a phone call from a man introducing himself as Robert Boshammer. He said he was relatively new to Kununurra. Originally a Queenslander, he'd been running a farm in South Australia and was lured north to manage a large vegetable farm owned by some friends. When Robert arrived, he found that the farm was rundown and desperately short of machinery. Now he was calling to ask if I could lend him some equipment. He struck me as a very polite, well-spoken man over the phone, but I explained that before I could give him an answer I needed to make some calls.

'Richard, I've just had a call from a Mr Robert Bosham-mer wanting to borrow machinery. Do you know him?'

'Yes, Frauke, he's a good fellow and very reliable, you can trust him.' Richard Titmarsh knew Robert and the family he was working for, and had no hesitation giving Robert my number when he called seeking Richard's help.

I phoned Robert back and said, 'Okay, you can come and meet me and talk through what you need.'

When the day arrived, a tall young man with piercing blue eyes was standing alongside Richard at my doorstep. He introduced himself as Robert Boshammer, and I was quite taken aback; he was clearly much younger than the deep, wise voice belied on the phone. His smooth, sun-kissed skin looked like that of a man barely in his late twenties. Robert was equally surprised. I think he was expecting to be greeted by a big old German hausfrau.

I made coffee and Robert explained that he wanted to borrow anything he could from me, as a matter of urgency. Shipping farm machinery up would take weeks he didn't have. If he missed sowing the crops now, he'd have lost a whole season.

I told Robert I was happy for him to borrow equipment, but it was up to him to go out to the farm and find it himself, and return it to me.

What struck me instantly was how gentle and refined he was. For a man who spent his days largely alone taming wild paddocks, he was worldly and well spoken, and most importantly, respectful. Not once did he show a sniff of condescension and not once did he treat me like I was just the little housewife, as many others had done. Robert and I talked farmer to farmer, eye to eye, and I appreciated his approach.

After Robert and Richard left, Helga suggested that in keeping with our tradition of welcoming new people to town, we should invite Robert along to a barbecue we were having with friends from the tennis club and our neighbours.

Robert accepted our invitation enthusiastically. He told me he looked forward to any opportunity to get out of his overalls and meet some new people.

But he never showed up.

We kept some food for him in case he was running late, but by 10pm I figured he'd either fallen asleep or had a better offer, never mind. A week later, at about 6pm, just as I was getting the children's dinner ready, a plume of dust rolled down the driveway. It was Robert. He knocked on the door, bottle of wine in hand, ready for the barbecue.

'You're a bit late!' I laughed. He blushed and apologised, then sheepishly started to walk back to the car.

'Come on in,' I said. 'You're here now. We're just having dinner; you might as well join us.'

Of course, it was Murphy's Law that the phone rang right then. It was Dorte calling from Germany. I signalled to Robert to sit down and help himself to food while I spoke with her.

When I glanced over my shoulder, I couldn't help but laugh. Here was this tall, strapping man, dressed up to have dinner with adults, nestled between Peter, five, and Maria, in her high chair, happily chatting away to them and helping Maria with a scoop of her food every now and then. I half expected him to politely make an excuse to leave, but he didn't.

Once I got off the phone and sat down to eat, we quickly discovered we had quite a bit in common. Robert's family was originally from Germany and he took great interest in some fine blue-and-white tiles from Lübeck that were on my wall. They were very precious to me because they matched the tiles at my grandmother's home. Each one bore an intricate picture of farms or farmers, castles, windmills or landscapes, and they told a story of the land.

Of the many people who'd been in our home, no one had ever taken any notice of them, but Robert did, and he understood their heritage and significance.

It wasn't the night that either of us had initially planned – after all, I wasn't even expecting visitors – but it turned out to be very pleasant and we enjoyed one another's company.

Over the following days I found my thoughts drifting to him and our accidental evening.

Robert Boshammer was someone I was interested in knowing more about. As it turned out, he was interested in knowing more about me too.

Chapter 18

About a month after Robert's impromptu dinner with us, he rang to let me know he'd finished with my equipment and would be returning it to the farm. To say thank you, he asked if I'd join him for a meal in town. He certainly had manners, and any excuse for an evening out with a handsome man was a good one, so I said yes.

Deep down, I was pleased he'd called; after being at our place during the mayhem of family mealtime I wondered if I'd ever hear from him again. He came out to Riverfarm Road and picked me up. He opened the car door for me and ushered me through the door of the restaurant before him. He was chivalrous beyond his years and I appreciated these little signs of respect. It showed he was raised with manners, and it felt nice having a man look after me, even just for a few hours.

Our dinner needed to be reasonably quick because Robert had to go back to water his crops, which suited me perfectly.

I'd be home in time to tuck Peter and Maria into bed. Even in our haste, we still managed to enjoy a lovely dinner and squeeze in dessert. We left suggesting we should catch up again. As an unofficial first date it had been a great success, which was lucky, because our official first date was almost a disaster.

Robert invited me for a picnic lunch and a swim with him at Black Rock Falls, on the outskirts of Kununurra. The falls come to life for a short time during the wet season but dry up fairly soon after the rains stop, so you have to be quick to see them in full flight. With the water now flowing, Robert was keen to take a look.

It sounded like a lovely idea so I packed some fruit and water, and with Maria in kindergarten for a few hours and Peter at school, we headed out to the falls. The red-dirt road was terribly rough and the ute bobbed and bumped its way over potholes and corrugated ravines until we came to an abrupt halt, landing plumb in a pool of thick mud.

No matter how hard Robert tried, the ute wouldn't budge; we were skimming and sliding around, getting bogged deeper and deeper.

Robert jumped out, got a shovel from the back of the ute and began digging the wheels out, but still the car wouldn't budge. After almost an hour of digging, I could see he was becoming more and more frustrated and exhausted. The temperature in the middle of the day was in the 40s and rising, and Robert was sweltering in the sun. We were about half a kilometre from the falls and time was ticking away.

'Robert, why don't we just leave the car for a bit and go and have a swim to cool down,' I suggested. 'We can walk the rest of the way to the falls.'

'Great idea,' he said.

We walked the rest of the way along the muddy track, quickly realising there was no way the ute would've gone any further in this bog anyway.

It was well worth the walk. A stream of white water gushed over the top of a towering black rock cliff face, forming a pool of pristine turquoise water at the bottom. The water was so deep that you couldn't touch the bottom and it was bone-chillingly cold. It was just what we needed to soothe our melting muscles.

Although Black Rock Falls is popular with locals, that day it was just the two of us splashing around, with the sound of the water rhythmically streaming down behind us.

We swam for a bit and Robert dived off a ledge on the cliff face into the water over and over again. We'd been at the falls for almost an hour and I was conscious of being back in time to get Maria, so I suggested we think about heading home.

Robert did one more dive then swam over to me. He wrapped one tanned arm around my waist and another under my legs, then scooped me up into his embrace under the water. He held me tight into his chest, then kissed me for the first time. I allowed myself to let go and be completely swept up in the moment.

It was so wonderful feeling the touch of a man's lips and the warmth of his skin.

It would've been very easy to forget about the world beyond the cliff face and spend the rest of the day with Robert at the falls, but I was conscious that Maria had to be picked up and our only mode of transport was ankle deep in mud. The realities of life interrupted a magical moment, but both of us knew this was just the beginning of something special.

The blistering midday heat had helped dry up the mud, so by the time we got back to the ute, a thin red dirt crust had formed and the wheels could find some grip. Our chariot was released from the sticky clutches of the Kimberley mud. We raced back into town, just in the nick of time. Robert dropped Maria and me back at home and gave me a kiss on the forehead as he left. Our visit to Black Rock Falls planted a seed, and from that day on our relationship began to blossom.

With busy lives, we didn't get to see much of one another during the week, but we tried to catch up most weekends. Robert had no qualms about dating a widow with four children – a widow who was eleven years older than him.

Everything Robert did was with the whole family in mind; he understood the children were my priority and he never made demands on my time. If he wanted to date me, he dated the whole family. Thankfully, that worked for us all, because he got just as much joy from the kids as they did from him.

They gravitated to his sense of fun and loved his attention. A natural with kids, he developed a wonderful rapport with them, and they looked forward to his visits. He never tried to be their father or replace their father, but he was definitely their friend.

Peter and Robert both loved fishing, and I'd often find Robert down on the riverbank with his little friend in tow, casting a line into the Ord. The two of them caught bags of barramundi together.

During their school break, I introduced Margret and Fritz to Robert. I was anxious about how they'd react to me having someone new in my life, but I need not have worried. Fritz shared Robert's love of farming and Margret was thrilled to see me so happy. Robert would arrange adventures for the whole family out to the various waterfalls – Middle Springs became a favourite – or camping trips on the banks of the Ord, or sometimes we went swimming at Lake Argyle.

Robert and I tried to keep our relationship reasonably private, but in a small town, word spread that I'd 'hooked up' with a younger man; it was quite the talk of the town. I ignored the gossip, as did Robert – it just didn't matter. Judy and John, Helga and our other close friends in town had welcomed Robert, and the children were happy. Theirs were the only opinions we cared about. None of my good friends blinked an eye that I was dating a younger man – in fact, they were all delighted to see me happy, as true friends would be.

Robert spent long days on the farm where he worked, so when we were able to get together I always made sure we had a special dinner and I went to extra effort to make things nice for us. We played tennis together some weekends, and when time allowed, we had dinner with friends. As people became accustomed to us being together, we were invited as a couple to go to dinner parties and barbecues.

One particular evening we were both very much looking forward to the birthday dinner of a mutual friend. Robert had spent weeks prior harvesting forty hectares of pumpkin crop. From dawn until well after dusk each day he'd cut, lifted, sorted and packed thousands of pumpkins that were headed for the markets in Victoria and New South Wales. Now he was down to the last load that had to be packed onto trucks.

When the truck doors were bolted he raced home and got himself showered and dressed up, thrilled to be out of his overalls. With the pressure to get the last of the crop off to market that day, Robert hadn't eaten anything since breakfast and we were both starving.

The dinner was at a beautiful country home and everything was immaculate. The table was set perfectly for a special dinner, the silver cutlery polished and vases of bougainvillea added a splash of colour to the table.

We sat down at the table for the first course to be served and out came bowls of pumpkin soup. Poor Robert! He'd been looking forward to a nice dinner all week but his stomach turned at the sight of the thick orange soup. He politely declined entrée but took up the offer of another drink, and another. By the time the main course arrived he was quite jovial and by dessert a little drunk, but nonetheless happy. We all had a terrific night but it took a long time before Robert ate pumpkin again.

We kept our space and independence, making sure we weren't in one another's back pockets all the time, but I soon knew we had something special.

Robert was wise beyond his young years. He wasn't flashy or showy, he appreciated the small things in life and he worked hard for everything he earned – all values close to my heart. When Friedrich died, I prayed to God to look after us, and I feel sure He sent Robert my way.

In August 1985 after the Coroner's report was handed down I was granted probate over Friedrich's will. Finally, legally, I was entitled to manage our financial affairs. It was a relief but came with immense sadness too because it was another reminder Friedrich was gone. With his life insurance payout I was able to pay down debt to the bank and put some money away for our future. It was a time of closure, and new beginnings.

Chapter 19

In early March the next year, Robert had a very rare weekend off from the farm and suggested the whole family pack up and go camping for the weekend. Helga insisted that the children stay home with her this time so the two of us could have some rare time alone.

This weekend was very much a test of our relationship, because I wasn't much of a camper. I preferred sleeping in my own bed, and I had enough of dirt and dust every day, but Robert promised it would be worth the inconvenience.

He organised everything, although I use the term 'everything' fairly loosely. Robert took a minimalist approach to his camping adventures: he was quite at home in the solace of nowhere, and loved nothing more than throwing the swag in the back of the car and spontaneously taking off, sleeping under the stars and eating off the land.

For the purposes of my comfort, he packed a tent, which he considered a luxury, along with swags and a few essentials like pannikins for billy tea, a couple of fold-up chairs and his fishing rods.

We drove north to Cape Domett, a four-hour adventure bumping along corrugated tracks and dodging potholes. It was definitely four-wheel drive only.

We wove our way along dirt tracks up through Carlton Hill Station, the place pioneered by the so-called kings in grass castles, Patrick and Michael Durack, in 1893. It was on these vast plains of waist-high Mitchell grass that the Kimberley as we know it was founded. At any given time, Carlton Hill Station could be home to nearly 40,000 cattle, including the somewhat strange-looking hump-backed Brahmans.

Carlton Hill Station led us into the Ningbing Range. I'd never been to this part of the Kimberley and enjoyed being a passenger taking in the spectacular surroundings. Ningbing is an important cultural area for local Aboriginal communities. On the drive through, you are greeted by magnificent limestone mountains and hectares of coastal vine thickets. Millions of years ago, this region was totally underwater – a barrier reef – and sea minerals, shells and marine fossils can still be found in the limestone.

We crossed creeks and rivers, bumped our way over dirt tracks hardened by the sun and split by erosion, and eventually found ourselves at Cape Domett. It was well worth the exhausting drive, because we had arrived at the very top of Australia. There was nothing but sea between us and Timor-Leste. We stood on a beautiful beach that stretched for miles. It was a popular place for locals, but not too many tourists found their way out here, and I could understand why. Luckily, we had the place to ourselves.

Robert warned me the waters around here were renowned for salties and sharks, so swimming was a no-no, but we pitched a tent high in a clearing in the dune scrub and while I set up camp, Robert scurried to throw his rods into the surf.

The pressure was well and truly on him, because if he didn't catch anything, we didn't eat!

Thankfully he hauled in quite a bounty, including a beautiful bream and a school shark and some other fish I'd never seen before. He'd kept his end of the bargain, and now I had to cook it all up for dinner on a campfire stove.

The barbecued fish was something of a triumph – more edible than I thought it might be – and I was proud of my efforts. Our dessert was a pannikin of tea and a few biscuits I'd smuggled into the hamper before we left home. We dined like royalty as we watched the sun set over the beach.

The night sky in the Kimberley is something to behold. It was truly breathtaking to watch the pink sunset roll into an inky blue then black sky which came to life with a million tiny stars.

I was worried I'd be a bit bored camping out, but Mother Nature was putting on a show that kept us captivated. We sat in silence underneath the twinkling sky, content and thoroughly in awe of this majestic region we call home.

The next few days were spent fishing, taking bushwalks into the hinterland and exploring. We caught crabs and fish, and Robert showed me fragile orchids and pretty grevillea plants native to the bush. He was so interested in nature and wide-eyed with wonder at every discovery that by the end of the weekend I was too.

One Saturday afternoon a few weeks after our camping trip, I was in the kitchen when a plume of dust from Robert's ute rolled down the driveway. I wasn't expecting to see him, because he'd planned a camping trip down the river with some farming mates, so it was a lovely surprise.

He strolled into the kitchen and gave me a kiss on the cheek then brushed past me to turn on the kettle. My hands were wrist deep kneading bread dough, so he made us both a cup of tea and leant back on the bench beside me, chatting about the crops he was currently planting. Out of the blue, mid-conversation about crops, he turned to me and said, 'Frauke, I was wondering if you'd like to marry me.' Just like that.

I smiled back at him and said, 'Yes,' and that was it, we were engaged, almost twelve months to the day since we met.

He gave me a kiss on the cheek, waltzed out the door and went off down the river. There was no bended knee or candlelight dinner, he didn't present me with a ring, there was absolutely no romance about it at all – but, like Robert, it was lovely and very authentic.

Soon after sunrise the next morning he wandered back in, ready for a hot shower and a decent breakfast. He'd celebrated the news over a few beers with his friends around the campfire and was a little worse for wear – nothing eggs and bacon couldn't fix.

We told Peter and Maria over breakfast, and afterwards I phoned Fritz and Margret, who were both terribly excited. Then we phoned Robert's family in Queensland and my family in Germany. Tante Banta was overcome and burst into tears. 'I'm coming to the wedding,' she declared there and then.

Sadly, not everyone was as overjoyed.

My father was very quiet when I told him. He made no secret of his wish to have us back in Germany, so my engagement was not happy news for him. However, he was gracious and offered to pay for Juergen and Ingrid to come to the wedding, which meant a lot to me. I would've loved my father to be there, but I guess he found it too painful losing a daughter for the second time.

The hardest task was telling the Boltens. They too still had hopes that we would all pack up and come back. They were still mourning the loss of Friedrich. The grief echoed in their voices and it made me terribly sad to think they were still hurting so much. They were concerned that this relationship was too quick and wanted to know who on earth this Robert Boshammer was and why he wanted to marry a newly widowed woman with four children. Friedrich's life insurance payment was substantial and Fritz Snr wanted reassurances that he wasn't out to grab our money, which I guess was fair enough. He was just trying to protect us.

I felt a great sense of unease after I hung the phone up from the Boltens. I'd always been incredibly close to them – in many ways, closer to them than my immediate family – and in my heart, I needed their blessing for this marriage. I couldn't marry Robert knowing they didn't approve.

Very hastily, I made arrangements to fly back to Germany. I wanted to talk to the Boltens face to face and help them understand that the children and I were fine and my engagement was good news. Robert was a man of great conviction, he would look after me and their grandchildren, and none of us would forget Friedrich.

Fritz Snr and Margarethe were as warm and welcoming as always, and we hugged and cried together. Clearly Friedrich's death had taken a toll. Margarethe, a robust and very stout woman, had noticeably aged. Fritz Snr's pale eyes looked like they'd cried all of their colour out. They still had some anger towards me that I'd told the truth about Friedrich's death. They argued that no one needed to know, and I had embarrassed them. I reassured them that I would've married Friedrich regardless of what had happened, and I would always love him.

It was a sad meeting. Their concerns were genuine and well-intended but a little misguided. I desperately wanted them to be happy for me and for the children, and we fare-welled one another on good terms, but I couldn't convince them to come out for the wedding.

A congratulations card arrived some time later, but none of the Bolten family came – not Friedrich's brother, Hartwig, nor his sister, nor his cousin Soeren.

Planning a wedding in Kununurra comes with its own unique set of challenges. We set a date in August, timing it around the harvesting of crops in the dry season, when it was less likely we'd be inundated with rain or flooded in, and Robert could get some time off afterwards.

We wanted the wedding to be quite low key, very relaxed and informal. Some friends offered to host the ceremony for us on their beautiful houseboat on Lake Kununurra, the perfect place. They could moor the boat in Lily Creek Lagoon, on the edge of town, where we'd be married with the lake in the background, and afterwards the guests would come back to Riverfarm Road for the reception. I would do all of the catering, and the food and drinks would be served out on the lawn, with a local band playing afterwards for dancing.

Normally the biggest challenge in the outback would be finding a dress, but during my trip to Germany visiting the Boltens, I came across a lovely dress by the designer Bogner in Berlin. I'd always considered it too indulgent to spend money on designer clothes, but this time I decided to treat myself. I had no choice but to wear my sister's wedding dress when I married Friedrich, but now I had a second chance and I wanted something special. It was a two-piece ensemble, a pretty top with loose sleeves that sat over a full skirt that fell to ankle length. The fabric, pale pink and embroidered with pretty pink and green flowers, was a beautiful feather-light batiste cotton, which would be perfect for a very hot Kimberley day.

For a week before the wedding, we were beating a path to the airport every day picking up guests. Fritz and Margret came home from school, Tante Banta arrived with Juergen and Ingrid, and we had an influx of Robert's family coming in convoy from Queensland.

With no florist anywhere close by, I had flowers flown up from Perth. The last trip to the airport, the day before the wedding, was to pick up my bouquet, the buttonholes and a halo of pretty white orchids and gypsophila that would be my headpiece.

The coolroom was stuffed full to the brim with food and wine. On the morning of the wedding we frantically put the finishing touches to the canapes and the desserts, and got tables, chairs and a dance floor set up. Maren was amazing; she worked tirelessly helping me.

By 2.30pm, the countdown was well and truly on for our 4pm nuptials and I was nowhere near ready – I was whipping cream for our desserts. Helga took over and shooed me off into the shower to begin getting ready. My brunette curls were carefully smoothed and tucked under the crown of fragrant orchids, then with one last dab of lipstick I was ready.

Helga acted as my witness, and Robert's brother-in-law Dick stood proudly beside him as his best man. The local Uniting Church minister married us with traditional church vows. I vowed to honour and obey; Robert promised to look after me in sickness and in health, 'til death do us part.

With a kiss, we were husband and wife. I looked around the congregation of friends and family, who were all clapping and cheering. When the formalities were over and a few pictures taken, it was back home to celebrate. Robert and I went ahead of the guests so we could have things ready as they arrived.

Fritz had got his driver's licence the day before the wedding, so he was tasked with being the official wedding car driver. He wore a suit of his father's. It wasn't entirely fashionable, with flared pants and long sleeves, but Fritz didn't care; he was very proud. He was so cautious driving us back to the house that a couple of times I said to him, 'A little quicker, Fritz, we need to hurry,' but he was a steady hand on the wheel and wouldn't be distracted from his official responsibilities.

When we arrived, I raced in the door and turned on the stove to begin heating up the food, but nothing happened. I flicked on a light switch and it didn't go on either.

'Arggh! Robert, quick!' I yelled. 'We have no power!' Robert found the fuse box and fiddled around, but nothing worked so he raced up the road to the neighbours and called his friend who was an electrician.

By that stage, our guests were beginning to arrive and we had to tell them all dinner would be a little later than planned. With plenty of cold champagne and beer and enough cold finger food to buy us time, no one seemed too bothered, but I was panicking that the coolroom would be slowly warming and our food getting ruined.

Sensing the urgency, the electrician raced out to us and within an hour had things up and running again. We invited him to stay for drinks and dinner.

I'd cooked a huge buffet of chicken, mustard-and-herb-crusted roast beef, salads galore, vegetables – enough food for the entire town. For dessert we had two types of traditional German cake, *Bienenstich* and *Donauwelle*, and cherry cheesecakes.

Our wedding cake was an extra-special *Baumkuchen* cake. This one had more layers of fine sponge than I'd ever attempted before, and I was particularly proud of how tall it stood.

As the sun began to set over the Ord, the band struck up and the dancing began. The wedding reception went well into the early hours, but Robert and I snuck off to bed around midnight. I woke the next morning in Robert's arms, pinching myself that I had found love again.

Among our wedding gifts was a beautiful tapestry that my dear friend Cynthia Titmarsh had made. It was an intricate, hand-stitched picture of our new family, all wearing traditional German outfits but accompanied by an eclectic collection of crocodiles, kangaroos, rosellas, waratah flowers, farming imagery and horses. Even our snake-catching cat, Midnight, and Peter's dachshund, Barbarossa, made the picture. It was a wonderful representation of our lives coming together as one. Above the image of our family are these words:

No matter what,
No matter where,
It's always home,
If love is there.

I treasure that tapestry and to this day it takes pride of place in our kitchen.

Chapter 20

After the last of our wedding guests had headed for home, we packed up the four-wheel drive with tents, swags, mozzie nets, pannikins and flyspray, and hit the road with Peter and Maria.

Robert's family were gathering in Queensland for a reunion, so we were taking a family road trip there, doubling as a honeymoon. Robert came from a large family: he had fifty cousins spread all over Australia, some of whom he'd never met. It wasn't too often that they could all get together, so this was quite a special event. The trip would take us five days of solid driving and we had planned very little. Instead, we would drive until we felt like a rest, pull over somewhere off the highway, unroll our swags and set up camp for the night. I generally like to know which pillow my head will rest on when I travel, but Robert's spirit of adventure was contagious and his idea of sleeping under a million stars sounded romantic. We would dine at roadhouses, so we would be sleeping like paupers and eating like kings.

We ambled our way through Katherine and on to Mataranka, in the Northern Territory; down to the Barkly Tableland, just on the Queensland side of the border. From there we followed the 'Overlander's Way', a pioneering stock route which is now a tourist drive, into the Gulf Country and on to Mount Isa, then stopped at Cloncurry, where the very first Royal Flying Doctor Service flight took off in 1928.

Australia never ceased to amaze me. In Germany, you couldn't drive for more than ten minutes without coming across a farm, a town or a city. Out here you could drive for hours and not see another soul. The northern country was hot and harsh; the sunburnt land stretched on forever, relentless and sparsely populated, and yet so beautiful. What courage it must've taken the early settlers to make their way across this inhospitable land on horse and foot.

By contrast to those pioneers, we were travelling in relative luxury, but after five days of driving with two children cooped up in the car I was relieved when the ocean came into view as we finally rolled into Townsville, on the eastern coast of Queensland.

Fritz and Margret flew in from school to holiday with us, and we spent our first day together in Queens Gardens. There were acres of green space for the children to run around in, which they did, swings, sandpits to roll in, birds to watch.

It was the first time in many months that I could recall all of us being together relaxing, with nowhere we had to be, nothing we had to do, no one to entertain. It was just us enjoying one another's company, just being a family. Complete harmony.

One of my absolute highlights of our time in Townsville was watching Peter and Maria trying to work out what on earth was going on when we came across an escalator at the local shopping centre.

The two of them stood at the bottom of the silver conveyor with puzzled looks on their faces, not game to step onto the metal belt. It dawned on me: they'd never seen an escalator before. It must've been like something from outer space.

We navigated it together and, of course, after their first ride they thought it was such marvellous fun that they raced down the other side and went up and down, and up and down, having a ball.

After a few days together, we packed up the car again and headed south to Toowoomba for the Boshammer family reunion.

I was a little nervous about meeting this huge clan I'd heard so much about, wondering how they would greet Robert's new family, but we were embraced like long-lost relatives and welcomed with open arms, literally. I think I was hugged a hundred times.

We gathered at the Lutheran church for a special service, then the whole family enjoyed a long afternoon lunch in the church hall. There were hundreds of people and I was especially thrilled to meet relatives who'd flown in from Germany. I spoke German to them and helped translate for others; we chatted about the old country and I felt a great sense of kinship. I was embraced by the Boshammers with such warmth, and I too embraced them.

Our trip home took us through the Queensland towns of Chinchilla, Roma, Mitchell, Longreach and Winton. It was a wonderful adventure, and Robert was a confident bushman who clearly loved the land. He was happiest with the sun on his back and the stars over his head. Every day was a new discovery with him.

After we were married, Robert and I decided that he would take over Oasis Farms and we would rebuild it. I couldn't think of a better way to honour Friedrich than to see his dream come to fruition. It would take a while for the lease to wind up, which gave Robert time to plan his crops and get organised. Running a farm isn't just about being out in the paddocks watching seeds grow, it is a business, and to be successful in farming requires financial acumen, knowledge of markets, yields and pricing, and strategic planning to ensure you have the right crops to maximise your return. I'd always taken a keen interest in the business side of our farms, and even though it was Friedrich running them day to day I'd learnt a lot along the way; what to do and what not to do. Robert was very different from Friedrich; he asked for my opinion often and he took the approach that this was an equal partnership. It was good to feel that we were building something together. We also decided to buy a little unit in Perth so I had a place to call home when I was visiting the children. It made good financial sense and I loved Perth. I'd made good friends there and enjoyed catching up with Doris particularly; it was so good to speak with someone who understood my heritage.

In June 1987 the peace and tranquillity of our beautiful region was shattered dramatically when a young local couple and their friend were murdered.

Phillip Walkemeyer, his fiancée Julie Warren and their friend Terry Bolt were camping at a popular fishing spot on the Pentecost River – a place we'd been to many times. It was a very popular spot for locals and tourists and in June, the height of the dry season, it was teeming with people.

Their bodies were found in the river; they'd all been shot in the back, executed. The entire town was rocked by these deaths.

Five days beforehand, a father and son had also been killed at a fishing spot along the Victoria River in remarkably similar circumstances. Police found matching boot prints at both scenes and suspected a serial killer was targeting people on the very roads we'd driven during our recent honeymoon.

For the first time, fear blanketed our town. Dozens of police flew into Kununurra, road blocks were set up around the town. Some people were asked to stay at home and keep their doors locked; others were evacuated. Roads were eerily empty across the whole region and we were told that if we were driving our cars, we were not to stop for anyone under any circumstances. We were terrified, and Robert slept with the gun next to the bed.

On 19 June, a helicopter pilot mustering cattle near Fitzroy Crossing spotted a car camouflaged under branches and tarpaulins. The tactical response group moved in and the gunman was shot after firing at police. What motivated twenty-six-year-old Josef Schwab to commit such horrors, we will never know. We breathed a sigh of relief when he was found, but our town would never be the same again. I was particularly devastated to learn he was a German man, who'd only arrived in Australia one month before. He'd broken our hearts and blackened the good name of every German.

It was during a conversation about this terrible tragedy that Doris broke the news that she and Karl were separating. I was very sad for her.

Doris had trained in gemology and diamond grading at Oeding and Erdel, an internationally renowned jewellery store in Münster, Germany. She married Karl, who was also a jeweller, and they travelled the world. They fell in love with Canada and set up a jewellery business in Vancouver. While living in Canada, they took a quick holiday to Australia to visit friends, and when they landed in Perth, they decided they never wanted to leave. Doris marvelled at how glamorous Perth women were. They paid attention to their clothes and appearance, and they liked the finer things in life, like she did. It was an emerging city with a very cosmopolitan air.

Perth was far away from the rest of Australia but awash with money from mining and vast farming enterprises. She knew there was a market for a luxury jewellery store, and so Brinkhaus Jewellers, in upmarket Claremont, was born.

Doris and Karl – or Kally, as he was known – worked hard building the business, which became successful very quickly.

Doris was a natural frontwoman for the shop: tall and very attractive, she looked as if she'd stepped straight off a

European catwalk. Doris wore her passion for fine things like a badge of honour. Her manicured fingers dripped with expensive diamonds, and her smooth European accent captivated the Perth social set. Everyone along the high street wanted to get to know the glamorous blonde or buy one of her pieces. She designed beautiful jewellery and showcased extravagant pieces from renowned overseas designers. Kally worked behind the scenes. It seemed as if they had the perfect partnership, but Doris was devastated when he dropped a bombshell: he was heading back to Canada and wanted his share of the business.

Doris loved Perth and wanted to stay, so that left her two options: sell the shop or find a new investor. Doris was a very good businesswoman and I knew this was a good opportunity to invest in a very strong business that was continually growing. Robert agreed, and now that the children were a little older, he encouraged me to develop my own interests.

Doris was overcome when I rang offering to buy out Kally's share with some of the money I'd put away from Friedrich's life insurance, and so we became partners in Brinkhaus Jewellers, Perth's finest jewellery store. Doris would remain the frontwoman for the store, while I was in the background learning the ropes. It was such an exciting time.

Doris behind the counter at the opening of my first shop.

With Robert in 1987, a year after marrying.

Peter and his best friend, Johnson Kirby, at Bullo station.

Fishing trip for Peter's 10th birthday.

Robert and Fritz walk Margret down the aisle.

Margret, Lance, me and Katrina, at Margret's wedding.

Fritz and Andrea's wedding day, cutting the collapsing cake!

Enjoying a BBQ with German TV star Blacky Fuchsberger and his wife Gundel.

Fritz and Peter on the farm, six months before Peter died.

Exhausted volunteer search team resting on the veranda after Peter went missing.

Fritz mounting the steel cross following Peter's death. Helga is comforting me.

Peter's Wesley friends Michael Gardiner (left) and Ben Cousins (right) at home in October after Peter died.

Katrina, Maria and Margret wig shopping with me after my cancer diagnosis.

Left: Maria and Chris on their wedding day.

Above: Reunited with Dorte, visiting our grandmother's house after my cancer treatment. I love these Delftware tiles.

Katrina and her partner Frankc with me at Kimberley Fine Diamonds.

All of the family (except Lance) gathered in Broome to celebrate my
70th birthday.

Our newest addition, baby Alexa, my 11th grandchild.

Outback women are resourceful because we have to be. We sacrifice many comforts our city sisters take for granted, but that doesn't mean we don't appreciate the finer things in life; we just don't get the chance to indulge ourselves very often.

Doris designed beautiful jewellery and she was one of the first to use Argyle diamonds. I was always complimented when I wore one of her creations. People would stop me in the street in Kununurra and ask, 'Where did you get that?'

I suggested to Doris that we organise a private showcase at Riverfarm Road for family and friends, to give them all the opportunity to buy something special. I invited quite a large number of women I knew to come over for champagne and canapes while they viewed a collection of pieces Doris brought up from Perth. We sold the lot and took orders for more.

Word spread around town and through every cattle station, and there was enough interest to arrange a second showing for the women who'd missed out the first time. This time we held it in a bigger space, the local leisure centre, and again we sold every piece.

Around the same time, there was noticeable growth in tourism in the town following the discovery of the Bungle

Bungles, now known as the Purnululu National Park. Some years earlier, a film crew flying over the Kimberley found a stretch of spectacular rock formations that looked like striped beehives poking up out of the earth. These domes were unlike any other ancient rock formation known in the world. The crew filmed them as part of a documentary which aired on national television and showed the Kimberley in a whole new light.

Travellers began arriving to see these fragile rock formations for themselves, and they came with bulging wallets and a desire to take a piece of the Kimberley back home with them.

One resourceful local woman began taking tourists out to the Argyle mine in her minibus twice a week. It was a hit, and she was booked solidly through the dry season. But the Argyle mine didn't offer diamonds for sale to travellers, only wholesalers. I seized on the opportunity.

I arranged to buy small batches of polished diamonds from Argyle, which was all we could afford, then we offered the tour operators an exclusive showcase. The minibus would bring the tourists from the mine to Riverfarm Road on their way home, and I would offer refreshments while the tourists viewed the sparkling gems from the mine they'd just visited.

My first showcase was at dusk on my back porch. I was a little nervous, because having tourists come to your home is different to inviting friends and family. I had lovely champagne well chilled and ready to serve, and an offering of beautiful food. Robert helped me set up tables with white linen cloths on the back porch, and I had the jewellery displayed in a glass case on the table, which was decked with fresh flowers.

The Ord was in her finest form, sparkling and sunset pink. The only trouble we had to contend with was the mozzies that descended in a thick cloud as soon as the bus arrived, but no one seemed to mind. They were more interested in snapping up the coveted diamonds.

A visit to Riverfarm Road became a regular part of the Argyle mine tour and proved very popular. The interest was strong enough to cement my belief that we could expand, so I began looking for opportunities to showcase the diamonds closer to town.

A friend of mine, Barbara, had opened up a small gift shop in the main street, and she was willing to stock some jewellery pieces there. Our diamond business was a small but blossoming business, in a small but blossoming town.

At the end of the school year in 1987, Fritz farewelled Wesley College and headed to Germany to begin agriculture studies. Before Friedrich's death, I had organised for him to undertake part of his farming apprenticeship with the Boltens in Germany. Fritz was proud to be following in his father's footsteps, and Robert and I hoped that when he returned he would work on the farm.

It meant the world to the Boltens that Fritz was returning to their farm for a time, and it helped us reiterate how important they were in our lives. Just because I had remarried didn't mean I'd forget our family roots: the Boltens would always have a special place in all of our hearts.

With the jewellery business growing, I made regular trips to Perth to see Doris, and also to support Margret, who was in her final year of school and preparing for her exams.

Boarding school hadn't been overly kind to her, and she missed her family and we missed her. We were so happy when school ended and it was time for her to come home.

The tourist season slowed down as we approached Christmas and the wet season, which gave me a chance to focus on preparing our annual Christmas Eve festivities. This year we had some new faces joining us.

Some months beforehand, Judy and John had quietly ended their marriage. There was no animosity; they'd simply grown apart and the spark that kept people glued together in this tough place was gone. They agreed it was time to move on.

Judy has a beautiful spirit; she lights up every room she enters. It didn't take long for her to realise that the love of her life had actually been right under her nose all along: agriculturalist Jim Hughes. We'd all come to know Jim through his work supporting farmers and developing the local sugar industry. He was a salt-of-the-earth fellow, passionate about the potential of Kununurra. From their first date they were inseparable, and they found happiness together very quickly. I couldn't remember ever hearing Judy laugh so much. The outback can be a terribly lonely place, but it's also a place where you can find love when you least expect it.

Also joining us was a group of retired German Rotarians on a driving tour around Australia. We always welcomed German travellers with open arms, especially at Christmas. While I prepared the Christmas dinner, the children took to the pool to cool off in the humidity. They hadn't been swimming too long when I heard a bloodcurdling scream.

'Crocodile!' Margret bellowed.

She'd dived under the water and found herself face to face with a smiling crocodile, a baby about half a metre long. The silver-haired Rotarians raced outside, absolutely beside themselves. Nine-year-old Peter thought it was marvellous and chased the little croc around the pool until he was finally able to fish it out. He burst out of the water, grinning from ear to ear, with the croc tucked under his arm. I'm not sure whether our guests were impressed or absolutely horrified, but none of them took up Peter's offer of a quick pat.

I wasn't overly fussed about all of this because it was the wet season, and we'd had baby crocs in the pool previously when we'd had big rains and the river had swollen. They were relatively harmless and often more frightened of us than we were of them. Robert would fish them out and let them go, and they'd race down the riverbank and slip back into the river without any trouble.

However, this poor little disorientated fellow didn't follow the plan. Instead of heading towards the riverbank, he raced right through the door and into the living room, where the Christmas tree and presents sat, perfectly decorated.

'Peter!' I yelled, as the little creature then zipped past me in the kitchen. 'Peter, come and get this crocodile out now!'

Peter ran in and chased the croc around the house, followed by Margret and Robert. Four-year-old Maria stood squealing with delight beside the Christmas tree. It was quite a sight, all three of them running around in circles chasing the slippery little beast that was faster than all of them combined.

It skidded under the chairs and behind the sofa, ran around the tree and under the kitchen table, where our German visitors were sitting with their feet up on the seats as they clutched the edge of the table in a death grip. They must've been wondering what on earth they had got themselves into. Eventually Robert caught the petrified little creature by the tip of its tail and walked the wriggling and writhing baby back down to the river, making sure it headed home.

When the little croc scurried off into the water, I dutifully returned my attention to our guests, offering them all a round of stiff drinks. No one refused. The crocodile circus only lasted a few minutes, but we'd given our travellers a lifetime of stories to take back home. I could only begin to imagine the tales they'd tell of the German lady with crocodiles in her outback kitchen! We really were quite a world away from Germany now and as much as I missed home, I couldn't think of a place I'd rather be.

Chapter 21

Our life had settled into a lovely, uneventful routine, the farm was ticking over, my little diamond business was bubbling away nicely and the children were growing. It was a time of such happiness for us all.

Midway through 1989, at the age of forty-one, I became noticeably tired, needing a little afternoon nap most days. I put it down to a hectic few months. Maria had started school and Peter was now in grade 5. I immersed myself in helping out at Kununurra Primary, volunteering with the parents' association, helping organise fundraising events and doing tuckshop duty – all of which I enjoyed enormously.

I'd also been travelling to Perth more frequently to be with Margret. She was commencing Speech Pathology at Curtin University so I was helping her settle in, and I would also catch up with Doris and see how the business was going.

Putting my weariness down to my hectic daily life and the extra travel, I didn't think much more of it, until I began to feel familiar waves of nausea. If I didn't know any better, I'd say I was pregnant.

Robert and I had been trying to have a baby since our wedding, but luck hadn't come our way. I'd suffered two miscarriages, which was sad, but I was resigned about it: I was getting older, and God had given me many blessings in life. Maybe a baby with Robert wasn't meant to be. We'd been to a specialist early on in our marriage to check everything was okay to have a baby, and it was – but it was very much in Mother Nature's hands.

Strangely, this time I felt the symptoms of morning sickness with far greater ferocity than in previous pregnancies. I was absolutely exhausted and could barely stand the sight of food.

By the time I got to the doctor, he confirmed I was indeed pregnant. I was about six weeks along, and this baby was growing very nicely. The heartbeat was strong and measurements good. All of the signs pointed in the right direction, but he gave me strict orders to take it easy and look after myself.

Robert was quite overcome when I broke the news we were actually having a baby. He was already a wonderful father to my children, and now he would get to experience having a little baby of his own in the house. Our world was about to be turned upside down, and we couldn't have been more thrilled.

We waited until I was beginning to show before we shared the news with our friends and family. I was paranoid about losing another baby and wanted to ensure this little one was safely through the first trimester. Given my age, some people greeted our news with raised eyebrows, but friends and family were openly happy for us and I watched my swelling belly with wonder.

It was a big year for family birthdays. Fritz was turning twenty and my Peter the ripe old age of ten. We celebrated every birthday with gusto, but Fritz's celebration would have to be postponed until he arrived home from Germany. Peter turning ten was cause for something special. When I asked him what he'd like to do for his birthday, not surprisingly he nominated a fishing trip.

Peter had become quite confident wandering downstream from home with his rods and a bucket of bait under his arm, fishing on his own. He'd happily spend the whole afternoon casting his rods and come back with a barramundi or two, which I'd cook up for dinner. His favourite fishing spot was Ford's Beach, a sandy little watering hole tucked away at the bend of the river downstream from us. Peter wanted Robert to take him there camping for his birthday.

This was intended to be a boys-only trip, but I wasn't going to miss out on the fun.

They left on Friday afternoon, and the next morning I made a special cake and a nice picnic lunch, blew up so many balloons they filled up most of the car, and with Maria helping navigate, we took off to drop in on them.

A few minutes from camp, I stopped the car and got out, tying balloons to the roof, the bumper bar and the side mirrors. I also tied a big bunch to the back of the passenger seat, so they floated out through the sunroof. Then I sticky-taped a plastic 'Happy Birthday Peter' sign to the bull bar.

I honked the horn several times as we arrived at camp, signalling our arrival, much to Peter's delight.

Overnight they'd reeled in quite a haul. Peter dragged an enormous barramundi up to show me. It was half the size of him, so big he struggled to lift it. He grimaced as his little arms fought to hold up the heavy fish for an all-important trophy photo.

Maria and I left after morning tea, and the boys followed us home later in the afternoon. For dinner, I cooked up Peter's giant fresh barra as he requested. The rest of the fish they caught were filleted and frozen, adding to a burgeoning store in my coolroom. I made sure we said grace before dinner that evening: it was a wonderful day and I was truly grateful for the food on the table and my growing family, especially knowing we'd soon have one more face smiling back at us.

Fritz was still in Germany, coming to the end of his apprenticeship, when protests on the street started growing as anger about the Berlin Wall reached boiling point.

The wall was built on 13 August 1961 – the date is etched vividly in my mind, as if it were yesterday. Such sadness descended on our country. We were torn in half, physically and emotionally. All of us, on both sides of the border, lived with fear in our hearts.

We were the lucky ones, because we were on the west side and all of our family was on the west side too. Plenty of other families were not so fortunate.

There was a border crossing near Zarrentin, and sometimes we would take visitors to go and see it. The tall razor-wire fence was a monument to fear. Armed guards and dogs patrolled the crossing day and night, and people were shot if they tried to cross the border to escape life in the communist East. We'd always keep a reasonable distance and we'd smile and wave to the guards, who carried machine guns. None of us was in any doubt that they would open fire in a heartbeat, so we did our best to show we meant no harm. Stern-faced, they never waved back or smiled at us – they weren't allowed.

Daily life was terrible in the east: little fresh food; bananas and oranges once a year if they were lucky; and a bag of coffee cost almost one month's salary. Aside from the impoverished living conditions, politically it was treacherous. East Germans had their phones tapped, they were spied on. The Stasi had detailed dossiers about everyone's movements, who they spoke with, who visited their homes, where they worked. Neighbours spied on neighbours, and anyone suspected of disloyalty was interrogated, even imprisoned.

The Bolten farm was close to the border, and as the protests intensified, I became terribly worried that Fritz and the rest of my family could be in danger. News from Germany generally didn't make it into the headlines here, but as tensions rose, the world began to take notice.

The East German leader, Erich Honecker, resigned, bringing real hope that this dreadful divide that had inflicted fear, oppression and sadness on Germany for almost four decades may at last come down.

Under immense pressure, with East German refugees flooding into neighbouring countries, the new head of the East German communist party, Egon Krenz, announced that from midnight on 9 November 1989, citizens could cross freely at the official checkpoints: Alpha, Bravo and the famous Checkpoint Charlie on Friedrichstrasse. Border troops could no longer shoot to kill anyone who tried to cross.

Well before midnight, more than two million people gathered along the length of the wall, and at the stroke of midnight, the crowds rushed the checkpoints, flooding the streets. Some ran into the arms of relatives and loved ones they had not seen for four decades. Others came with picks and hammers and began the task of knocking down the brutalist wall.

The will of the people to be one united country again far outweighed the oppressive ideals of the East German government, and they had no choice but to effectively concede defeat. Some say it was the world's biggest street party that night, a celebration to rival no other.

I tried to phone our family as soon as news began to filter out that there was an uprising, but all of the lines were jammed; I think the entire world was calling Germany right then. I tuned in to the coverage on TV. Tears streamed down my face. I was ecstatic, euphoric and overwhelmed.

I was a long way from Germany but my heart was with every one of those people celebrating on the streets. This was a wonderful moment in time, one I truly thought I may never see. Hours later I was finally able to get through to Fritz and

Dorte and my father. They were exhausted from the celebrations but utterly elated. I wished I could ring Friedrich in heaven and tell him the good news.

Whenever I visit Seedorf now, I make a point of driving over the old border, because I can. It's my way of honouring those people who lost their lives running for freedom, and a reminder of how lucky I am.

I will never forget what it was like to live in a divided Germany. Watching the wall come down remains one of the greatest days of my life. One year later, East and West Germany were finally, formally reunited as one country. Today I have two pieces of the Berlin wall framed in my living room to forever remind us never to take freedom for granted.

Fritz arrived home in time for Christmas. He'd changed physically and emotionally: my boy was now very much grown up.

It was clear his trip to Germany had been a great success, because this normally reserved boy could hardly wait to tell us about all of the things he'd seen and done. Words spilled out as he and Robert chatted enthusiastically about farming techniques, crop rotations, fertiliser and the potential for the Ord River region.

If I closed my eyes, it could've been Friedrich speaking.

From the time he was a small child, farming was all Fritz had ever wanted to do, and yet, after Friedrich died, some family members tried vehemently to encourage him to do something else, afraid of him following in his father's footsteps.

However, farming was in Fritz's blood, and regardless, he didn't make any decision lightly. If Fritz followed his heart, it was because his head said it was the right thing to do.

'Mutti, I just think Dad was ahead of his time,' he said over a belated birthday dinner. 'He was right about this place, the potential is infinite. Dad was just a few years too soon.'

Maybe Fritz was right. The consequences otherwise were unthinkable.

Chapter 22

At my age and with all of the complications I'd had previously, I wasn't taking any chances with this baby's arrival. I flew to Perth for the last few weeks to ensure I was near help if the baby decided to arrive early. Robert came down a few days before the due date and arrived in time to be with me when I went into labour. On 10 March 1990, we welcomed Katrina Olga Boshammer into the world. She arrived safely after a relatively good labour, with a smile that melted her daddy's heart. After the nurses had cleaned and wrapped her, he cradled the sleeping little doll in his arms. 'I thought it would be much harder,' he said.

'Speak for yourself, Robert. It's easy from where you're standing!' I replied.

A week after Katrina's birth, we packed our bags and headed home to Kununurra. As we were checking out of the hospital, my doctor, George, said, 'I'll see you again next year, Frauke.'

'No, George, you most definitely won't,' I assured him. Robert and I felt very blessed to have Katrina. Our family was already complete, but she was the icing on the cake. Neither of us wanted to take any more chances.

Not surprisingly, Katrina very quickly became the centre of attention at home. Everyone adored her and she barely spent a minute alone. There was always someone lined up to have a cuddle with her or rock her in the bouncinette.

From the moment she was born, to Fritz, Margret, Peter and Maria she was always their little sister – never a stepsister. We are all very much one. Katrina is a constant reminder to us that life is full of wonder and that from heartbreak, happiness can come.

While we were celebrating Katrina's arrival, in Germany my beloved sister Dorte was suffering the collapse of her marriage. It was a very sad time and I encouraged her to come to Australia to have a holiday with us. It took a bit of convincing, but eventually I twisted Dorte's arm. I arranged a trip to Broome for us. A walk along Cable Beach at sunset would be a wonderful tonic and I'm convinced a little sunshine on your bones does everyone the world of good.

She arrived with her daughter Iris, who was twenty-one, and after a few days to settle themselves and shake off the jet lag, we packed up the four-wheel drive and hit the road. This was a girls-only trip. Katrina came with me but Robert was busy with the farm and offered to look after the others so I could have some time with Dorte.

It was a ten-hour drive from Kununurra to Broome. We planned to drive to Halls Creek first, stay overnight then continue on to Broome.

For most of the trip I drove, but there were times when I needed a break or Katrina needed to be fed, so we'd pull over and I'd hop in the back seat and feed the baby while Dorte or Iris drove.

The road between Kununurra and Broome was pretty rough. It was virtually unsealed with a very thin strip of bitumen through the middle. If a car, or heaven help, a truck, came in the other direction, you had to pull off onto the dirt or scrub to let them pass. We had some very hairy moments with B-double trucks barrelling towards us and nowhere for our car to go. For much of that drive we were two wheels on the road, two wheels in the scrub. I was very glad when Broome appeared on the horizon.

We had a week at Cable Beach, spending many long days talking, swimming and walking along the sand. It was very healing for Dorte to be far away from the troubles at home – the sun, sand and endless blue sky will soothe anyone's fractured soul – and very special for me to be with my sister when she needed me.

The only one who didn't have a good time was Katrina. She hated the sand and cried and cried.

Dorte and Iris were marvellous, often taking her so I could go for a walk along the beach or have a nap. They were long, lazy days I still cherish.

At the grand old age of seven, Maria took to the task of being a big sister with particular gusto and loved looking after 'her' baby.

Ten-year-old Peter never did things by halves; he played hard and he was utterly fearless. He was born an outdoors boy, and didn't sit still. There was always a bike to ride, a cubbyhouse to make or a fish to catch. I never had to encourage Peter to get off his bottom and go outside to play. It was the opposite: I had trouble keeping him indoors, finding him only when dinner was ready.

At school he was active too, always kicking a ball, running around or climbing a tree. He had a very strong natural athletic ability and was the first one called on to join the footy team, athletics team and cricket team, and he did it all.

He'd been chosen to compete in the state athletics competition in Perth. He was one of a team of eleven kids from his school, the Kununurra Barras, and the parents worked hard raising money to send them. I'd become quite a dab hand at making doughnuts at every fete and fundraiser, and I happily volunteered again.

They trained hard each week and with the funds we raised, we booked their airfares and accommodation and had enough left over to get special T-shirts made as their team uniform. Peter was so excited, and we were excited for him.

On the Saturday afternoon a week before the big athletics meet, I was in the kitchen when I heard Peter scream. Peter never screamed at anything – he was as tough as nails and nothing fazed him – so I instantly knew that something was wrong.

I found him at the base of a tree on the front lawn, writhing in pain, holding his left arm. He was crying. For Peter to be so distressed meant he was really hurting. 'What happened Peter?' I yelled as I raced to him.

In between deep heaving sobs, he gasped, 'I fell into the tree.'

'Into the tree?' Hmm.

My motherly radar thought it more likely that he had fallen from the top of the tree, where he'd been spending a lot of time recently and where he'd been warned not to go because it was too high and too dangerous.

His right arm was cradling his limp left wing, and it wasn't the time or place to quiz him further. I needed to get him to the hospital quickly. We'd discuss how one falls 'into a tree' at some other time.

Robert helped me bundle him into the car, and as gently as I could, I drove him to the Kununurra hospital. X-rays confirmed he had indeed broken his arm and he was placed in plaster from his wrist to above his elbow.

Robert and I assumed this was the end of his trip to the state championships, but Peter insisted he could still run. 'No, Mutti, please don't cancel,' he begged. 'I'll be right by then,' he said.

We kept a close eye on him, and a few days before the team was due to leave, the doctor gave him the okay to travel and race, as long as he was careful. The doctor strapped the plastered arm up in a special supportive sling, and off we all went to Perth.

This was a big adventure for the kids from Kununurra. For some of them, it was their first time on a plane and the first time they'd ever left the Kimberley. Perth was a big place by comparison and it was a feast for their senses.

Over the weekend of the competition, it became clear that this was a pretty serious event; these kids who'd come from all over Western Australia were racing to win. Peter had been able to jog rather gingerly in the last few days before we left Kununurra, but sprinting with a broken arm was something else.

We had reassured him many times that he didn't have to run, that he could pull out at any point. When it came time for his race, he slowly moved up to the starting line. In that moment, as the kids all bent down on their marks to get into position, it dawned on Peter that this really wasn't going to work too well. He couldn't kneel into the starter's block, because he couldn't put his hands down on the line to support himself.

Peter backed away from the line and spoke with one of the marshals. He'd decided to pull out. It didn't matter to us – we were proud of him for wanting to be there and proud that he'd still made the effort to go along and support his team. But to Peter, there was no way in this world that he was going to come last. To him, it was better not to run at all.

My little diamond interest had been going and growing quite nicely, until Barbara rang to tell me she was changing direction at the shop and no longer wanted to stock jewellery.

This was a blow and posed a big dilemma: I didn't want to stop selling the jewellery; I felt in my heart that this was just the beginning of a strong business with so much potential, but we needed to do something more than selling from the back porch.

Robert and I discussed it and agreed it was all or nothing; it was time to open up our own shop. I spoke to Doris: although this was my shop, it made sense to source jewellery through the Brinkhaus store and suppliers.

It was a major turning point and from that moment, a whirlwind engulfed our lives.

One of the small shops I owned was becoming vacant soon, so that seemed the logical place for the business to begin. While waiting for the tenants to vacate, I began getting ready. I commissioned Doris to make some pieces and ordered stock from diamond suppliers. I had business cards and letterhead made, as well as signature velvet jewellery pouches and boxes for clients to take their precious purchases home.

The day the shop was free we swooped and began a week-long transformation. Robert and I gave the walls a fresh coat of creamy white paint to complement the soft grey carpet I'd had flown up from Perth. New shelves were hooked up on the walls to showcase art from local artists. Doris flew up with the last of the jewellery and helped me do my first stock-take. Carefully we arranged the precious gems in a beautiful long glass cabinet she'd helped me order. Individual studio lights hanging from the ceiling flashed little sparkles off the diamonds from every corner of the shop. Inside, the store was gleaming.

Thankfully, a late wet season storm subsided long enough for me to wash the Kimberley dust off the front windows. I polished them until the reflection of the shops across the road was gleaming back at me. The final touch was a new sign Robert hung above the door.

On 19 April 1991 Kimberley Fine Diamonds was officially open for business.

We hosted a grand opening party and invited people from the town and friends and family along and started selling pieces that very day. The shop was open six days a week to cater for the tourists who were coming in ever-increasing numbers, and I was there every day.

Thankfully, an au pair named Karoline from Germany came over to Australia to help us. She was a godsend. Karoline would look after the children in the morning while I was at the shop, then I'd go home at lunchtime to breastfeed Katrina and have some lunch, returning to the shop in the afternoon. Friends would fill in if I needed to be out for an hour or two.

Running a business came very naturally to me. I did everything from selling beautiful diamonds to cleaning the shop, vacuuming the floor, ordering stock and balancing the books. Being in town each day was quite an eye-opener for me. It was such a change to be around people and I enjoyed getting to meet new townspeople and the passing parade of tourists.

Every dollar we made was invested back into new stock and I purchased Argyle diamonds whenever we could. Our budget strategy was very simple: we only spent money we had.

I was so happy being in the shop – I just loved it. My life was suddenly so very different, but Robert supported me and encouraged me the whole way, and it was exciting for all of us to see Kimberley Fine Diamonds slowly grow. The business gave me a new inspiration and a sense of purpose beyond our kitchen, and the children were really proud of what I'd done.

I thanked God every day for answering my prayers and looking after me.

Of course, life at home went on as busy as ever. We regularly welcomed travellers and guests, especially Germans. The consulate often sent people our way, and weary tourists were welcomed into our home with a hot meal and a bed to rest in.

One such was Hans. The consulate gave our details to this young Lufthansa pilot headed to the Northern Territory and we were happy to be a pit stop for him on the way through. He'd travelled the world with the airline and visited many amazing places, but he was still overwhelmed by the beauty of the outback he'd experienced by the time he landed on our doorstep.

Hans was only in town for a few days on his way to Uluru, but we wanted to make a good impression and ensure that he left telling the whole world what a magical place this was.

We went to great efforts to show him the sights and sounds of the Kimberley. Robert took him out to Lake Argyle and to the Ivanhoe Crossing and we all hiked to the top of Kelly's Knob to soak up the rich colours of an outback sunset.

On his final night with us, Fritz and Robert thought a boat ride down the Ord at dusk, when the crocs come to life, would be just the thing to give him a taste of real Aussie adventure.

I prepared a lovely meal for us all and after second helpings of my mango cheesecake, we all made our way to the pontoon and hopped into the boat.

Robert cruised down the river and we all kept our eyes peeled for crocs to impress Hans. I spotted the first one, a huge salty stretched out on rocks on the opposite riverbank.

'Good God!' Hans said as the prehistoric creature put on a show, lunging into the water and thrusting its thick tail from side to side. Hans was impressed; the croc wasn't.

As night fell, the boys moved the boat closer in along the riverbank. A croc had been terrorising farmers further downstream, so we knew there was a biggie around. Robert had a rifle tucked underneath the spare life jackets just in case.

A sudden rustle among thick reeds ahead of us caught our attention as the tip of a croc's tail disappeared into the water. Robert motored over to the muddy spot, cutting the engine as we neared, so we drifted along.

No one was game to make a move. In silence we sat, waiting for a ripple or splash as the croc resurfaced, but other than the night song of the river, a cacophony of frogs and insects, there wasn't a movement to be seen or heard. We knew we weren't alone; this river was filled with hungry crocs, and in the darkness crocodiles' eyes open up to give them virtual night vision. They can see us long before we can see them.

Fritz shone a torch to the river side of the boat while Robert focused his torch towards the bow, but the river was eerily still.

'I think he's gone,' Robert said.

Then quick as a flash from nowhere, the giant beast jumped straight up out of the murky darkness and lunged at the side of boat. 'Fuck!' Hans screamed, splintering the silence, his heart must have been almost jumping out of his chest as the boat rocked unnervingly from side to side.

Water licked our faces as the beast thrashed around and whacked the boat with such force it felt like we would capsize. After a frenzied few seconds, it dropped back into the river as quickly as it had come.

'He's a biggie!' Fritz yelled with excitement. Poor Hans was too scared to speak.

Robert quickly put the motor back in gear and headed to the middle of the river, away from the bank. 'What about that, Hans!' he said, teasing the poor ashen-faced man.

'I think it's time to go home,' I quietly suggested to Robert. Our guest had had more than enough adventure for one night and that croc was only just getting warmed up.

Our little boat was really no match for his prehistoric force. We would barely be his entrée if he decided to lunge at us again.

Poor Hans barely said a word during the ride back. Judging by his greyish pallor he was close to vomiting but, I imagined, not game enough to put his head over the side of the boat to do so. The boys had well and truly delivered on their promise of Australian adventure.

Chapter 23

Peter enjoyed the first few years of secondary school at Kununurra High, but we wanted him to finish his education as Fritz and Margret had done. We enrolled him at Wesley, in Perth, to begin in 1993, following in his big brother's footsteps. Because Wesley had been so good to me and Fritz after Friedrich's death, I felt a special affection for the school. I knew Peter would be in great hands.

It was always hard saying goodbye to my children. I didn't have children so I could send them away to school. With each of them, that farewell hug almost killed me. I'd take in great gulps of their air to keep me going until I could wrap them up in my arms again.

There was an obvious void around the house with Peter gone. The hum of activity when he was around, whether he was getting up to mischief with his little sisters or planning his next great adventure, was gone and I never warmed to the silence.

Ten-year-old Maria missed him terribly, because he was her partner in crime. She adored her big brother and they got up to all sorts of things together. She wandered around rather aimlessly for a little while, until she realised she was a big sister now. Katrina was the beneficiary of her extra attention.

Sometimes I'd sneak into Peter's room and smooth down his bed, even though it was already made, just to soak him up for a few minutes.

Margret wasn't overly happy away at university and wanted to return to Kununurra. At twenty-two, she was old enough to make her own decisions. She always loved helping out in the shop and had taken to jewellery like a duck to water, so after a trip to Germany to study gemology, she began working in my store. For some months she had been dating a very lovely young helicopter pilot, Lance Conley. Robert and I had come to like Lance a lot – he was a very thoughtful and well-mannered young man. Although quiet, he had a very cheeky sense of humour once we got to know him, and he fitted in with our lively family very well. But winning her heart hadn't come easily.

My pretty caramel-haired daughter had first caught his eye at the annual Rotaract Round-Up dance in Kununurra.

She was serving behind the bar and stone-cold sober; Lance, however, was full of Dutch courage.

He beat a path back and forth to the bar, ordering more and more drinks, trying to chat to her and catch her attention – but as the night (and every drink) progressed, Lance's chances of winning Margret's affection were getting slimmer and slimmer. It probably wasn't the best tactical move on his behalf. At the end of the evening, when he was a little worse for wear, he asked her out for dinner. Not surprisingly, he got short shrift, but Lance was persistent.

In an effort to shoo him away so she could clean up and get home, Margret, who was the spitting image of me at the same age, rattled off her phone number and told him he could call her sometime. She figured that when he woke up the next morning with a guaranteed hangover, he'd be lucky to remember her, let alone her phone number.

She was wrong.

The very next day, Lance Conley phoned to ask her out for dinner, and Margret, despite being impressed that he remembered her number, said no again.

'Mutti, I don't even know this man!' she said.

In the weeks that followed, Margret bumped into Lance several times around town. Each time, they stopped for a chat, talked a little more and began to get to know one another.

When the handsome pilot asked her out for dinner again, it was third time lucky. She said yes, and romance began to blossom.

I was at home one Saturday afternoon when an almighty noise descended on the place. Outside, dirt was whipping around the garden as though a dust devil was racing through.

'What on earth is going on?' I muttered, tossing off my apron as I ran out the back door.

It was Lance. He'd flown in to visit and was landing his helicopter on our front lawn. It was a tiny thing with no doors, just enormous blades slowly thumping away and nothing but a way-too-thin Perspex shield between the pilot and the ground.

'G'day, Frauke,' Lance yelled. 'I've come to take you for a ride.'

What in God's name is going on? I wondered.

He hopped out, ran over to me and said, 'Come on, Frauke, hop in. I'll give you a bird's-eye view of Kununurra.'

I went back inside and turned the ovens off. Robert was sitting at the kitchen table grinning from ear to ear. 'Go on,' he urged. 'Looks like fun.'

Lance gave me a leg-up to climb into the tiny cockpit of the helicopter, which was only marginally bigger than the one Friedrich had bought. Lance was a pilot with a good reputation. He'd been building up his own business heli-mustering for the various cattle stations and I trusted him, but I was still a little nervous.

I clicked on the seatbelt and we lifted off, hovering high above the house and the Ord. I'd never seen the property from this angle before and with the river in the background, Lance was right, it was a wonderful view.

With the slightest turn of the joystick, the nose tilted down and off we flew. My fingers gripped the seat as Lance zipped the doorless machine over the town, then accelerated up over the sharp rock face of Kelly's Knob and down into Hidden Valley. Tiny blue pools of water dotted the earth and I felt I could almost reach out and touch the waterfalls as we weaved through the red rock canyon and out the other side. As we turned for home, Lance swooped down low over acres of farmland, we stirred up cattle in paddocks and gave a few farmers a hell of a fright, I think, but we had a great time, chatting all the way. Lance was a very good host, and just a few minutes from home he got to the real point of what this roller-coaster ride was all about.

'Frauke, I'd like to ask Margret to marry me,' he said. It was the first time I'd ever seen Lance nervous.

He'd fallen in love with Margret the moment he saw her, and although it took her a little longer to warm to him, they were a good couple and brought out the best in each other. I knew he would look after her and that together they would build a wonderful life, so I gave him my blessing.

The wedding would take place in August 1994, with Lance and Margret marrying at the local church, then everyone coming back to our house for the reception.

We went into overdrive getting organised. Margret had seen a dress she loved in a magazine, and luckily we had an excellent seamstress in town who could make it picture perfect. The two of us drove ten hours to Darwin to find the right material, then it was down to business ordering flowers and getting the invitations out.

The wedding was in the dry season, which is peak tourist time. It was a busy time to be organising a wedding, but also a very busy time in the shop. To cope, I had all hands on deck, including the bride-to-be. She was my best salesgirl and an absolute natural.

On the morning of the wedding – with the town swollen with campers, Winnebagos and tourists stocking up on their way through – I planned to close up after lunch and go home to prepare for the late-afternoon nuptials.

A lovely French family who were visiting town had been in and out of the shop several times. They had six children and had brought them all to Australia for a holiday. Each time they came into the store Margret had served them, talking them through the various diamonds, cuts and quality. They were smitten by a particular Argyle diamond and had been trying to negotiate the price for several days, requiring quite a bit of individual, undivided attention, which they deserved.

As luck would have it, they decided to come back into the shop on the day of the wedding, just as we were beginning to close up. Margret attended to them again, nervously keeping an eye on the clock.

This time, though, they'd made up their mind that they were going to buy. They paid cash for a stunning $30,000 diamond. This was a very big deal and Margret was as pleased as punch with the sale, but when she should have been at home getting ready, she was instead counting an enormous pile of cash in the back office of the shop.

We were all quite bemused by this couple. There are very few banks in the middle of the outback, so they must've carried around a huge amount of money with them in their camper. I couldn't imagine carrying all of that cash through the outback – it was so dangerous.

The money got locked up in the vault for the weekend and we raced home to get ready, intent on celebrating Margret's successful sale later in the evening.

Robert and Fritz walked Margret down the aisle, and the local Uniting Church minister, Val Bock, married them. Val was a recent newcomer to town, and as she was on her own and never married, our small congregation took her under our wing. She was regularly invited to family dinners and special occasions all around town, and she became a good friend to us, often popping in for breakfast or dinner. She was a wonderful woman and a trusted confidante, and it made the day even more special having her officiate. It was a time of absolute happiness for us all.

Early in 1995, I flew back to Germany to celebrate my father's eightieth birthday. It had been quite a few years since I'd seen him, and our relationship had thawed somewhat. He had come to accept that Australia was my home, and he was always pleased to see me whenever I came back, which I did as often as I could.

Robert, Maria, Peter and Katrina came with me. Margret and Lance were setting up their home in a small house on the property at Riverfarm Road and settling in to married life, and Fritz was busy looking after the farm. It was February and we'd left 40-degree days in Kununurra to arrive in the middle of a bitterly cold German winter.

Father had organised a lovely dinner for family and friends at a restaurant near his home. We went to great effort, getting dressed in our Sunday best for this very special occasion. Katrina, now five years old, was meeting him for the first time. Because it was so cold I made her wear a very heavy velvet dress, just like the ones I wore as a child, with thick stockings, and matching shoes. She was a very outdoorsy young girl; she lived in shorts and a T-shirt and absolutely hated every minute of the starchy German clothes. Nonetheless, she quickly became the centre of attention and had a lovely time meeting her Opa and all the relatives and friends she'd heard us talk about.

The birthday dinner was a lovely affair. We dined on Father's favourite chicken soup and dumplings, and big platters of beautiful meats, cheeses and roasted winter vegetables. Afterwards, all the traditional German desserts were served in a very extravagant buffet.

It was wonderful to see my father happy. I felt for the first time that he was proud of what I'd achieved and the life we'd built. He was a man of few words, but there was a warmth to him I'd not known before, an acceptance which I hold dear.

Twelve months after Margret and Lance's marriage, we repeated the wedding celebrations for Fritz and his fiancée, Andrea Sunderland. I felt quite sentimental seeing my baby boy becoming a husband. They too were a lovely couple and we were so happy to welcome Andrea into the family.

The wedding was on a terribly hot July day. Peter was home from school, and Fritz and Robert had been working hard at the farm on the eve of the harvest. I was looking forward to us all taking a break together to enjoy the wedding celebrations.

As she had for Lance and Margret, our friend Val, the Uniting Church minister, married Fritz and Andrea. The bride was absolutely radiant as she walked down the aisle on her father's arm – remarkable, considering she'd been suffering a dreadful bout of chickenpox in the lead-up to the wedding.

At the church, I felt so proud looking at Fritz standing at the altar. I wished Friedrich was there to see it too. I know that Fritz thought about his father a lot that day and felt his father's loss terribly. Special occasions always reminded us of the hole in our hearts that suicide created. We said a prayer for Friedrich and absent friends; he would never be forgotten.

After the ceremony, the newlyweds were greeted by a polished Fendt tractor parked outside the church. It was covered in love hearts and a sign that read 'Just Married'. It's an old German farming tradition to take newlyweds on a lap of the town in a tractor, and we had a lot of fun watching them roll off in their rather unusual bridal 'car'.

Back at home we'd prepared a lovely buffet dinner for more than one hundred people. Once everyone had eaten, the speeches began, after which we cut the cake. Fritz and Andrea had opted for a traditional French wedding cake, a towering croquembouche. It looked magnificent and we had the cake very proudly displayed on a separate table.

Midway through one of the speeches, much to my horror, the cake collapsed before our very eyes. What had been a grand tower was now a towering mess. In the heat of the evening, the spun sugar holding the cake together had been slowly melting, setting the little balls of custard-filled choux pastry free.

We watched, frozen, as each delicately made ball slid down, bounced off the edge of the table and rolled onto the lawn. Initial gasps were followed by a long silence, only broken by Robert's giggles. We had to laugh, what else could we do?

It gave me such joy to be able to host these occasions at home, collapsing croquembouche and all. After losing Friedrich the way we did, I always felt there was a little sadness hanging over the place. Hosting weddings gave a great sense of new beginnings, of joy and togetherness.

During the night, Margret and Lance let slip that they were having a baby, my first grandchild. Happy memories at home now far outweighed the sad, and I felt incredibly blessed.

Much to our delight, Margret's baby Liesa arrived six months later, just after Christmas, a darling granddaughter and the best Christmas present we could ever receive.

Chapter 24

In the five years since we opened, Kimberley Fine Diamonds had grown beyond my wildest imaginations. From the day we opened our doors we had been profitable, so much so that after our first year the tax office had come to investigate why we were doing so well.

What they found was a well-run family business that thrived on the principle of reinvesting every dollar back into new stock, special pieces and only the very best-quality diamonds. Through trial and error, I had worked out what our customers wanted to buy, and that's what we delivered.

The taxmen had congratulated us and that was the last we heard from them.

The secret to our success was the great pride we took in our personal service. Everyone who walked through the doors of Kimberley Fine Diamonds was a VIP and given the red-carpet treatment. From day one, I kept a record of every diamond sold. I photographed each piece and logged the purchaser's details; I can tell you what every customer who ever purchased a diamond from Kimberley Fine Diamonds bought and when.

I wanted us to have a reputation for being the very best, and it became apparent that to achieve this we needed a jeweller on hand to make pieces for us, rather than sending away to Perth. In 1996 we joined the Jewellers Association of Australia to secure our credentials as a purveyor of very-high-quality diamonds.

Over time we built a very strong relationship with Argyle, and as the mine grew and they unearthed more and more amazing gems, our business grew too. When the Argyle mine opened, it was estimated that the diamond deposits would be exhausted in 2006. They were producing 30 million carats of diamonds annually, including the famed champagne, cognac and pink diamonds.

In 1994, their production peaked and 42 million carats of diamonds were produced in one year. This rather dry and dusty, very unglamorous-looking open pit mine was hiding a sea of priceless gems underneath.

The pink diamonds were the rarest and were becoming increasingly popular – and increasingly valuable. The tiny number of pink diamonds unearthed each year were sold at the annual Argyle diamond tender, the most exclusive diamond sale in the world, and they won record prices.

A handful of the world's best jewellers were invited to the Perth tender, a special showcase of the very best pink diamonds of the year. There's only ever between fifty and sixty diamonds on offer, and each diamond has a reserve price. Potential buyers place bids in a sealed envelope and the highest bidder gets to purchase the rare diamond.

We were stocking pinks from Argyle but my goal was to work towards earning an invitation to the tender. That was the big league.

I didn't help my cause, though, when I lost a precious pink diamond in the shop one day.

These blessed little gems are full of static electricity and they 'jump' around. You have to handle them ever so carefully with tweezers or they can flick right out of your fingers. This day, I was putting a little pink away in the glass cabinet when I caught it on the wrong edge with the tweezers and it 'jumped'. I didn't panic. I got down on my hands and knees on the floor, and scoured every inch of the carpet, but I couldn't find it. My three staff came to help me, then Robert and the children. For days we searched the floor millimetre by millimetre, even using a magnifying glass. I wouldn't let anyone vacuum or sweep. We searched every corner and turned the shop upside down, but we never did find that diamond.

We'd invested so much money buying a small stock of pinks, so losing one was a big blow. That tiny diamond was worth about $3000 at the time.

As far as I know, it's still in the shop somewhere. Maybe one day some lucky person will find it.

By that stage, we had outgrown our shopfront. We needed something that really reflected the gravitas of the business and what was happening inside. There was a building going up for sale around the corner. It needed a lot of work but it was a bigger shopfront on a very prominent corner location, near the major shops. It had the space we needed to showcase our diamonds and to put in a bigger vault, an expanded jewellery workshop and offices.

Robert and I discussed it, but there wasn't really much to discuss: he was wholeheartedly behind the decision to buy the building. It meant borrowing from the bank, which I didn't like doing. I always worked on the belief that you should only buy what you have the cash for. However, this was too good an opportunity to expand the business, so we took the plunge and the deal was done.

It was a beautiful store with a huge retail showroom, which meant we could extend our range, so along with our collection of diamonds we stocked pearls from Broome and exquisite art, glassware and wooden sculptures from local artisans. Big glass windows looking out onto Konkerberry Drive gave us more opportunity to showcase the jewellery to passers-by. Handcrafted blond wood counters with glass display insets stretched around the store and every available inch of wall space housed artworks and imagery from the Kimberley. We turned it into a truly beautiful space, more like an elegant gallery than a shop.

With our expansion, I wanted to bring in someone to handle the shop day-to-day so I could focus on developing the collections and running the business. Helga had been managing the local hotel and doing a fabulous job, but she was getting a little bit bored and wanted a new challenge. She was just the woman for the job, and I was ecstatic when she accepted. I sent her to Germany to formally train in diamond grading and valuation, and she returned full of ideas from the European masters.

We had a big opening celebration and invited half the town along to herald a new chapter for us.

Tourists loved coming in to wander and browse. They were often quite overwhelmed to find this very cosmopolitan oasis in the middle of the desert – something so fine and lovely in an otherwise very harsh environment.

Not long after we opened our new doors, we received the news that we'd been offered our first invitation to the exclusive Argyle pink diamonds tender. Not only did we go, we were successful in buying. We beat out established jewellers from London, New York and Geneva and were now one of only a handful of jewellers around the globe stocking the finest pink diamonds in the world. To cap off a wonderful few months, I was honoured with a Self-Achievement in Business Award from WA Tourism Week. Kimberley Fine Diamonds had arrived.

Towards the end of 1996, the phone rang at home quite late in the evening. We always jumped when a call came through late. On the end of the line, a very distinguished German voice said, 'Could I speak with Mrs Frauke Bolten-Boshammer please?' I half recognised the voice; it was familiar but not immediately identifiable. Then the man added, 'My name is Joachim Fuchsberger. Do you know who I am?'

'Of course I do!' I said. 'Blacky Fuchsberger! I've watched you on television since I was a child.'

Joachim 'Blacky' Fuchsberger was a household name in Germany as a major film star and radio host. He made his name playing Gunner Asch in a war-movie trilogy, but really became a star as the voice of the 1972 Munich Olympics; he was the stadium announcer for the opening and closing ceremonies. During the games, Palestinian terrorists killed eleven Israeli team members, and during the closing ceremony, there were reports that a hijacked passenger aircraft was being flown towards the stadium. Fearing he could trigger a fatal stampede, Blacky held his nerve and decided not to tell spectators to evacuate the packed stadium. His split-second decision proved to be the correct one, as the reports of the rogue aircraft were found to be false.

He went on to star in eighty films and became an ambassador for UNICEF.

Blacky had fallen in love with Australia after filming a television series of his travels around the country called *Terra Australis*, which more than 160 million people had watched. He loved Australia so much he even bought a holiday house in Hobart and an apartment in Sydney, and divided his time between Munich and Australia. He'd heard about me through German friends and wanted to come and visit.

'Come on up!' I said. 'We'd be thrilled to have you.'

Blacky arrived a few weeks later with a film crew in tow. We very happily entertained them, my banana curry successfully feeding twenty of us at dinner out on the lawn. Blacky spent a few days filming us for a pilot of a new season of *Terra Australis*.

A few months later, he phoned to say he'd been given the green light and he was on his way back to Kununurra. Blacky and the crew stayed and filmed for about a week. We showed them around, and they filmed interviews with our family and friends, and in the shop. They also visited some of the beautiful places around Kununurra, and Lance had a ball zipping Blacky around in his helicopter.

On Christmas Day 1997 in Germany, *Terra Australis: Zwischen Zuckerrohr und Diamenten – Terra Australis: From Sugar Cane to Diamonds* – went to air.

Two million people watched the documentary. In the middle of winter, as Germans were huddled around their fires over Christmas dinner, the deep blue skies, rich red earth and endless Kimberley sunshine warmed their hearts. The phone rang off the hook, and we were inundated with lovely letters and cards, which were swiftly followed by dozens of tourists. It had a remarkable impact.

The episode, which has been replayed many times, was one of a series Blacky filmed covering every corner of

Australia. He was a wonderful ambassador for Australia and put the sunburnt country on the map for many Germans. Years later, a German man came into the shop, stopped in his tracks, pointed to me and said, 'I know you!' He didn't, of course – he'd just watched the show.

By 1997, Kimberley Fine Diamonds was recognised around the world, and we were invited to participate in the pink diamond tender each year. For consecutive years we were successful bidding against the biggest jewellers from Hong Kong, Tokyo, Geneva and London, and we were building a collection of pink diamonds second to none.

With Helga in control of the day-to-day running of the store, I was able to spend some time building my knowledge of the industry and extending my network. I went to Central Europe to train in the trade, and to workshop designs and ideas with jewellers and designers I admired.

We held art exhibitions at the shop, one particular favourite being the works of the painter Elizabeth Durack. Then my jeweller and I began designing our own pieces of jewellery. The Staircase to the Moon necklace, with pink diamonds leading to a stunning Broome pearl, was nominated for a prestigious jewellery award.

The success of the business made my heart sing. We were now able to invest money back into the local community that had done so much for me and my family. We supported every local event we could, every local sporting team – the footy club, swimming club, netball team, water-ski club and cricket club – and organisations like the hospital. Local clubs and charities are at the heart of every community, but are essential for those of us who live so far away from anywhere.

My cheeky husband was making something of a name for himself too. Robert has a wicked sense of humour and loved playing a practical joke on anyone gullible enough to fall for his tricks.

He played tennis regularly with Judy's husband Jim Hughes, and dear Jim made the mistake of leaving his tennis racquet in Robert's care momentarily each week when he was getting dressed in the change rooms. For some time, Robert had been plotting a prank.

Unbeknown to poor Jim, Robert took his racquet and slipped a condom inside the cover. Jim took the racquet home none the wiser.

A few days later, Judy grabbed the first racquet she could find from the cupboard and threw it in the car for Ladies Day. She realised when she got to the courts she'd grabbed Jim's racquet. *Never mind*, she thought. But as she removed the cover, the slippery little condom, still in the wrapper, dropped out onto the court in front of the Kununurra ladies tennis team. Judy was mortified.

Luckily for Jim, he was working 100 kilometres away in Wyndham that day, too far for Judy to confront him, but when he got home at 2am, she was sitting up ready and waiting, and all hell broke loose.

Poor Jim was perplexed and professing his innocence, but Judy gave him the rounds of the kitchen and tossed him out of the house. Judy was on the verge of ending the marriage. 'Who was this woman?' she demanded to know.

Jim eventually twigged who might be responsible and rang Rob. Clearly realising this had caused more fuss than intended, Rob visited Judy with his tail between his legs and a bunch of flowers under his arm and apologised.

Chapter 25

My babies were growing up very quickly. Fritz and Andrea welcomed a son, Rick, followed by a daughter, Kimberley. Margret and Lance added baby Hannah to the family, and my own baby girl Katrina settled into primary school.

Peter had never warmed to Wesley the way Fritz did. He missed home terribly and would have preferred to be on the riverbank with a line in rather than stuck in class. Despite his longing for home, he did well at school, and his boarding house-mother, who wanted to have a baby of her own, said to me, 'If I could have any child, I'd have a boy like Peter.'

Things got a little easier for him when Maria arrived in Perth to board at St Mary's in his final year of school. They'd always been close and they found it reassuring to have one another to rely on in Perth. Still, he was counting down the days until he finished.

During the holidays, Maria would catch up with Judy's daughter, Julia. Peter's buddies Johnson Kirby and Clint

Slingsby would whisk him off on fishing trips when they weren't playing football and cricket with the local teams. At Wesley, Peter had become good mates with Ben Cousins and Michael Gardiner, who would go on to have professional AFL careers. Peter didn't have the natural talent of Ben and Michael, but he had the heart of an ox and he never gave up on the footy field.

When he finished year 12, Peter decided on furthering his education in Germany, as Fritz and Margret had done. I was thrilled he'd be immersed in his German heritage; he was thrilled he'd be immersed in new rivers and lakes, and have the chance to hook types of fish he'd never caught before.

He stayed with family for part of his trip but mostly with my friends Arno and Sigrid, whose son Jochen was the same age as Peter. As Germany was still in its school year, Peter went to school each day with Jochen rather than staying home alone. It was good for him to polish up his German, and a little bit sentimental for me because it was my old school, Klaus-Harms High School in Kappeln/Schlei. Whenever Jochen went to his French lessons, Peter would slip out and visit my father, who by then was in a nursing home just down the road. It brought my father immense joy to see him, and Peter loved regaling Grandpa with tales of the giant barra he caught at home – I think the fish got bigger and bigger with every retelling of the story.

$\sim$

Peter loved his time in Germany but after six months away, he was happy to be home in the sunshine, and we'd all missed him terribly. The night he returned we sat on the veranda together overlooking the river, chatting, and I said to him, 'What did you miss most?'

'This view, Mutti,' he said.

We had a big dinner to welcome him home and spent the night catching up on the six months he'd been gone. Peter was a quiet boy, and very sensitive. He was a deep thinker with a wise soul. The other children loved him. I could tell them to do something ten times and no one would listen to me, but Peter would say one word and they jumped. He was never loud or boisterous, so when he spoke, we knew he had something important to say, and we all listened.

It was the simple pleasures that he enjoyed. He never got caught up wanting the biggest and best of anything. Happiest with his rod in the water, a campfire and his friends for company, he never wasted money on the latest labels. At one stage, his footy boots started to come apart and his team-mates at the Ord River Magpies ribbed him: 'C'mon, Peter, time for some new boots.' He wasn't fussed, he kept playing on them until every last stitch was gone, and only then did he go and buy a new pair.

After his return from Germany, Peter went to work on the farm with Robert and Fritz. They loved having him around, because he was tough, reliable and got on with the job. The three of them also had a lot of fun together. It wasn't long before Robert felt that Peter was ready to take on more responsibility. He tasked Peter with looking after the irrigation for 400 hectares of sugar-cane crop on the property.

Peter treated the crop like it was his baby. He did whatever was necessary, often going out at all hours of the night to water it. He was determined to make it work and bring home the best sugar yield anyone had seen – he was terribly competitive. The only thing that got in the way of the sugar cane were his friends and footy: Fritz and Robert were quite amused to see Peter setting up an elaborate irrigation system so that he didn't have to leave the pub on Saturday nights to water, or to come on Sunday when he had a footy game on.

In 1998, his beloved Magpies made it through to the grand final. He played a good game, but the team lost. But in 1999 when they went through to the grand final again, Peter was so fired up, we knew this time they wouldn't lose.

Peter took the field again that day, and this time the team brought home the trophy.

Peter loved working with Fritz and Robert as much as they loved working with him, but his heart was always near the water. He applied to study aquaculture in Perth, and I could see him spending his days farming rivers and lakes; he would be completely at home. We had a nervous wait until the New Year to see if he got in. It was a popular course: more than two hundred people applied for only thirty spots. I crossed fingers, toes and everything else I could for him.

Helga, who was still handling the day-to-day operations of Kimberley Fine Diamonds, was a beautiful woman, always immaculately groomed. Every day she came to work looking like she'd stepped straight off the pages of a magazine. Despite our distance from the rest of the world, she managed to keep up with fashion trends and she always wore the most beautiful clothes, lipstick perfect. Amid our desolate surrounds – a lifestyle of dirt and dust – she was miraculously unweathered, never a line on her face, never a hair out of place.

That was why I knew something was seriously wrong the morning after we'd celebrated our 1999 staff Christmas party. We'd all had a wonderful time, and Helga was the life of the party, as always. The next day, she turned up for work looking very dishevelled, wearing the same clothes she'd worn to the party the night before.

I pulled her aside into the office, shut the door and made us both coffee.

'Helga, are you okay?' I quizzed.

She broke down and told me very honestly that after she arrived home from the Christmas party, she'd tried to gas herself in her car in the garage.

'Oh, good God, Helga!'

Thankfully she'd come to her senses before it was too late. I couldn't imagine what would prompt her to do such a thing: there was no sign she was depressed. We hugged and cried together and talked. Helga told me she wasn't unhappy but that she didn't want to get old. She wanted to stay forever young.

'But you must be feeling so sad to do something like this,' I said.

'No, Frauke, that's the thing, I'm not unhappy. It was just a feeling I had to follow, a moment in time,' she said. Yet she must have planned it ahead of time, as she had packed up her house. It was shocking to think this was going on behind the scenes and I had no idea.

Robert and I rallied around her. We hugged, we laughed, we ate together. With Helga's blessing I spoke to Val, our

Uniting Church minister and friend, who offered great support too. We made sure that Helga knew she was very loved. And I was relieved when she went to a doctor to get the help she needed.

With the clock about to tick over to the year 2000, Robert and I were heading off for a break. We hadn't had a holiday for a long time and this particular year marked such a big moment in history, we had made plans to do something special. We had booked ourselves a trip to Perth for the Hopman Cup, then afterwards we would fly to Noosa and all of the children would join us.

On the Saturday night before we were due to fly to Queensland, we had a special dinner with several of our closest friends, including Doris and Val, who was also on holidays in Perth. It's always tricky getting a table at a restaurant on a Saturday night in Cottesloe, but I'd booked our favourite Italian restaurant well in advance. Over fine wines and a beautiful meal, we toasted love and laughter, and good health and happiness in the New Year.

Now that Robert and I had celebrated with good friends in Perth, we would soon be celebrating again with all of our family around us in Noosa. I couldn't think of anything more perfect.

Chapter 26

Maria woke startled by the phone. The clock said 5.30am. *That can't be right*, she thought. *Who's calling at this hour on a Monday morning?* It took a few seconds for her consciousness to kick in before she jumped out of bed and ran to the phone.

'Maria, is Peter there?' Fritz asked.

'Hang on, I'll just get him.'

She knocked on Peter's door, then walked in, noticing immediately that his room didn't have the telltale fisherman's smell that usually greeted her. His bed was empty. He hadn't been home the night before, either, but that was nothing unusual. Peter spent most Saturday nights with his mates and often stayed over at their places.

From the kitchen window she could see that his car was parked outside on the lawn. She wandered out the back door and around to check on the boat – if it was gone, he'd probably left for an early-morning fish. His boat wasn't there.

She ambled back inside, still half-asleep, and told Fritz that Peter's boat was gone, hung up the phone and went back to bed. Several hours later, Fritz rang again.

'Sorry, Maria, is Peter back yet?'

She got out of bed and proceeded through the same checklist: bed, car, boat. Nope.

'Well, when you see him, tell him to get off his lazy arse and get to work like everyone else!' Fritz snapped.

Bored, alone and now rudely awake, seventeen-year-old Maria wandered over to Lance and Margret's for breakfast. We'd recently moved a transportable home onto the property at Riverfarm Road for Margret and Lance and their girls, who were also looking after Katrina while we were away.

'Margret, have you seen Peter?' she asked, propping herself up at the kitchen bench.

'No, should I have?'

'He's not home. He never says where he's going,' Maria moaned, as Margret put a fresh plate of toast in front of her. 'He just goes off with his mates and leaves us in the lurch!'

Margret tried to remember the last time she'd seen him. She recalled something about him saying he had a barbecue to go to and wouldn't join them for dinner as he'd done every other night while Robert and I were away.

But whose barbecue? She trawled her brain but nothing came to mind.

It's not easy trying to get hold of a farmer in the middle of a paddock, but she managed to get Fritz on the two-way radio.

'I've talked to all of Peter's friends – Kaylen, RB, Lon, Kym, Johnno,' said Fritz. 'Margret, he never made it to that barbecue.'

It had been thirty-six hours since anyone had seen Peter.

Robert and I both woke early that Monday morning with the intention of going for a walk along the beach before packing our bags to head to the airport, but just as I was walking up the steps to the bedroom to put my runners on, Fritz rang. It was 7.30am.

'Mutti, Peter is missing,' he said.

'What do you mean, missing?'

'He hasn't turned up to work this morning and no one has seen him since Saturday,' Fritz said.

Word had quickly spread around town that Peter was missing. Bad news travels fast in the country. Fritz reassured us everyone was on the case. He'd already called the police, and they were doing everything they could to find him. Peter would turn up somewhere, Fritz said, and 'then I'll bloody well kill him!'

In my heart, I knew it wasn't good, and I was worried. But I couldn't let my mind drift to the dark places for even a second. I kept positive and hopeful that Peter would turn up like he always did.

I told myself: *It isn't unusual for Peter to take himself off fishing down the river for a few nights. He'll be fine. He'll be fine.* Robert and I boarded our flight with fingers crossed that by the time we landed in Brisbane, Peter would be found and we'd put this down to one of those fishing adventures gone too far.

Margret and Fritz weren't so confident. Lance began organising an air search. Lance's former boss, Kerry Slingsby, ran an aviation business from Kununurra airport, mainly taking tourist groups out to the Bungle Bungles and heli-mustering around the Kimberley. He lived nearby and his son Clint was Peter's friend. Kerry called in all of his pilots, and every available aircraft was soon up in the air.

Maria and another neighbour had taken a boat out on the river to check out Peter's favourite fishing spot – the very spot where Maria, at the age of eight, had landed a 20-pound barra, smashing Peter's record of 10 pounds. As they made their way down the Ord she smiled, remembering Peter's disgust that the fish *she'd* caught was almost longer than him.

After an hour with no sign of Peter, they headed back home.

Every minute of the five-and-a-half-hour flight from Perth to Brisbane ticked over painstakingly slowly. The hands on my watch didn't seem to move. I kept my eye out the window the whole time, crazily hoping to spot him a thousand feet below.

Robert squeezed my hand. He didn't say much, other than reassuring me: 'Don't worry, Frauke, you know what Peter's like. He'll drift back in with a bagful of fish and wonder what all of the fuss was about.'

Robert's brother met us in Brisbane. It was late in the afternoon, and there was no good news to greet us. By then the story was running on the ABC news, and we hoped that someone might spot him somewhere.

Word had well and truly got out in Kununurra that Peter Bolten was missing, and ute after ute of people began arriving at home to help search for him. Fritz coordinated the search logistics with the police, then headed down the river in Robert's boat. Margret set up food and drinks for all of the volunteers and manned the base, instructed new arrivals where to start searching, and fielded endless phone calls. Lance led the air search.

As dusk was settling, Peter's upturned boat was found lodged among rocks in rapids quite a way downstream from our house. This news was devastating, but I prayed that he was stuck on the riverbank somewhere, maybe injured, waiting for someone to find him. I couldn't let my mind drift to the unthinkable: that he'd been taken by a crocodile.

He's a strong swimmer, I told myself over and over. *He's fit, and he knows the river better than anyone.* They were weasel words of comfort.

We were stuck in Brisbane, feeling utterly helpless. The phone kept ringing. I think I heard 'They'll find him, Frauke, don't worry. We're praying for you' a thousand times.

We didn't sleep a wink that night. Waves of nausea washed over me, and my legs were stiffening as if someone had poured slow-setting concrete through my veins. Inch by inch, I felt paralysed. Not even the warmth of Robert's arms could thaw the chill running through me.

At dawn on Tuesday morning, we headed to the airport to fly to Darwin. By that stage, I would've walked barefoot over broken glass to get home. There were no flights from Darwin to Kununurra, so Kerry Slingsby chartered a private plane from Kununurra to pick us up in Darwin and get us home as quickly as possible.

It was the middle of the wet season and a fierce thunderhead was rolling across the East Kimberley sky, dumping rain all around the region. Technically, Slingsby Air wasn't supposed to fly in these conditions, but Kerry made a decision from the heart to help us in an emergency. He assured me he'd worry about any repercussions from the authorities later. From the plane we could see lightning splitting through a rolling wall of thick black clouds; I wondered if we were flying into hell.

By the time we arrived home, scores of people had gathered at Riverfarm Road to help search. We counted at least fifty cars parked on the lawn, up the driveway and around the house, jammed into any spare spot.

Looking for my boy were the police, the State Emergency Service Search and Rescue team and more than sixty volunteers: Peter's friends, our family friends and the entire Kununurra football team. All around Margret's veranda and scattered across the lawn, people rested their bones, some having cups of coffee, some downing a well-earned beer after hours scouring sodden bush tracks and muddy riverbanks in the rain. Some had searched all day on Monday and had slept at the house, setting off again at dawn. I hugged them all and thanked them for their help.

We were humbled by how many people were helping us. Maria went around and took photos of them all so she could show Peter just how much inconvenience he had caused everyone. He'd be in so much trouble when they found him.

A foot search had begun at daybreak along both sides of the rushing, wild river, which was swollen by the rains. A flotilla of boats was slowly making its way up and down. Around mid-afternoon, the Search and Rescue people came to tell us the search had to be temporarily halted because a huge and aggressive saltwater crocodile was stalking the search party downstream. The croc was putting the searchers at risk, so they all had to take a break until wildlife officers came and removed it. They shot the croc and took it away for autopsy.

While no one said it aloud, the obvious assumption was that this croc may have taken Peter and they were expecting to find his remains. God help us.

I tried to be strong, but every hour we were edging closer to a precipice I couldn't bear to acknowledge. Sporadically I gathered enough strength to keep myself engaged, but there were moments when the world was zipping around me and I felt like I was sitting in the middle of a glass bubble, unable to hear or process what was being said, unable to reach anyone, in a world of my own. Maybe I didn't want to hear.

Judy arrived back from Queensland, where she'd been on holiday, totally unaware of what was going on. As they approached Kununurra in their car, Judy had said to Jim, 'Let's stop in town and grab some things on the way home.'

She went into the post office to pick up the mail, and the postie asked, 'Have they found Peter yet?'

'Peter who?' she said.

'Peter Bolten. He's missing, haven't you heard?'

She dropped everything and raced over to us. Jim joined the search, while Judy kept me company. Val was still in Perth, so the locum minister came out to be with us. I had a house full of people – wonderful people – but I felt so alone.

After many hours, Judy went home to change clothes and get supplies. Watching the search from her window, she saw Lance flying up and down the river, then she noticed that he came in low and circled the same spot. He landed at the bottom of her yard. She went down to find out what was happening, but by the ashen look on Lance's face, she knew straightaway. 'Have you found him?' she asked.

'Yes.'

From my window, I saw Judy's car pull up. She came inside, hugged me and went to put the kettle on. Then a few moments later, Lance's helicopter landed on the lawn and he came inside. A handful of family and friends was gathered there, and he asked us all to sit down on the sofa.

'Frauke, there's no easy way to tell you this, but we've found a body and we're sure it's Peter,' Lance said. 'I'm so sorry.' Lance had already spoken with the police.

Maria gripped my hand and my body began to shudder violently. *'Nein, nein, nicht Peter! Nicht Peter!'* I screamed. I stood up, but in a split second my heart and my head gave way and my legs collapsed from underneath me. I don't remember clearly, but apparently it was Judy who grabbed me before I hit the ground. I sat on the sofa with my head in my hands – howling, numb – then eventually someone took me to bed. Peter was gone.

Lance had flown over that stretch of river several times during the past two days, from varying heights and directions, making sure he'd scanned every inch of the waterway. He had spotted nothing until today, when Peter's body had risen to the top.

Because of the storms, Peter's body couldn't be retrieved straightaway. Later that evening, when there was a break in the weather, a team of boats went out to bring him home. It was pitch black and the rain had drawn out all sorts of the river's creatures, but the rescuers all put their own fears and grief aside to bring Peter back to me.

Much of the period after that is a blur, and to be honest I don't wish to recall it. I know I was sedated and the world happened around me. I could've had a thousand pills – they still wouldn't make a dent in my sorrow. My world was black. Colour had been drained from the sky. Lightness and joy were gone. The sun rose and set, but I didn't care, Peter was gone.

When Friedrich died, something innate clicked on inside me: a survival instinct. I knew I had to keep going because I had children to look after. But this was my child, my flesh, my blood, my bones, my heart and my soul. It's not the natural way of things for a child to die before a parent. I wanted to die too.

Chapter 27

In the days immediately after Peter's body was found, Robert was a rock, as was Judy. And Fritz's and Margret's iron spines carried me through the fog.

Katrina was just nine years old; she couldn't understand at first when Robert told her, 'Peter is gone.' Gone where? When she realised he wasn't coming back, she hid herself in her room and cried.

Maria was utterly bereft. She and Peter were peas in a pod, twins born a few years apart. She was his alter ego; she would finish his sentences and hung off every word he said. I have some recollections of her crawling into bed with me, the two of us howling ourselves to sleep, but still waking in hell.

Everywhere I looked, pictures of my family graced the walls, the sideboards, the bedside tables, and there was Peter, at the centre of every photo, with a grin so wide you could stuff a 10-pound barra in it. I could not comprehend or accept that he was no longer alive.

Sometimes I'd find one of us, if not me, lying on his bed or sitting in his room, soaking him up. Visitors came constantly; the house was full of people, flowers, friends and family. People dropped off food; they hugged us, cried with us. Days melted into nights and again into days. Some days I didn't know whether it was dusk or dawn. Peter's death brought me to my knees – physically, emotionally, spiritually. I questioned God, but mostly I questioned why he had died.

Peter's body had been taken to Perth for an autopsy. I wanted to see him, but the doctors said no. After being in the water for so many days, he looked nothing like the boy I knew, they said. It would only add to my grief. Thankfully Robert convinced me that was not how I wanted to remember Peter.

Sometime during that week, I can't remember exactly when, the police called and asked us to come to the station to answer some questions. We were met by two detectives. They weren't local police; they'd been called in from Broome.

Peter's death was being treated as suspicious, the detective told us. By all accounts, he was a healthy, happy boy. His death didn't make sense. They were investigating possible murder and needed to ask some questions. Murder. My God.

We sat through hours of interrogation: how did Peter seem before he died? Did he have any enemies? What were his last known whereabouts? What time did you last see him? What did you discuss?

I had trouble remembering what day it was at that moment. If I could remember my last conversation with Peter, I would've seared every single word of it into my soul, never to be forgotten. But I couldn't.

It didn't take long for whispers to circle around town that Peter Bolten may have been murdered, and we fielded calls from many people who were well meaning but only added to our grief.

I wondered who would possibly want to kill him. It was ghastly and I couldn't begin to entertain the thought. But for many days, until the autopsy report was released, we simply didn't have answers to any questions. We were subjected to scurrilous rumours, gossip and the awful thought that our precious boy was involved with something sinister. Nothing added up.

The autopsy revealed the truth. Peter died by his own hand, and the crocodile suspected of killing him was found to be totally unconnected to his death.

An investigation was to be conducted by the coroner, which meant we would have to wait about three months for the official findings. In the meantime, Val and I visited the coroner's counsellor to hear what they had found in the autopsy. We learnt that Peter had died on the Saturday evening. He had weighed himself down with rocks. There were no symptoms of a struggle, and no drugs or alcohol in his system. The counsellor told us that it would have taken about thirty seconds for Peter to die.

A lifetime of joy, of love, a life so precious to so many, gone, his life force extinguished in just thirty seconds.

They told us that twenty-year-old males have a high rate of suicide, and that although suicide can be planned it is still an impulsive act. But Peter? Why? He did not have depression; I know what depression looks like only too well.

And yet obviously he'd been thinking about this for some time to go to such lengths.

There were no signs, no warning bells, not for any of us. I discussed it over and over again with family members and Peter's friends: did he say something to someone? Did anyone have a clue as to why? No answers. He was happy, healthy, with his whole life ahead of him. Nothing made sense and there were no explanations.

Ironically, postmarked the day after we found Peter's body, a letter came from the university congratulating him on being one of just thirty people to be accepted to study aquaculture. We hadn't opened any mail until now; it was the last thing on our minds. It was his dream come true. The final cruel blow.

With so much unease in the community about Peter's death and so many questions unanswered, Robert and I thought it best to hold a gathering at our house – a debriefing of sorts – so we could share what we knew. We were worried about some of Peter's mates, who'd taken his death very badly. We wanted to get them all together to embrace them and thank them for what they'd done for us. Everybody needed to talk, clear the air and somehow begin to heal. It was as much for our family as for Peter's friends and the local community.

We decided to hold a memorial service at home, even though Peter's body was still with the coroner in Perth. Eleven days after he died, we gathered on the lawn at River-farm Road, overlooking the river, Peter's favourite place, where we'd farewelled his father. The weather was unbearably hot and humid at the height of the wet season, so the service began at 6am, just after the sun had come up.

Chairs were placed all over the lawn and we set up an altar, on which we placed Peter's number 9 Ord River Magpies premiership jumper, the premiership footy, some of his trophies, his favourite photo from a fishing trip he took with his friend Johnson Kirby, and those blessed footy boots, falling apart at the seams. Three hundred people came.

They brought food, sunflowers to lay at the altar and good wishes. We all dressed in white – I couldn't stand us being in black. Friends and family had flown in from all over the world. I hoped Peter and Friedrich were somewhere together watching on.

Fritz and Maria both spoke, paying tribute to their brother, as did Lance and a friend of ours, Peter Letchford, who'd been there to retrieve his body. Robert's father Claude read a poem with the line 'Miss me but let me go.' Andrea sang a beautiful song, after which Robert and I both spoke. I actually can't remember what I said, but Robert's beautiful eulogy lives with me to this day.

'When I came on the scene, Peter was already five years old, and he already had a reputation for having a mind of his own and a love for the outdoors, particularly the river,' he began. 'While I fell in love with, and married, Frauke, I really fell in love with the whole family. Peter's passion was fishing and I loved going with him. He was with me when we caught our first 20-pound barra – I won't tell you where!' he joked.

'When he was younger, Peter would throw a paddy whenever he got beaten, just like any normal kid, but he grew out of this. Later, I can only remember two times when he really lost it. The first was on a trip to Port Warrender.

Just before dark he hooked a very good fish and played it for the best part of an hour before losing it beside the boat. The other was when the Ord River Magpies got beaten in the '98 grand final. Flashes of pain and anger were only momentary, then he got going again. The next day at Port Warrender he caught a few big mackerel, and in 1999 the Magpies came home with the flag.

'Peter was always disappearing down the river or off to a mate's place. Sometimes this drove his mother frantic. Secretly, I loved and envied him for going out like this. Once, when he was sixteen, Peter was out somewhere along the river well after midnight. Frauke was worried and woke me.

'The boat was gone, so I walked up along the riverbank 'til I saw a campfire up over on the shingle bank. I walked back and borrowed Jim's boat and slipped over there. Then I walked quietly and sat in the shadows at the edge of the firelight. I sat there for almost half an hour, just enjoying their youth and remembering mine. I really loved that short period. I headed back home without letting him know I'd been there, reassuring Frauke he was just fine.

'Where is Peter now? It's a philosophical debate. I believe Peter is with God. I imagine he's checking out the best fishing holes and camping spots, waiting for us to join him. I also believe Peter is in the river he loves, in the environment he was so passionate about. And to honour him, and because I share his passion, I will do my best to preserve this environment and look after it.

'Finally, I believe Peter lives on in each of us. I know we all have very mixed emotions when we think about Peter. Mostly I just miss him. Our family has a strong belief in God. In this God I find love and hope. However, in the early mornings, when I am walking around thinking, often I can only repeat the thought of King David of the Old Testament when he heard of the death of his son Absalom. And I cry out: "O my son Peter, my son, my son Peter!"

'Since Peter died, the question asked of us, and that we asked of ourselves constantly was why. Why would a young man, who had everything going for him, and the world at his feet take his own life? Peter left no note so we will never truly know his reasons but we have our own theories.'

Robert surmised that maybe Peter believed life couldn't get any better than this. Peter had enjoyed two brilliant years, travelling to Germany then home working on the farm with Fritz. His footy team the Ord River Magpies had won the flag, and he'd been catching fish many people only dream about.

'He'd just been in Darwin for the New Year with a great group of friends. He told them, "I've had the time of my life." He lived on the Ord River, a place he loved. So maybe like a great sportsman, he could retire while he was ahead,' Robert said.

I clung to this theory and the belief that he'd ticked off everything he wanted to do in life. Anything less was unbearable. Robert's words were the warm blanket I needed.

Fritz and some of Peter's friends made a steel cross as a memorial for Peter. Over a few beers, they had got together and welded some fencing steel to create the cross, then attached a plaque that read 'RIP Peter Bolten'. At sunset, a few days before the memorial at home, they erected the cross at a lovely grassy outlook high above the river, overlooking the spot where Peter's body was found, with a view all the way down the Ord and past Peter's favourite fishing spot. About thirty of us gathered and watched as Fritz, Robert and Peter's friends dug a hole and stood this wonderful tribute in its place. They worked in silence – no words needed to be said – with their hearts and minds in unison. The 4-metre-tall structure stood majestically as the sun set over the Ord. It was quite breathtaking – rustic and industrial, but very beautiful.

We then flew to Perth to attend another memorial at Wesley. By then Peter's body had been released by the coroner; he would be cremated after the memorial and we would take his ashes home. Our first stop when we arrived in Perth was at the funeral home, to see Peter's coffin. Grief affects people in many different ways. My senses of sight and smell were heightened. Before us, Peter rested in a lovely white coffin, peaceful – but around the room at the funeral home were bunches of dreadful plastic flowers that had a musty smell about them. I had to leave.

The service at Wesley had a very different feel to our memorial at home: it was a more traditional church funeral. Peter's coffin was carried in covered with a wreath of fresh, fragrant lilies, yellow and white, with sprays of purple irises throughout.

Val officiated and delivered a lovely eulogy along with Peter's boarding house-mother, Janelle McCann. Robert and I also spoke. When it was my turn to take to the altar, I struggled to get the words out, until Robert stepped up behind me and placed his arm around my waist, gently encouraging me to keep going. With a tissue gripped in my fingers to mop up tears, I thanked everyone for coming and shared a few favourite stories about Peter's fishing adventures, and how he went missing with Barbarossa as a two-year-old. Then I told a story Maria had shared at the service in Kununurra, about how Peter had taught her what to do if she was ever chased by a crocodile on the river.

'Head for that tree and climb it,' Peter had told her, pointing to a towering eucalypt. She had stretched her arms as high as she could, but she could barely reach its lowest branches.

'How am I supposed to reach?' she asked him.

'Maria, when you are scared, you can do anything,' he replied.

Then I repeated the words Maria had spoken at the memorial at home: 'Peter was my teacher and my protector.'

We sang hymns and recited prayers, then Peter's body was taken to the crematorium, where we said our final goodbyes. As the coffin was taken away, the priest said, 'Peter, into the freedom of the world and the sunshine, we let you go.'

But we will never let him go.

Chapter 28

Maria was adamant that there was no way she was going back to school in Perth. 'Not without Peter,' she said with a heaving sob. It was her final year and terribly important that she finish school, so I suggested to Robert that I fly back to Perth with her and stay for the first term, helping her to get resettled and focused on her studies. Katrina would come too.

Robert encouraged the idea. He thought it would do me the world of good to get away from Kununurra, where I was struggling, my mind lost in a tangle of thoughts about Peter. Most days, I'd get only a minute's break from the heaviness of my mind; on a good day, maybe an hour before the sorrow would seep through again. There was little respite from the grief. I could barely look out the window. The joy and beauty of the river was gone; ripples of misery and darkness spread out with every ebb and flow.

Robert was my backbone. He was grieving too, but he quietly picked up the pieces around me. Saying goodbye to him was hard, but we both felt it was the best decision for Maria, and he would fly down to be with us as often as he could. In Perth, I immersed myself in the small comforts of motherhood. The little things – packing lunch boxes, school drop-offs and pick-ups – gave me moments of joy and usefulness. I desired nothing else in life but to wrap my girls up in love and soak up the normality of their routines. I missed normal.

I dreamt of Peter often. On the rare nights I was able to get some sleep, he trickled into my thoughts. Always a vibrant little boy with his mop-top of blond curls, buzzing around the place, so lively and so alive. The same dreams repeated over and over, night after night, until one evening when twenty-year-old Peter came to me.

He said to me, 'Mum, this is the last time I will come to you,' and leant over and gave me a kiss. This was very precious to me because the boys at Wesley used to tease him when he gave me a kiss goodbye. Then he said, 'Now I'm not coming back to you, goodbye.' He felt so real it was as though I could reach out and touch him.

Peter had been with me. Never have I been surer of anything. His presence was so powerful that I felt him. After that night, just as Peter had told me, the dreams came only every now and then, and never again with Peter as a twenty-year-old, only ever as a child.

Katrina missed her brother, and missed her father when we were in Perth. I know Peter's death had a deep impact on her, and in hindsight I'm not sure I was present enough to be a great support to her. I was too distraught.

Maria was really struggling. She had idolised Peter, and I was at a loss as to how to help her come to terms with his death. We went and saw a counsellor, who recommended hypnosis. Initially I was sceptical, but by this stage I was prepared to give anything a go to help her. The process of hypnosis was very gentle, and when she fully woke, she had a calmness I hadn't seen for some time. She said that she'd met Peter under hypnosis and the two of them talked. Peter said he was sorry he upset her, and he said goodbye.

I asked, 'But Maria, did he tell you why he did it?'

'No, Mutti.'

I feel it's important to be very honest about how we coped with Peter's death: it was not easy, and we took every available bit of help we could. My doctor prescribed antidepressants for me, which helped. I walked along the beach at Cottesloe every day, finding solace in the cool sand under my feet and the gentle waves washing up onto the shore. I've always found water very soothing; maybe Peter did too.

Some days were better than others, but some days I could barely get out of bed.

There were still so many questions unanswered about why it happened, and I've slowly accepted that I will never know – but I still struggle within myself that I didn't know.

My relationships with my children have always been very close. How could I not have known? My faith is deep, and I believed that if something was wrong with one of my children, instinctively, my heart or my sixth sense would tell me.

It upsets me to think I didn't feel anything the moment Peter died. I had no idea. It distresses me to think I was at dinner with my friends, with no hint of my son taking his own life. I believed that if one of my children was hurting or in trouble, God would send a sign. I believed that, as a mother, you just know. But I felt nothing the moment my precious child – my flesh and blood, my soul – left this earth. I struggle with that still.

At the end of first term, we went home. Our plane touched down, and the familiar heat that I'd once loathed was warm and comforting as we stepped onto the sticky tarmac. Brilliant purple bougainvillea was blooming all around town, and the sugar cane was trying its hardest to stretch to the sky. I saw beauty in the rich kaleidoscope of Kununurra's colours, and I felt Peter's spirit here. It was good to be home.

The time away had helped. I wouldn't say we were beginning to heal, but we had accepted Peter wasn't coming back and we were learning how to live with the grief. I felt I could cope with walking past his bedroom or seeing his car or his clothes hanging in the cupboard, bumping into his friends or reading the Ord River Magpies footy scores in the paper.

Small steps, just one foot in front of the other.

We started going to church again on Sundays. Fritz and Andrea, Margret and Lance and all of the grandchildren would gather at our house for breakfast, then we'd go to the 9.30am service together. Faith and family helped.

My first few trips into town were hard. Some people didn't know how to react or what to say. There were times I walked into a shop and people I'd known for years would look intently into their shopping trolleys and scurry off in another direction. Some avoided me. Most wouldn't make eye contact. There really are no words that offer comfort in a situation like this, but a 'hello' helps. It's much better than saying nothing – saying nothing hurts far more than saying something silly.

After Peter died we had left his room pretty much as it was. I went in there one morning to begin sorting a few things out, and from the moment I stepped inside I could feel a presence; something was in the room with me. There was a little scratching noise, which I thought could've been rats or mice, both of which I absolutely detested. I sat very still on Peter's bed, trying to identify where the sound was coming from. It was coming from the corner of the ceiling and as I looked up, a little bird poked its head over the top of Peter's air conditioner.

It had obviously been living there for some time, having made a nest. The bird wasn't frightened of me at all – in fact, it was quite curious and hopped around, getting closer to me.

The little bird was strangely comforting and I wondered if it was a sign of Peter.

At times I can feel Peter's presence very strongly, and coincidentally on those occasions the little bird always appears around the house. It often turns up on family occasions, and we've come to believe that the bird is in some way connected to Peter.

Every now and then someone will ask, 'Have you seen the little bird?' The Peter bird, as we call it, is very special to us all.

$\sim$

Life goes on. There were crops to harvest and a shop to run. Day by day I got stronger. I went back to work; I'm not sure how helpful I was, but the distraction was certainly helpful to me. I cried often and wasn't ashamed to let my emotions out.

Maria settled back into school with a renewed focus for term two, and I was very proud of her.

I was frightened that people would forget Peter and was looking for a tangible way to honour his memory. Fritz came up with the idea of sponsoring a trophy at the football club in Peter's name. That idea blossomed into something much bigger: a big celebration to mark what would have been Peter's twenty-first birthday in October 2000. Two weeks beforehand, we placed an ad in the local paper inviting the entire district to come and join us for an afternoon of cricket and swimming followed by a barbecue.

It was the tail end of the dry season, and the weather was perfect. Riverfarm Road was filled with people young and old; they spilled over onto the lawns and the riverbank, the whole community coming together.

It was a way for us to not only remember Peter but also acknowledge the wonderful community spirit that had carried us through the past nine months. And it was a chance to be reacquainted with people who'd drifted away from us in that time. All of the people who'd searched for Peter came, and over many hugs, kisses and a lot of beer, we reminisced and shared happy memories and cheeky stories about Peter. For one evening, he came alive again. His spirit was with us; we felt his presence, and we soaked up the joy he had brought to so many others. It was a wonderful evening and a fitting way of honouring our lost boy.

Maria finished school and we flew down for her valedictory dinner and graduation. Despite all she'd endured, she did well in her exams. Like Margret, she travelled to Germany to study gemology in Idar-Oberstein, a famous jewellery town in Germany's Rhineland region. A pretty place with tiny streets and buildings that date back hundreds of years, Idar-Oberstein is a village tucked into the side of a mountain, with a lovely homely feel about it. It was a world away from Kununurra, and she had a wonderful time and returned for Christmas ready to study a commerce degree the following year.

I normally love the preparations for our big Christmas Eve celebrations, but this year it just didn't feel right. Fritz and Andrea offered to have Christmas at their house, and the change of scenery was a good idea. We still did our best to maintain our traditions and give the impression that life goes on, but sadness was never too far from the surface. An empty chair, a picture frame, lemon sorbet – Peter's favourite dessert – all prompted tears, but the tears were better out than bottled up inside.

Ten-year-old Katrina wrote out her wish list for Santa. In pencil, in her prettiest handwriting, she listed the things she wanted. Number one was 'Peter back'.

Sadly, not even Santa could deliver that Christmas miracle.

Chapter 29

It felt good to be immersed in the business again, and I could feel my focus and energy slowly returning. My staff were more precious to me than any diamond, and I loved their company and their shared passion. I was learning as much from them as they were from me, and distraction proved the best medicine.

In 2000, we'd again been successful in the annual Argyle pink diamond tender, and a range of sparkling new pink diamonds were now on display in our showroom: pink champagne diamonds, pink rosé and exquisite purple pinks with a depth of colour and clarity I'd never seen before.

Our sales had been a little soft in the middle of 2000, which we put down to tourists heading to the Sydney Olympics rather than to the Kimberley, but with the new pinks in the collection, by the New Year our figures had bounced back up and the business was in good shape. So much so, I employed a third jeweller to help keep up with demand.

The rare pinks tickled the interest of people from faraway corners of the world, and international tourists were an increasingly large part of our clientele. We created a multi-lingual website, which was cutting edge for the outback in the early millennium. Not long after it went live, we had our first major internet sale of an Argyle diamond, worth nearly $30,000. Along with the pinks, the shop now stocked an extensive range of traditional diamonds and jewellery, rings, bracelets and earrings, but by far our most popular pieces were the designs our jewellers created in-house, mini works of art that reflected the local landscape. I loved the design side of the business and wanted us to showcase signature pieces that were unique to the Kimberley. We designed a gorgeous little boab tree, crafted in platinum, silver and gold, which became the centrepiece of earrings, charm bracelets and rings. My favourite is a stunning pendant made of polished Kimberley rock with a pretty gold boab set into its centre and Argyle diamonds reflecting stars in the sky of the rugged landscape. Many hours went into creating the piece; it is a work of art.

It warms my heart to think that all over the world, strangers are united by a little piece of the Kimberley. The business remained very much a family affair. Maria was taking a gap year at university and working with us almost full time after completing her gemology studies, and Margret worked whenever she could in between commitments with her busy young family. Helga had done a wonderful job managing the store, especially after Peter died. My absence had put a great weight on her shoulders, which she handled effortlessly, but I knew we couldn't keep her forever. She was a free spirit and ready for a new challenge.

The right opportunity fell into her lap when the magnificent El Questro cattle station outside of Kununurra expanded its tourism operations, opening up its beautiful homestead and station surrounds to more guests. With Helga's background in hotels and customer service, it was a terrific opportunity to use all of her skills. I was sad to see her go but thrilled for the new adventures she could sink her teeth into. Thankfully her office was based in town, just down the street, so we could still see one another almost every day.

Every now and then I think back to my childhood in Germany. I think about those school teachers who belittled me and made me feel stupid. In many ways, I have to thank them, because subconsciously they've driven me to be the person I am today.

When I opened the doors of my first shop I had no background or training either in business or the jewellery trade; I'd been a mother for twenty-two years. But I had a vision of creating a touch of European sophistication in the middle of the outback, an oasis to show the world the gentle refinement that coexists with this dusty, harsh, often cruel landscape. Seizing fate, luck and opportunity helped me achieve that dream.

So it was a huge honour and a big thrill when I was nominated for the prestigious Telstra Business Women's Awards in early 2001. It was also terrifying. As a nominee for the state of Western Australia, I had to put a presentation together about my business and contribution to the community, and go through interviews with the judges.

Robert and the children's pride and encouragement helped me put my fears aside. The awards organisers asked people from local businesses and the community to give references for me. People were so kind and once again the spirit of Kununurra lifted me and carried me along. The town's support propelled me right out of my comfort zone.

The following month I was invited to speak at another business dinner in Perth. I found myself sitting next to Janet Holmes à Court, a woman I'd long admired from afar. Because Janet rebuilt her family business after her husband Robert's untimely death, her story had resonated with me and inspired me to keep going during some very difficult days.

When it was my turn to speak, I took a few deep breaths to compose myself. I was conscious of needing to speak very slowly, because sometimes when I get nervous, I speak too fast and it can be tricky for people to understand my accent. I'd laboured over the right words to say, and I knew there was only one way to begin: I carried a German *Stehauffrauchen* doll to the lectern. A 'Stee-off' doll is a roly-poly toy that you can't knock down. No matter how you roll it, it always gets back up.

Everyone could see the toy in front of me. With a flick of the fingers, I knocked the clown down, and it rose back up again smiling. And that was how I introduced myself: as a living *Stehauffrauchen*. I might get knocked down, but I'll always get back up again.

I took the audience through my journey to Australia and all of the things that had happened along the way, with the culmination of my work creating Kimberley Fine Diamonds with my family. As each chapter of my life unfolded on stage, the nerves melted away.

After the speech, Janet Holmes à Court hugged me, gave me a kiss on the cheek and said, 'Congratulations, Frauke, what an achievement.' Her words meant a lot. I didn't go home with an award that day, but it didn't matter: the real reward was just being there among so many wonderful women, each of whom inspired me in some way.

While I was in Perth, back home preparations were well underway for the very first Ord Valley Muster. A group of locals had come up with the idea of hosting a gala dinner for the entire community to come together for one night and celebrate the Kimberley, and catch up with friends old and new. This was especially important for the men in our community, who didn't get together often. Money raised on the night would support local charities, so Kimberley Fine Diamonds happily became one of the sponsors.

The organising committee wanted this to be something special: a night for us to leave the overalls at home and dress up. The invitation said black tie, and we would enjoy a beautiful meal in the sheds at the Hoochery, a sprawling sugar-cane farm that local man Raymond 'Spike' Dessert had turned into a distillery. The rusty corrugated sheds looked a million dollars, and stockmen, miners, sugar-cane farmers, cattle wranglers and beef barons came dressed in their finest for the evening – with a touch of Akubra, of course.

The sweet warm smell of the rum distilling lingered in the air as we stood around enjoying our pre-dinner drinks. I found the blend of molasses and baked-bread smells from the fermenting yeast quite pleasant.

A team of the most beautifully groomed horses cantered up to the sheds, their riders mustering us to our tables. Then shortly after we were seated, formalities began with a wonderful Indigenous corroboree. The sound of the didgeridoo echoing around the sheds was haunting, and the Kununurra primary school choir that followed sounded almost operatic in the warm, still air. The Australian cricket legend Dennis Lillee was the special guest of honour.

Not long after dinner, a sudden cold snap whipped an unusually icy wind through the place, and all of us in our strappy cocktail dresses were freezing. The temperature plunged dramatically and what had been a balmy night was suddenly outback arctic.

Those of us with farms nearby raced home and gathered up every coat, jumper and blanket we could find for guests who had travelled to the event from far away. Fashion went by the wayside as denim jackets covered bare shoulders, and satin skirts were covered in oilskins and Driza-Bones. By the time the band began, we were all happy to dance to warm ourselves up a bit. Even the old bow-legged stockmen joined in.

Robert took my hand and led me to the dance floor, swirling me around with all of the other couples. I had a smile on my face the whole time, but it was plastered on – underneath I wasn't smiling at all. To the outside world I put on a happy face, but I struggled emotionally. This was how I'd been living my life since Peter died. I felt guilty about being happy or having fun. I felt that I shouldn't be, and I didn't want people thinking that all was okay, because nothing could've been further from the truth. Our lives were very much a day-to-day struggle; some days we coped better than others. I spent most of the night fighting off the urge to run away and hide. It would take about five years for that feeling to wear off.

Chapter 30

Just after lunch one afternoon in early October 2001, I got a call from the office of El Questro.

'Helga hasn't come to work today, Frauke. Would you know where she is?'

'No, I haven't seen her since last week.'

My heart skipped a beat. I rang Robert straightaway and asked him to drive out to her house as quickly as he could. She'd bought herself a lovely little acreage at Crossing Falls, about 20 kilometres out of town, surrounded by natural bush, boab trees and beautiful mature frangipanis. It was her little piece of heaven.

Robert swung by the shop and picked up one of my jewellers, who was friends with Helga too. In the meantime, I frantically called Helga's house. When I received no answer, I rang anyone I could think of who may have seen her. At every turn, I came up with nothing. She hadn't been seen at all over the weekend.

I racked my brains trying to recall my last conversation with her. She'd been busy at work and I'd been busy with the shop, so we hadn't spoken for about a week.

I now had a terrible gut feeling. I made coffee, paced up and down in the office, and waited and waited.

When Robert phoned, I knew straightaway. Through tears, he could barely get the words out: 'I'm so sorry, Frauke.'

I collapsed into the chair at my desk and threw my head into my hands, howling. 'But she promised,' I cried.

Helga had hanged herself. Robert found her in the garage.

I was so sad, but so mad with her too.

Only a little while after getting treatment from the doctor, she had got back to being her vivacious self. In fact, within six months of her first suicide attempt, it was impossible to imagine that she could've done such a thing. And she had said so herself.

Peter's death just weeks after her first attempt had been a big wake-up call for her. After he died, she was an amazing support to me, and she promised me that having seen the widespread grief Peter's death caused, she would never do something so silly ever again.

I believed her. It was a heartfelt promise because she'd witnessed the absolute devastation suicide brings to those left behind, and I knew she was hurting over Peter's death too.

Life was a precious gift, she knew that now. But she broke her promise.

The grief rolled in like a tsunami all over again. At times, I felt almost catatonic, unable to speak or process the images in my head of her final hours. The town was in shock. There was no note, no explanation.

Was it just another 'moment in time' that took her to this place? We will never know.

Her body was taken away to Perth for an autopsy. Robert and I flew to Perth with her, because I didn't want her to be alone. We held a service for her there with a few of the friends she had made during her travels and adventures.

Then we brought her ashes home and had a service at her house. A huge number of people came; Helga had touched many lives.

I think about Helga often. She is in my prayers, and I still miss her terribly. I regret sending Robert out to find her. It should've been me. I wish I'd been there to cradle her at the end, to comfort her soul and remind her how much we love her.

Sometime after Helga died, I noticed that I could no longer hum. Often when I was shopping or in the car or in the kitchen busying myself, I'd hum — not consciously, it was just a reflex thing. After Helga died, I stopped.

I physically couldn't hum any more. I needed help and was prescribed antidepressants.

Suicide has touched our lives way too often. Sadly, in the Kimberley region we have a terrible problem with suicide, which seems to impact every generation, young, old and particularly our Indigenous community.

Beautiful hearts, gone.

It's a difficult issue to discuss, and some say we shouldn't for fear of triggering the vulnerable. But I'm choosing to talk about this in the hope of saving others.

Our family now knows that there is a familial link with suicide. If somebody in the family has committed suicide, there is a greater risk that other family members may take their own life. I wish I had been aware of this before Peter's death.

If Peter's story or Helga's story can save one life, it is worthwhile sharing it. We must talk about this. We must support each other. We must encourage each other to seek help, because help *is* available. And life is a precious gift.

Chapter 31

In 2005 Robert and I decided it was time for change. We wanted to build a new home of our own, a modern fresh place for our family to gather. I wanted a new vista to wake up to each day, a new space in which to create happy memories and start afresh. It would've been easy to sell up and move to a new house, but that wasn't the answer. My soul and my heart are here, where my husband's ashes are buried and my son's ashes scattered.

Robert and I agreed we had an abundance of land at Riverfarm Road, and we could build a new home on the empty paddock at the side of our house, which offered better views of the river and a sweeping outlook of the imposing Cockburn Range.

We'd keep our existing house as a guest house for when friends and family came to stay. In the back of my mind, I was also keeping it for Maria. She was 22 years old and in the final stages of completing a commerce degree at Curtin

University where she had met her boyfriend, Chris Magnay. Robert and I had our fingers crossed that they would marry, and this could become a home for the newlyweds.

I eagerly threw myself into the project of building our new home. For much of my life I'd had to accept other people's decisions about where I lived, mainly Friedrich's. Now together Robert and I would build a house that reflected the two of us, something that was intrinsically ours.

We worked with an architect to design a light, modern, airy space. The house would sit higher up on the riverbank than our current home, with floor-to-ceiling windows to capture the extraordinary Kimberley views and a rolling wavelike rooftop to cope with the rain. The bones of the building were to be of the strongest steel, able to weather any storm – no more flooded carpet! Extra-high cathedral ceilings would allow the heat to rise and dissipate.

The humidity of the wet season brings plagues of little insects and midges: you can't sit outside for two minutes without bugs landing in your food. But we wanted to be able to sit on the veranda and soak up the views all year round. The answer was metres of netting that was layered like a cake underneath the deck so the bugs couldn't come up through the cracks in the wood. We would also have floor-to-ceiling panels made of an extra-fine mesh. Up close, you can see and feel that it is super-fine steel, but step back and you could be looking through a window. We would feel the sun on our backs and soak up the view bug-free.

The most wonderful luxury was being able to design my own kitchen, which to me was always the centre of my home. Windows looking onto the river and Friedrich's resting place would mean that the breathtaking pink dawn would greet us at breakfast every day.

Margret and Lance had welcomed two new children, Joseph and Phillip, to the family, and with our numbers swelling I wanted an open-plan living room and lots of space for my grandchildren to play.

A project like this takes time to build, especially in the outback. Materials generally have to be freighted in from Perth or Darwin, and if a crucial nail, screw, bolt or beam is missing, the builders may have to wait more than two weeks for it to arrive. Delays are part of the deal, but our castle slowly began to rise from the earth.

By 2006, we'd been building for almost a year when Chris and Maria became engaged. Chris was a pilot, flying mainly tourist flights over the Bungle Bungles and Lake Argyle. Maria had a very quiet nature, but she was noticeably more confident around him, and they made a lovely couple. We were thrilled when he proposed and even more delighted when they accepted an offer from Robert and me to host the reception at home. Maria's wedding would be the first major event at the new house and I couldn't think of a better way to christen it – we just had to get it finished! The race was on and we had a very clear deadline: 15 July 2006.

The builders worked furiously to get the house completed in the nick of time, and we finished moving in the week before the wedding. We had people flying in from all corners of the globe, many staying with us, so Robert and I worked around the clock unpacking furniture and crockery and making beds.

The garden was a mess. Well, it wasn't a garden at all – it was bare dirt all around us. On the morning of the wedding, after a quick cup of coffee, I was out in the garden planting sago palms and birds of paradise, while Robert gave the lawns on the riverbank one last mow and set up tables and chairs.

I was so engrossed that I totally lost track of time and at 2pm Robert found me up to my elbows in potting mix.

'Frauke, hurry up! People will be arriving soon.'

I raced into the shower and made a mad dash to get ready. I'd chosen a strapless gown and when Robert zipped me up in front of the mirror, I realised you could still see the bra marks from where I'd been out in the sun all day. There was no time to worry. We managed to get ourselves dressed and ready, then we each took a huge deep breath as we welcomed the first guests to our home. When the living room was full, Robert said, 'I think it's time to get the bride.'

I looked around, amazed at how well the house adapted to 120 guests. The river sparkling in the background made the perfect backdrop, and I couldn't have been more thrilled.

My heart skipped a beat when Maria appeared on Robert's arm at the door. She was radiant in a raw silk gown with a beautiful flowing skirt. It was clear from Robert's face how proud he was to be walking her down the aisle. For all intents and purposes, he was her father. He had been there for her in good times and bad, for as long as she could remember. During our Christmas Eve celebration just days before Peter died, he and Maria had surprised Robert by asking him to formally adopt them. It was the best Christmas present Robert could ever have wished for. I've sometimes wondered if it was Peter's way of saying a final thank you to Robert for being a father to him, an expression of how much he loved him. Robert had never tried to replace Friedrich; he had become the children's confidant and friend. In doing so, he had won their respect and their hearts, as he'd won mine.

Watching Robert walk Maria down the aisle in the home we'd built together was one of the happiest moments of my life. I felt like we were writing a new, happy chapter in our lives. Robert gave Maria a kiss on the cheek and sat down beside me.

The guests were all sitting quietly listening to Val go through the formalities when, out of the corner of my eye, I caught a glimpse of movement, a flicker up in the ceiling. It was a tiny little bird perched high above us.

The wren plunged off the ledge and swooped down over us, soared across the room and went out through the front door. Guests giggled at the cheeky wren momentarily stealing the spotlight. It was the little Peter bird. Maria saw it too.

Tears welled in my eyes. The guests were oblivious of the special meaning of this little bird, but I was overcome. Peter was with us, the little bird told us so.

The wedding was better than any house-warming party we could've thrown, and it was the first of many happy family times that have made this house a home. And every now and then when we are all gathered together, our lovely little Peter bird joins us. It's of enormous comfort to me knowing that he's found his way home too.

Some months after the wedding, Robert and I were driving out to Carlton Hill Station, northwest of Kununurra, to visit friends when we came across a car pulled over to the side of the dirt road.

'Are you okay, mate?' Robert asked the dishevelled driver, who had a dog-eared map spread across the front seat.

'I'm looking for a house and I think I've got myself a bit lost,' he said.

'Which house?' Robert asked.

'Well, not one specific house,' he said.

Curious and slightly confused, we got talking with the young man. A location scout for a film company, he was looking for potential houses for a movie that was going to be made in the area next year. He'd gone off the main road and couldn't find his way back to the highway, which was understandable given that every dirt road looked the same out here.

There had been all sorts of talk around town that a big Hollywood movie was going to be made here. I'd thought it was just gossip, but maybe I was wrong.

We pointed out where he was and showed him how to get back into town. Then Robert asked, 'What sort of houses are you looking for, mate? We might be able to help you.'

It turned out that he was looking for nice places for the cast and crew to stay.

'Well, you'd better come and have a look at our place!' Robert joked.

Sure enough, the next day he was on our doorstep for a tour.

'This place is lovely,' he said, poking in and out of bedrooms, furiously taking notes. 'This is exactly what I'm looking for. Would you be interested in renting it out? You won't need to pack anything up. I'm looking for a residence that's fully furnished.'

'Who would be staying here?' I gently fished.

'Sorry, that's confidential.'

The look on his face said 'and don't ask any more questions', but cheeky Robert couldn't help himself. 'I'd be very happy for Nicole Kidman to sleep in my bed,' he joked.

His comment was met without so much as a grin.

The money they were offering was incredibly generous, but aside from that, if this movie was a big blockbuster, as promised, it would be a wonderful advertisement for the town and could really put Kununurra on the map. That would be good for everyone.

We signed an in-principle agreement, then kind of forgot about it. The shoot was months down the track, so we just got on with our lives.

$\sim$

Back in 1995, it had been a huge development for the region when CSR established a sugar mill in Kununurra. Sugar was a commodity with a guaranteed market around the world, and Robert and Fritz had the foresight to transform the farm from rotational crops that were planted each year with hope and fingers crossed, to more reliable sugar cane.

After each harvest, sugar cane naturally regrows from the roots. A crop can last five years and it grows all year round, which was revolutionary for us. The long days spent ploughing the backbreaking earth every few months were over.

The government had supported the building of the mill, largely thanks to the work of Judy's husband, Jim Hughes, who fought tirelessly for the farmers of the Ord River region. Much had been promised to them for many years, and it felt like the government had at last come good with its word. At its peak, the mill produced 60,000 tonnes of sugar each year, and it revolutionised farming in the Ord Valley.

For us personally, sugar was transformational. It brought stability, which meant banks were finally willing to open their doors to us and we could invest and grow the farm. We employed local workers and had very successful yields. There were no more headaches of living crop to crop. Robert and Fritz were a wonderful team. They worked well together, and I knew in my heart that Friedrich would've been so proud to see them realise his dream.

But trouble began brewing in the early 2000s when the mill was sold to a Korean company, which, despite its best efforts and a huge amount of support from local growers, couldn't make the mill profitable. They had bought the mill in good faith, with lots of promises of government support, which sadly never came to fruition.

After twelve years of farming sugar cane successfully, we were devastated when we got word that the company was shutting the mill. The 2007 crush would be the last. This was a massive blow. Suddenly we had nowhere to take our crop, and the cost of transporting it to another mill thousands of kilometres away made that a totally unviable option.

We, like many farmers in the region, had more than 1000 hectares covered in sugar cane and nowhere for it to go.

Robert and Fritz crunched the numbers every way they could – backwards, forwards and inside out – trying to figure out how they could continue to grow sugar cane profitably. But they couldn't. The only option was to get rid of it and start all over again with a different type of crop.

The trouble was, by the time we received notice that the mill was closing, we were perilously close to missing the planting season for new crops. If we didn't get a crop in the ground immediately, we'd lose not only the sugar cane but the next year's income too.

We had a three-week window to remove over 1000 hectares of sugar cane, plough, fertilise the ground and plant a new crop. With no time to waste, it was all hands on deck: every available worker we could employ, plus our seven regular farm staff, was seconded to dig up the sugar cane. It was a wretched thing to remove. The root systems penetrated deep into the earth and stuck in the soil like glue. The fields had to be ploughed repeatedly to get rid of it all. Even then, new shoots would emerge overnight, sucking every last nutrient from the soil. Robert and Fritz, along with our team, worked around the clock, day and night, battling the sugar cane. It was a momentous challenge for them to keep going, but they won. Finally, after weeks of work, huge expanses of bare earth, ready for a new lease on life, lay before them.

As our farm had been covered by lush green sugar cane for more than a decade, it was startling to see the paddocks stripped back to red bulldust, but it wasn't long before the first sprouts of chia began to emerge and a tinge of green softened the blow of the sugar-cane loss.

Once again, we would start from scratch, and Oasis Farms would rise from the ashes.

Chapter 32

In August 2007, Hollywood actually did come to Kununurra.

A Boeing 737-200 touched down at the airport with many of the cast and crew of the film *Australia* on board. The flight itself was big news for our little town: it was the first time a plane of that size had landed at Kununurra airport. The director Baz Luhrmann was on board, and media from around the world mingled with locals outside the airport waiting to catch a glimpse of him. The film's stars, Nicole Kidman and Hugh Jackman, would arrive at a later date and would spend most of their time filming around Carlton Hill Station, which would be transformed into the fictional Faraway Downs cattle station.

The whole town was buzzing about this film, the sense of excitement palpable. More than a hundred cast and crew were employed on it. From its budget of $120 million, $4 million was expected to benefit the Kununurra economy, through feeding and accommodating the influx of people.

Every hotel, house and caravan had been booked up. Even the racecourse had been converted into a caravan park with dozens of motorhomes lined up.

As we got the house ready for the cast or crew who would be staying, there were paparazzi camped at our gate. I can only imagine their disappointment when they realised the strapping farmer they'd snapped in his tattered overalls and battered Akubra wasn't Hugh Jackman in costume but real-life farmer Robert Boshammer on his way to work. A photographer even anchored a boat in the river in front of our house, snapping close-up pictures of our living room that were splashed across the *West Australian* newspaper.

Once the house was absolutely immaculate, Robert and I packed a few bags and headed over to Fritz and Andrea's to bunk in their spare room. We were inundated with calls from media asking us who was staying in our house. Friends and family were desperate to know too. In truth, we didn't know who was staying in the house: we had signed an iron-clad confidentiality agreement and it was better not to know. The town and its people went to great lengths to accommodate the film production. Many locals gave access to their properties to allow filming to take place. Public roads that were vital during the busy dry season were closed. Waterways were lowered to allow the filming of cattle scenes. Tourists were shut out of many of our most picturesque sights. And the town agreed to all of this happily, for the greater good of showing Kununurra to the world.

The pubs were full, cafes busier than they'd ever been and we were run off our feet at the shop. *Australia* was great for business.

We were suffering something of a heat wave for Kununurra: day after day of 43 degrees, with no respite at night. I was worried that my garden would shrivel up to dust, and didn't expect our house guests would be worried about watering my birds of paradise.

We'd been given the phone number of the butler who would be looking after the guests in the house. Sheepishly, I rang to ask him if it would be okay for me to pop over sometime and water my plants. He was very official and told me he needed to check the schedule of the resident. Ten minutes later, he called me back and said I could come over between 5pm and 6pm that day – not a minute before, not a minute later – because the occupant would be out on set.

I rushed over right on 5pm, grabbed the hose and raced around the garden giving everything a good drink. I was just about to turn the tap off when a voice from behind me said, 'I do like your bed.'

I turned to find a very handsome silver-haired man standing with his hand outstretched. 'G'day, I'm Baz,' he said.

'Oh, hello, I'm Frauke,' I said, shaking his hand. 'I'm so sorry, I was told to come now because you wouldn't be home. I hope I haven't interrupted you. I'm just finishing up.'

'No, please don't hurry, it's fine,' he said.

He stopped and chatted for a few minutes, explaining that he'd come back from the set a little earlier than planned so he could have a rest from the heat before heading back out to film some night scenes.

We would later learn that both Nicole Kidman and Hugh Jackman had spent time at our place too. Robert has got plenty of mileage out of his evergreen 'Nicole Kidman's slept in my bed' joke. Nicole came into the shop several times during breaks in filming, as did Hugh, and we made pieces for them to remember their time in the Kimberley.

A few weeks after the cast and crew had left town, a package arrived in the mail stamped from a Sydney address. Inside was our copy of the book *The Kite Runner.* Baz had been reading the book while he was staying and took it home by accident, and didn't want us to think he'd stolen it. It was returned with a lovely note, thanking us for our hospitality. I can say with all honesty the pleasure was ours.

In November 2008, *Australia* was released on the big screen, an event that was highly anticipated by the people of Kununurra. Those who had scored parts as extras were busting to see themselves on film, and the rest of us were busting to see how the Kimberley scrubbed up.

A special open-air premiere screening was organised for about two hundred people. You could've heard a pin drop for the first twenty minutes, and then out of the blue the famous Ivanhoe Crossing appeared on screen and the crowd erupted. It was only a fleeting glimpse, but Kununurra had made it to the silver screen.

The movie was a great success for our business, because many people came to town to see where it had been filmed. We were invited by Rio Tinto and Argyle Diamonds to showcase our work at the 2009 G'day USA celebrations in New York. We designed some exquisite pieces to take with us: cufflinks for Hugh Jackman and a beautiful tiepin set with a pink diamond cut in the shape of Australia for Baz Luhrmann, who was the star of the event. *Australia* would never be too far from his heart, nor ours.

Chapter 33

For several years, our life in Kununurra rolled on very happily. At sixty-seven and fifty-six respectively, Robert and I were growing older and found ourselves delightfully immersed in the lives of our growing grandchildren, the rolling seasons of the farm and shop and the new arrivals to the family; with no intention of slowing down.

However, in July 2014, completely out of the blue, I began having vivid dreams about my mother. I'd never dreamt about her before. Now sometimes she'd touch me on the shoulder in the night. Sometimes she was talking to me. Her presence always felt so real I'd wake up startled and would struggle to settle again, often only nodding off as the pink dawn was creeping under the curtains.

During the day, I was tired and lacklustre, which wasn't like me at all.

Fitness had always been important to me, and a few times a week I rode my bike home from the shop. It's a relatively easy ride on the flat, hot bitumen and dirt roads out the back of town, past irrigation channels and crops of lush green mangoes. I know the roads like the back of my hand – even where to look out for the shiny-backed king brown snakes that regularly sun themselves on the red dirt shoulders of the road.

But increasingly I arrived home from my ride exhausted.

One afternoon, when I lifted my helmet off there was a little sore patch on the back of my head. Maybe my helmet was rubbing and I needed a new one? After several weeks and some adjustments to the helmet, the sore patch hadn't subsided, prompting me to visit the doctor.

She gave me a thorough examination and thankfully everything seemed in good shape. There was nothing that warranted worrying about. She thought my upcoming holiday would do me the world of good. We'd had a busy season in the shop, and Robert had been working terribly hard with Fritz cultivating a new sandalwood crop. We had a trip to Germany planned for November.

But by the time we returned home in December, the pain hadn't subsided and the sore patch had swollen into a lump on my skull, so off I went to see the doctor again.

Robert loves tennis as much as I do, and every year after Christmas we travel to Perth to the Hopman Cup, so the doctor gave me the details of a specialist I could see while I was there, but she said there was still no need for concern.

Our Christmas was a wonderful affair. Along with our neighbours and friends, there were ten grandchildren, including Lance and Margret's latest additions, Nikita, five, and Sarah, three, and Maria and Chris's two children, Peter, four, and Georgia, two. My grandchildren now spanned from teens to toddlers and I adored having them around.

Twenty-four-year-old Katrina, who was fast becoming the most adventurous of my children, was the only one missing. She'd been dating a very handsome young man, Frankc, a kitesurfing instructor she'd met during her gap-year travels. They were having Christmas in Peru. We had thirty-five people for a feast of apricot chicken, beef rouladen – thin slices of beef rolled up with bacon, onions, mustard and pickles – and more salads and roast potatoes than you could count. I was quite proud of my efforts at making the German desserts that year; my cakes were almost too good to eat.

From the dining table on our deck, we watched the heavens put on quite a Christmas light show: an enormous thunderhead rolled across the ranges, giving a spectacular display of lightning. Sure enough, it was followed by a downpour. Christmas Eve storms had become something of a tradition too.

Despite the rough weather, miraculously, 'Santa' arrived after dinner and everyone got to sit on his lap and receive a present. Every year we had great fun watching Lance sit on Santa's knee. A strapping man, he bristled when his name was called out. 'No thanks, Santa, I don't need a present this year,' he said, trying to wriggle his way out of the fun and games.

But the children egged him on, and after a little arm twisting, he reluctantly played along. 'Lance, have you been naughty or nice this year?' Santa asked as we all giggled.

The next morning, we woke to the wonderful scent of Kimberley pine through the house and the sounds of excited grandchildren busting to open the last of their presents. Having the family all together was the best Christmas gift.

Robert and I flew to Perth and at the end of January, I saw the neurologist. He sent me for an ultrasound the next day to get a good look at what was going on, though he too said it probably wasn't anything to worry about. The nurse performing the ultrasound echoed the doctor's reassurance. However, she found a strange patch in my skull that needed further examination.

By now I was becoming very worried. The lump was about the size of a small apple and seemed to be growing quite quickly. I knew in my heart something wasn't right.

A further MRI showed a large mass, and I was told I needed to see a neurosurgeon.

A year or so beforehand, Robert and I had met a lovely man, Paul Bannan, a Perth-based neurosurgeon, on a cruise around the Kimberley. He struck me as having a gentle, wise manner. If I was going to have someone poking around inside my brain, Paul was the man for the job.

The specialist phoned his receptionist, who explained that he was away on leave. When the specialist told her that we knew Dr Bannan personally and the matter was quite urgent, she promised to call him. Thankfully he was holidaying at home in Perth and offered to see me first thing the next morning. I barely slept a wink, worried about what was going on inside my skull. But the strange dreams of my mother now made sense. I felt sure she was giving me some sort of warning.

Robert was right beside me when we walked into Mount Hospital. He held my hand and rubbed my arm, but even Robert's warmth did little to ease the nausea that was rising in my stomach.

We chatted with Paul for a little while and reminisced about our voyage through the gorges and waterfalls of the Kimberley, then he put my brain scans up on his screen. 'Let's have a look at what we've got here, Frauke,' he said.

As his fingers came to the ugly mass, he took a long deep breath. 'Frauke, this part here looks like it could be cancer,' he said. 'You'll need an operation to remove the tumour.'

My heart sank. He talked us through the details of the operation. It would take around eight hours and be gruelling.

The catch was, because he'd been on leave he didn't have any operating theatres booked. His nurse spent the afternoon on the phone trying to find a theatre available as soon as possible.

In the meantime, he sent me for a biopsy to see exactly what we were dealing with.

The biopsy was terribly painful, but after a very anxious wait, it revealed I had non-Hodgkin lymphoma, stage four. Although a serious cancer, it could be treated without invasive brain surgery. Instead I would undergo a course of chemotherapy to shrink the tumour.

Non-Hodgkin lymphoma has a relatively good prognosis, with a survival rate of 70 per cent beyond five years. At least we knew what we were dealing with now and I could get cracking on getting better.

Once you've been diagnosed with cancer, you want to get it out of your body as quickly as possible. I wanted to begin treatment right there and then. There was no time to waste; I wanted every little molecule of this bugger gone.

Robert rang the children in Kununurra and told them what was happening, and they all flew to Perth to be with me. Katrina, however, was still travelling through South America with Frankc and they were miles from anywhere. It took some time for Robert to get hold of her.

'Where have you been, Katrina?' he asked. Poor Katrina had seriously hurt herself kitesurfing in Peru. She prattled on with the whole story of what had happened, and Robert couldn't get a word in. Apparently, the wind had moved the board from under her in the surf and she had gone crashing into the ocean, hitting a piece of concrete under the water. She'd gashed her foot very badly. She took a breath long enough for Robert to say, 'Katrina, Mutti has cancer.'

There was silence on the end of the phone, followed by tears.

'Why didn't you tell me! How could you let me go on about myself?'

She insisted on coming straight home, but it was a long journey back to Lima, especially with a badly cut foot. The trip home to Perth took almost three full days, and she was exhausted by the time she arrived. I was so pleased to see her.

When the oncologist came to visit me in hospital, all of the children were with me, and I think he was shocked to see so many people in the room. My children gave me great strength, as well as a darn good reason to hurry up and get rid of this cancer.

The oncologist explained that I'd lose my hair, which was a daunting thought but a small price to pay.

My darling teenage granddaughter Kimberley offered to cut off her long blonde locks so I could have a wig made out of her hair, but I'd never had long hair and I'd never been blonde, so that didn't feel right. It was such a touching gesture, though. A young woman willing to make such a sacrifice melted my heart. Later, she still cut her hair off and donated it to be made into wigs for children with cancer.

The girls decided we'd all go on a shopping trip together to buy some wigs. We had a ball trying on wigs of all lengths, shapes and colours. We tried curly ones, straight ones, blue and purple ones. We laughed so much we cried. By the end of the day, I'd tried on every wig in Perth and decided they just weren't for me. I'd rather go bald and be done with it.

I've always been a very proud mother: my children and grandchildren are truly wonderful. Now I soaked up their courage and strength. Our laughter, little kisses, a squeeze of the hand reminded me why I would fight this with all of my might. Each of them is a life force unto their own. Their courage was my courage, and they would carry me through this.

The first chemotherapy treatment was worse than I thought and the impact was immediate. I began vomiting virtually straightaway, then every half an hour through the night, and my appetite went almost immediately. My heart felt like it was on fire, and I tossed and turned until the sunrise brought me some relief.

The next day, the hospital gave me tablets to cope with the nausea, which helped a bit.

As expected, my hair began to fall out. It washed away in the shower. It fell out in clumps at the kitchen table. Robert and I went for a walk along Cottesloe beach to get some fresh air, and my hair was literally blowing off my head into the sea.

By the time I went back for my second treatment three weeks later, I was completely bald. At least there was no hair left to lose.

Every now and then I'd run my fingers over my head and be surprised to feel bare skin. It was so strange, and a few times I got teary about it. But I kept reminding myself it was a good sign because it meant the chemo was working. I wanted that poison to gobble up every last cancer cell in my body. Dorte came from Germany for five weeks. She was a wonderful help and we walked along the beach together whenever I was well enough.

I had treatment every three weeks for six months. My last treatment was 2 June 2015, the day of my grandmother's birthday.

About a month later, little tufts of hair began to appear again, and eventually it all grew back. It was silver-grey and finer than before, but I loved it. It was me. I no longer worried about what people thought: if a hair was out of place, it didn't matter, because I was happy just to have hair.

In August 2015, a PET scan showed there was no more cancer in my body.

I've since had a course of antibody therapy, which is given like a chemotherapy infusion in hospital, and I am now in remission.

Having cancer forced me to reassess my life. I spent a lot of time reflecting on my family and my friends. I realised just how thankful I am for my life, and grateful for the opportunities God has given me. I prayed a lot, cried a lot and laughed more than I ever imagined I could.

Cancer reminded me of what was important and what wasn't. It was a cruel and unusual gift.

Epilogue

3 OCTOBER 2017

The cool water instantly softened my brittle bones. I relished the swell that gently lapped at the back of my neck as the Indian Ocean rolled in, touched the sandy edges of Western Australia then waved farewell again.

It was the end of the tourist season and the streets and hotels of Broome were still buzzing with travellers, but out here, surrounded by turquoise ripples, you could all but hear a fish breathe.

Every now and then I dipped my head back into the surf, let the salty water wash through my fine curls, and thought: *It is good to be alive.*

Around me, people bobbed up and down with the high tide, buoyed by the waves. They were all mine: my children and their husbands and wives, my grandchildren with the odd boyfriend or girlfriend. We were human corks, never much more than an arm's length from one another, floating, chatting, laughing and reconnecting.

Others played on the long stretch of pristine white sand: the little ones too young to join me for a birthday swim. One day soon. Our newest addition, Alexa Annika Magnay, was just three months old. She was cradled in her mother's arms under an umbrella on the beach, blissfully content. Alexa has been here before, I feel sure of that. She's the spitting image of Maria as a baby. Her big chocolate eyes melt my heart.

We had come to Broome ten years before to celebrate my sixtieth birthday, and it was such a happy time. All of our lives were becoming increasingly busy, but everybody made a special effort to be together in one place. We experienced the togetherness that becomes so much more important to me as I get older. I don't want gifts or platitudes, I want time.

As seventy approached, the pressure was on to organise another family adventure. But all I wanted was to gather at Cable Beach again and just be. The family flew in from everywhere. Margret and her family from Victoria, where she now lives; grandchildren from Perth; a carload or two came across from Kununurra. The only one who couldn't be there this time was Margret's husband, Lance, who was fighting bushfires in New South Wales. We'd make it up to him.

Our days were long and lazy, just as I'd intended. Often, we'd have breakfast together, and the intention was that we'd do our own thing then meet again for a family dinner. But each day we all seemed to naturally gravitate to one another, the thickness of our blood binding us together.

Some afternoons when the tide was in, I'd have a swim on my own or with Robert; other days everyone would join me. When the tide was low, we'd walk for hours along the vast stretch of sand, delighted when we found the fossilised dinosaur footprints that Gantheaume Point is known for.

We went whale watching and dolphin spotting. We even went to a crocodile park, because it's quite different seeing these majestic creatures in a safe environment. You don't get to appreciate their beauty when it's just a tail slipping into the river.

This was my heaven.

We arrived in Kununurra as five, and I can say now with confidence that my tree has truly been planted. Today we are twenty and growing, three generations who now call Australia home.

Each one of my children has made their own mark in their own way, and I couldn't be prouder. They contribute to their families and their communities, and they are good people.

My family is the essence of everything, the salt of my earth, and I thank God every day.

So much has changed since I arrived here thirty-seven years ago. What was a dusty outpost is now the thriving heartland of northern Western Australia.

With endless blue sky and earth, and the rich soul and community backbone of the outback to comfort you when you need it most, I am convinced this is the most wonderful place on earth to raise a family. Among the dirt and dust and beyond the endless horizon is a place where spirits can soar, where you can be truly free. I'm sure children are born here with resilience in their blood.

Some things don't change. Farming life remains a test of wills. The best farmer in the world can forecast and future proof right down to the last digit on a spreadsheet, but still so much rests on the shoulders of Mother Nature and forces that are at work beyond the farm gate. Hard work, hope and luck are essential.

As I am writing this, the Ord River region is suffering because of the collapse of sandalwood company Quintis, of which we are a shareholder and supplier. Sandalwood is a popular crop across the Northern Territory and Western Australia. In 2014, it was trading at $14,000 per tonne, with a promising forecast.

Oasis Farms has 400 hectares of sandalwood planted, earmarked for future sale. The aromatic wood and essential oils are used in the manufacture of perfumes and cosmetics all over the world, so we are hoping we can ride out this latest hiccup and find a place in the global market. We've had success with chia and hope the market for that crop remains strong.

In 2017, Rio Tinto announced that the Argyle mine will close in 2020. This means the production of pink diamonds, already impossibly rare, may be finite. It's a mixed blessing: Kimberley Fine Diamonds will need to change and adapt to new markets, but we have one of the largest collections of pink diamonds in Australia and these precious gems will only become more valuable over time.

As the miners depart the region, the fabric of our town will change once again, and we will need to adapt and welcome a new wave of opportunity.

Tourism is now a staple. The Ord Valley Muster is now an important annual event on the community calendar. People come from all over the world to dine under the stars and enjoy a touch of the Kimberley. Sir Bob Geldof has attended the muster, and I had a particularly enjoyable evening sitting next to the Hon Julia Gillard MP, who, three weeks after the muster, became our nation's first female prime minister.

The muster is a wonderful showcase of the spirit of the outback and we are proud to have supported the event every year.

Each Sunday the family gathers around my table for breakfast or brunch before we go to church. It gets a little noisier with every new arrival at the table. A hum of happiness.

Much of our breakfast is sourced locally: fresh mangoes, chia bread. I can't get enough of Kununurra mangoes; the freezer is full of them, and all year round we have mango smoothies, cheesecakes, muffins. We have everything we need in abundance now.

I thank God every day for bringing Robert into my life. This year we celebrated thirty-two years of marriage, and I am in no doubt that I would not have weathered the storms without him by my side. We may be a little older, our skin a little thinner, but he has not lost the twinkle in those big blue eyes when he's up to mischief. His cheeky sense of humour brings joy and lightness at the times we most need it.

A few years back, he came wandering into the house with an enormous black-headed python wrapped around his wrist. He'd found the harmless snake on the side of the road and it looked injured, so he was taking it to the vet, but not before bringing it in the house for show and tell with the wide-eyed grandchildren. Robert was in awe of the creature.

It was thicker than his arm, and as it coiled itself up towards his shoulder, the grandchildren shared his excitement. Every day he finds beauty in this landscape.

I travel to Germany at least once a year. Whenever I am home, I soak up the sights and sounds and smells, to carry me through until my next visit. I will always long for Katjes licorice and Lübeck marzipan.

My father passed away in 2001, and last year I lost my brother Juergen. As we get older, life begins to take this course. I miss them both dearly.

My heart will forever play tug-of-war between my homes. I'm happy for my kids that I came to Kununurra, but I remain divided. I miss the European culture and I miss my family.

I adapted, I accepted and I learnt to find the beauty in this place, but part of my heart is still in Germany, and it will always be home.

My cancer diagnosis prompted me to think long and hard about my final resting place. I came to the conclusion that as long as my ashes are mixed with some of Peter's ashes that I'd kept in reserve, they can do whatever they like with me. Fly us over Kununurra and scatter us, wash us down the river – I don't mind, but I don't want to forever be in a little box in a wall or in a coffin underground. I want to be set free.

People often ask me how I've kept going, especially after Peter's loss. I feel my faith has carried me through at times.

I have lived my life by the adage 'never begin to give up, and never give up beginning', because even during the most difficult days, you can always find a diamond in the dust.

Acknowledgements

Many twists and turns have made up my life, and along the way many people have stretched out a hand of friendship when I was alone, picked me up when I felt I could no longer keep going, hugged me when I needed comfort and warmth.

This book is my way of saying thank you.

I am very grateful to the team at Simon & Schuster for bringing my story to life with such care, compassion and enthusiasm. Thank you, Dan Ruffino, Fiona Henderson and Roberta Ivers.

To Sue Smethurst for believing in my story and faithfully retelling it; Selwa Anthony for her expert guidance and continued support of Australian authors and Australian stories, and Bronwyn Dove for introducing us.

Thank you to Teresa Bytschkow at the *Kimberley Echo* and the staff of the Kununurra Historical Society for liaising with Sue to fill in gaps when my memory failed me!

To the teachers in Germany who believed in me and encouraged me – Erwin Petersen, Frau Hoop and Frau Holz – and my classmates in 10B who skipped beside me and made me smile, and Frau Korf in Hamburg.

To my family in Bunsoh – it was my paradise in my young years.

To Hermann Effland. Without him, we would not have come to Kununurra.

My heartfelt thanks to the Bolten family for welcoming me with open arms, Maren, Hedi, Wiebke; also to Soeren Petersen, Hartwig Bolten and all of their family members for lasting friendship after Friedrich died. We will always be family. And to Hans and Elfriede Thomsen (Margarethe Bolten's sister), for introducing me to the Boltens.

Although they are a long way away, my friends are always in my heart and my prayers: the Koetting family, Marion and Fritz Junge, Renate and Carsten Struve, Yvonne and Stephan Struve, Achim and Trude Schnaak, Willem and Hedi Raak, Arno and Sigrid von Spreckelsen, and Birgit and Klaus Nevermann.

To George and Lynn Matsukis and the Hennebergs in Zimbabwe for helping us navigate such a wild and wonderful country. I am filled with nothing but happy memories from our time there.

When we arrived in Australia, I was so grateful to have the help of au pairs who became the backbone of the family. These girls packed their bags, left their homes and joined us on the greatest adventure of all of our lives. Thank you so much, Steffi Eppler and Maren Henk for being there when I needed you most; and Karoline Went, Ulle Jakob and Silke Sievers, who came into our lives a little later but have also become a much-loved part of our family.

To the late Harry Perkins, an extraordinary man. Harry, I cursed you when we first arrived, now I thank you for your vision and support. Your passion for the Ord River has changed many lives.

The outback can be a barren and at times despairingly lonely place, but when life takes a turn for the worse there's nowhere else I'd rather be. The Kununurra community sweeps you up and carries you on red-dust wings when your legs can't take you another step. I will be forever indebted to the friends and families that welcomed us with open arms, rallied around us in our darkest days, and have continued to make us laugh and smile. Thank you John Caratti, Judy and the late Jim Hughes, Robyn and Trevor Mildren, Dean and Francis David, Peter and Belinda Letchford, Debbie and Phil Rogers, Cynthia and Richard Titmarsh, Neil Townsend, Laurie and Trish Harvey, and Lou and Mike Hamshire. And to my special friend Py.

And the Mock family: without them I wouldn't have met Robert.

Just before he died, Peter spent treasured time with friends in Germany, and I am so grateful to them for treating him as one of the family. Thank you, Jochen, Simon, Lennard, Nis Peter, Soeren and Christian. And to Peter's friends in Kununurra: Johnson, Lincoln, Ben, Clint, RB and Steele, whom he adored and his friends from Wesley College. His life was too short but he packed a lifetime of adventures into every day.

To Doris, thank you. You started me on a journey I could never have imagined and I will cherish our friendship forever.

Thank you to Dr Peter Tan and crew at Hollywood Hospital, who nurtured me through cancer.

My very special friends Rob and Val Kilderry are not only the best neighbours in the world, they introduced me to Alicia Molik and Lleyton Hewitt, my heroes.

To Val Bock, my special friend, I miss you.

To Rainer and Renate Erler, who got my lifelong friendship with Blacky and Gundel Fuchsberger started, thank you.

Thank you to the staff at Kimberley Fine Diamonds, who are family too. Helen Thorne and my team have effortlessly picked up the pieces when times have been tough. They equally share my passion for the rare beauty of the Argyle diamonds our Kimberley backyard creates. Kimberley Fine Diamonds is testament to the friendship and loyalty of my wonderful staff.

But the most important recognition is left for my darling, cheeky, treasured husband, Robert my 'Professor', who has weathered every storm with me and made me smile when I least expected it. And for my children and grandchildren – who are the reason for being – my sister, Dorte, my dear late brother, Juergen, and his wife, Ingrid, and my beloved Tante Banta, whose love filled a hole in my heart.

Dienen lerne beizeiten das Weib nach ihrer Bestimmung;
Denn durch Dienen allein gelangt sie endlich zum Herrschen,
Zu der verdienten Gewalt, die doch ihr im Hause gehöret.

Early a woman should learn to serve, for that is her calling;
Since through service alone she finally comes to the headship,
Comes to the due command that is hers of right in
the household.

Johann Wolfgang von Goethe,
'Hermann and Dorothea', 1797

Services and Help

If you or someone you know needs urgent support, talk to someone you can trust, or contact a crisis support service such as those below.

beyondblue: beyondblue.org.au or call 1300 224 636

Lifeline: lifeline.org.au or call 13 11 14

MensLine Australia: mensline.org.au or call 1300 789 978

Northern Territory Mental Health Line: call 1800 682 288

The Samaritans: call 135 247